*"I am
honored
to be
here
today..."*

"I am honored to be here today..."

COMMENCEMENT SPEECHES BY NOTABLE PERSONALITIES

Compiled and edited by
DONALD GRUNEWALD, D.B.A.
Distinguished Professor

OCEANA PUBLICATIONS, INC., NEW YORK • LONDON • ROME

Library of Congress Catalog Card Number 84-063087

ISBN 0-379-11252-3

© Copyright 1985 Oceana Publications, Inc.

Manufactured in the United States of America

Table of Contents

Introduction

In the early days of American colleges and universities, it was customary for each student to speak (usually in Latin) at Commencement. With the growth in the size of graduating classes this custom gradually fell into disuse. In some colleges and universities this custom persists through a representative student speaker — usually the class valedictorian.

Over a period of time, most colleges replaced most or all of the student speeches at Commencement with an address given by some well known person — often from outside the institution. The college or university president also usually addresses the graduates but at many colleges this is a secondary address.

The commencement address has gained prestige over the years. Some commencement addresses have had a great impact. For example, the Marshall plan was announced in a commencement address given at Harvard University by Secretary of State George C. Marshall.

Commencement speakers are chosen in a great variety of ways. At some institutions, the president chooses the speakers. At others, a committee of the board of trustees or a faculty committee choose the speaker. Sometimes the students choose the speaker. Regardless of the method of choice, when the speaker is announced there is often controversy on campus as the commencement speaker serves as a symbol for many on campus.

This book is a representative collection of recent commencement addresses. They have been selected from over 500 recent commencement addresses obtained as a result of requests to the presidents of selected colleges and universities to submit a recent address from their own or another institution.

Speakers come from many walks of life although college presidents, authors, government and business leaders tend to predominate. Topics vary from major contemporary issues to more classic themes. In many ways, the commencement address gives a picture of what concerns America in a given period of time. Study of these addresses is of value to sociologists as well as to educators and those involved in American studies. A review of contemporary commencement addresses often is of value to the person faced with having to give a commencement address for the first time.

As someone who has served as a college president for more than twelve years, I have heard hundreds of commencement addresses. I am convinced that the commencement address is of value both the the new graduate (if they are not too excited to listen) and to society at large.

I would like to acknowledge with thanks and appreciation the help I have had in preparing this book. Mrs. Doreen LeMoult read each of the addresses and was of great help to me in deciding which addresses to include although the final decision was mine. Ms. Irene Buckley typed the manuscript in various drafts and secured permissions to use the addresses from both the speakers and the colleges and universities where the addresses were given. The staff at Oceana Publishing Company was helpful with editorial and other practical advice. I would like to thank my wife, Barbara S. Frees, my son, Donald F. Grunewald, and my colleagues at Mercy College for allowing me the many hours of time to complete this manuscript.

Donald Grunewald
Irvington, New York
May 1984

Edward J. Bloustein

Edward J. Bloustein

COMMENCEMENT ADDRESS
UNIVERSITY OF CONNECTICUT
May 23, 1982

THE SHOCK OF RECOGNITION OF THE PERIL
OF A NUCLEAR HOLOCAUST

I confess to being unabashedly sentimental when it comes to academic ritual. That is why I am so pleased to be present at this your 99th commencement. It is a privilege for me to participate in the award of honorary degrees to some of the luminaries of our time, and in the award of advanced degrees in course to you graduates, among whom are sure to be found luminaries of days to come.

These exercises bring to an end the first full century of education at the University of Connecticut; they also inaugurate the second century of this university's educational venture. The occasion provokes consideration of continuity; consideration which, with your indulgence, will take me beyond this campus and your time and mine, to continuity of the race of man on earth.

If you are shocked at this sharp transition from celebration of the end of your education at Storrs, Connecticut, to contemplation of the end of the race of man, that is fine, because that was my intention. For, as much as any other single factor, we are menaced with our extinction as a race, because we are insufficiently mindful of the threat to our lives and to our posterity which the nuclear arms race presents. We desperately require a national shock of recognition of that menace. Although I pretend to neither sufficient eloquence, nor wit, to provide it, perhaps today I can lay a bare framework for it.

But first I owe you some explanation of why a teacher and educator, without any special training in world affairs or nuclear armament, should address himself publicly to the danger of a nuclear holocaust. The reason is instructive of, not merely my psychology — because, of itself, that would not be worth talking to you about — but of the general torpor which besets the national consciousness on this issue.

Of recent months in the State of New Jersey I have been speaking out on the deplorable state of our public schools. What I have been saying is remarkable only because it took so long for a president of a state university to say out loud what is so obvious. The fundamental reason so many of our children are being so poorly educated is, not because they lack discipline and shun the hard work of learning; nor because we lack a sufficient number of well trained and well motivated teachers — these are causes, but not the basic one. The root of our difficulty must be traced to the fact that the public school system is society in microcosm. It can teach effectively only those skills, it can inculcate effectively only those habits, which the society esteems. It cannot create its own moral and intellectual climate; it is rather the creature of the culture in which it finds itself.

Unfortunately, the condition of our contemporary culture is grievous: the supermarket is our cathedral; the television set our omnipresent baby-sitter-teacher-preacher; the soap opera our moral liturgy; while overhead there lurks the ever-present terror of mass nuclear destruction. My conclusion — one which leads me as an educator to share with you my views on nuclear disarmament — is that a society which hovers between moral ambivalence and decadence, and is under the ever-present terror of mass nuclear destruction, cannot really hope to educate its young to sound habits of mind and behavior.

I have elsewhere spoken about the other aspects of our contemporary condition which impinge on education, and what we can do about them. Today I address the issue of the impact of the nuclear peril.

The primary consequence of the threat of nuclear disaster on the consciousness of our students is one which is also apparent in the population at large. Students, all of us, are simply numbed by it. It befuddles and confounds us. We obliterate it from our conscious thought, but it remains behind working its insidious effects. Teachers in the classroom report that they teach their students through a barely noticeable fog of fear; as a result, they are difficult to reach and easily distracted. Politicians find their constituents passive and inert when confronted by the issue of nuclear disarmament. It is difficult to get them to think about the issue; even more difficult to get them to take any action about it.

Jonathon Schell, in three recent articles in *The New Yorker* magazine entitled, "The Fate of Earth" — articles comparable in their significance for alerting us to the perils of nuclear war to Rachel Carson's "Silent Spring" in warning us of environmental hazards — describes our condition in this fashion:

> ". . . in spite of the immeasurable importance of nuclear weapons, the world has declined, on the whole, to think about them very much. We have thus far failed to fashion, or to discover within ourselves, an emotional or intellectual or political response to them. This peculiar failure of response, in which hundreds of millions of people acknowledge the presence of an immediate, unremitting threat to their existence and to the existence of the world they live in but do nothing about it — a failure in which both self-interest and fellow-feeling seems to have died

— has itself been such a striking phenomenon that it has to be regarded as an extremely important part of the nuclear predicament as this has existed so far."

What are the causes of our passivity, of our failure of response? One is that mankind has never been faced before this nuclear era with a peril of such an apocalyptic character; the very magnitude of the disaster we face paralyzes us. A second cause — especially instructive of what course of action we must take in the matter — is that each of us, as an individual, feels impotent to deal with the terror we feel. The third ground of our inaction again an instructive one —is that the issue seems veiled behind impenetrable complexity, technical obscurity, and military secrecy.

The history of the last two decades should have taught us at least two things, however. The first is the power of public debate to enlighten us collectively on issues which were beyond the ken of most of us individually. The second is the power of democratic public opinion, when widely enough held, and persistently enough expressed, to affect the course of political events. These lessons of the recent past, seen in the context of our current sense of impotence, hold a plain message which should embolden us as we confront the nuclear peril: If we discuss and debate the issue collectively we will indeed be able to react to it intelligently and responsibly. Thereafter, by expressing our collective will, we can be certain of our power as a people to determine our own destiny, rather than having it determined for us.

The position of minorities, of women, and of our youth, are unquestionably improved today over what they were in the 1950's. These changes were not handed down from on high; they were wrought in the cauldron of public debate and democratic political action. They prove that we are a Nation where the emphatic and responsibly articulated concerns of large numbers of people, acting in concert, can alter the course of public affairs.

I do not mean to suggest that popular opinion is necessarily progressive, or that a mass movement is always on the side of the angels, or that it will always succeed. Still less do I mean to say that cherished goals, once partly attained, are immune to reversal or erosion when their supporters disperse or their opponents gather fresh energies. My intention is rather to urge that no individual of good conscience is entitled to withdraw from the arena of public concern over nuclear war, and that it is unworthy of a free people to abdicate their responsibility for public debate and social action when confronted by an unprecedentedly grave source of concern.

We can all be thankful that the beginning of an end to our sense of impotence about the nuclear threat seems to be emerging at last. Not only have there been numerous protest demonstrations in western Europe in recent years, but expressions of acute concern have recently taken shape in this country as well. I allude to the efforts of the nuclear freeze activist organizations. I allude as well to the numerous articulations of our plight, and of possible ways to remove ourselves from the brink of the abyss, by Jonathon Schell, and other national spokesmen and leaders.

The illustrious historian Barbara Tuchman, who we are honoring here today, has suggested, for instance, that our fear itself, now that we have begun to admit to consciousness the extent of it, may provide the motive power we need to override humanity's warlike history. She recommends that every political candidate this fall be asked to state his or her position on the nuclear arms race. "When control of arms becomes a goal of the mainstream, then it will prevail," she has written.

We can also adduce the testimony of George F. Kennan, former Ambassador to the Soviet Union, on receiving the Albert Einstein Peace Prize in May of last year, when he urged that an immediate 50 percent across-the-board reduction in American and Soviet nuclear weapons be undertaken. "There is no issue at stake in our political relations with the Soviet Union, no hope, no fear, nothing to which we aspire, nothing we would like to avoid, which could conceivably be worth a nuclear war," he said on that occasion.

We have as well the observations of retired Admiral Noel Cayler, former commander-in-chief of United States forces in the Pacific, former director of the National Security Agency, taking the Kennan proposal a step farther with a suggestion for implementing it. Cayler urges that we cut through the impasses of the negotiating table — the issues of verification, of weapons classification, of what is "fair and equal" — by having each side simply turn into a joint Soviet-American commission an equal number of explosive nuclear devices, each side to choose which devices it will give up, each device to count as one, and to be converted, under safeguard, to nuclear power for civilian purposes.

And, then, most recently, President Reagan has responded to these evidences of the unease of the American people about the possibility of nuclear war by changing his own views. He earlier had expressed the conviction that it would harm our national interest to even discuss disarmament until we had greatly strengthened our nuclear arsenal. He has now abandoned this refusal to even talk to the Soviets about the issue, and has, instead, offered them a concrete proposal for disarmament, one, we must note that they turned down out of hand.

Whether the President's proposal was a debater's tactic in a world war of words with Chairman Brezhnev, or a realistic attempt to find accommodation is open to skeptical question — as is, indeed, the immediate, seemingly reflexive and unduly hasty, response of the Soviet Union to it. Nevertheless, the President has taken a distinct first step forward. He must be congratulated for it — and, of course — urged to continue down the same path, as speedily and as effectively as possible; a course of action, which must also be urged upon the Soviet Union.

I mention only a sample of the recent outpouring of analysis and recommendations for dealing with nuclear weapons. There are other critiques and other strategies to be examined. Some commend themselves more to me than others, but it is not my intention here to persuade you of the merits of any particular proposal. I only want to emphasize that this issue is, above all, one that can be dealt with only by thinking about it; that, once we begin to bring the issue to consciousness and think rationally about it, solutions will suggest themselves even to men and women like those of us gathered here today who are of ordinary intelligence, without any special expertise in the netherland of nuclear armaments and the diplomacy of disarmament.

The reason this is so is because, although there are those who would have us believe otherwise, the politics of nuclear disarmament is at root a generalist's, and not a specialist's, intellectual conundrum. Once a critical mass and variety of weapons became available to both the Soviet Union and the United States — as it now has — disarmament cannot be achieved by building more weapons. That course involves an endless spiraling cycle in which each side expends more and more of its resources to achieve either parity or superiority over the other.

We learned in the 60's that simply throwing money at social problems does not cause them to go away. The same is true of the perils of the nuclear arms race; more money spent by each side only adds to the other side's sense of military insecurity. The consequence is that we come not one step closer to disarmament, while each side further impoverishes its people, whose real needs are more and more neglected.

Nor can disarmament be achieved by force, since the use of force — the kind of force we are discussing, the force that nuclear physics has placed at our disposal — can only extinguish the problem along with life itself. If the intelligence of the human species has presented us with the nuclear dilemma, it is only through the application of human intelligence that we can find a way out of it.

Thus, it seems to me that universities have a special responsibility and a special role to play in this issue. The experience of the recent past has taught us that, though universities may not always be able to solve problems, they can and do perform the very, very useful function of bringing attention to them. In the process of debate and discussion thus engendered, a variety of policy imperatives are clarified, and new alternatives for action emerge to be considered.

In my own State I am currently attempting to organize a coalition of college and university presidents to initiate discussions of nuclear disarmament on their campuses this fall. I am also urging university presidents across the Nation to bring all their campuses, which have thus far been relatively inert on the issue, into this vital dialogue.

There is no clear answer, no demonstrably certain way to achieve nuclear disarmament; there is much to debate. But I am convinced that increasingly large expenditures for nuclear arms by both powers, constitutes acceptance of the status quo, a *de facto* resignation to a state of helpless waiting for the world as we know it to end, and that such a course of action is not worthy of us. The process of debate, however unsettling, is healthier than the passive acceptance of a world-wide death sentence.

You graduates assembled here today have grown up under the shadow of the possibility of a nuclear death sentence. Your earliest conceptions of the future must in some sense have included the awesome possibility of there being no posterity to follow you, no future for thc human race. Consciously or not, this prospect must have colored your serious thoughts and your frivolous ones, your beliefs about life's continuity and the worth of planning, your ethos of social responsibility.

Whether your early introduction to the possibility of extinction may make it easier or more difficult for you to confront it, than it has bcen for those of us who came of age before Hiroshima whether that possibility is more or less paralyzing for you than for us — that I do not know. I do know, however, that you have a new vantage point, a set of difficult insights, and that we badly need that new perspective today.

I will spare you a recital of the numbers of people here in Connecticut who would be killed or dismembered in a nuclear holocaust, or who would survive it, only to die later more tortuously, or to live out dismembered and disfigured lives. I will also spare you a recital of the names of towns familiar to you which would be destroyed in a hypothetical ground zero analysis.

But I hope *you* would not spare *yourselves*. I hope I have shocked you into recognition of our peril. I hope you will think about this issue, talk about it, act on it. It needs our best minds, our varied perspectives, our keenest insights, our deepest commitment. It needs them now, before it is too late for thought and united action to work their wondrous ways in avoiding a nuclear holocaust.

William G. Bowen

William G. Bowen

COMMENCEMENT REMARKS
PRINCETON UNIVERSITY
June 8, 1982

"NO LIMITS"

By long custom, the President is given the privilege of ending the Commencement ceremony by making a few personal remarks. It is a privilege, and I am grateful for it, even as I recognize how difficult it is to express adequately the feelings that so many of us share as we come together today, with family and good friends, united in this hour by our ties to Princeton. May I ask the graduates to join those of us on the platform in a round of applause for the parents and relatives assembled here, to whom all of us owe so much.

Commencement is, of course, a time not only to look back on what I hope are many warm memories, but also a time to look ahead. This is especially so when the country is in the midst of an important debate over priorities and future directions.

Let me quickly reassure you. I do not propose to use this happy occasion to impose my own views about the desirable shape of the budget, what should and should not be done about national defense, the right level and mix of taxes, the desired rate of growth in the money supply, and so on. That would be inappropriate — even in Paul Volcker's absence and even if I were confident that I had the right answers. In any event, I am reminded of what Keynes once said: "Only one man in a thousand understands the currency question... and I meet him every day." I suspect Mr. Volcker meets him at least twice each day!

Still, I think it is appropriate — perhaps even obligatory — to say directly what I believe about certain values fundamental to our nation that are at the core of university communities. Specifically, I am concerned about our commitment, as a people, to the idea of opportunity — to the proposition that education of the highest quality ought to be available on the basis of individual qualifications, not simply financial means.

It is surprising, frightening in some respects, to see how fast national moods and norms can change. It wasn't long ago — less than 15 years — that Edward Levi, then President of the University of Chicago, was warning us not to sacrifice educational quality in our efforts to pursue an overly simple notion of what constitutes "opportunity." Excellence and opportunity were then, and are now, powerfully complementary goals. As John Gardner observed: "The good society is not one that ignores individual differences but one that deals with them wisely and humanely."

Now, just a little more than a decade later, we face a very different kind of danger. There are signs that we risk reverting to a situation in which educational opportunity is more a function of family circumstances than of qualifications. On one of my visits to Washington, I was taken aback when a Congressman told me in almost casual tones that he didn't see that it would matter much if Princeton again became a school attended largely by those of means; others, he suggested, could go elsewhere.

Why do I react so strongly — so negatively — to that way of thinking? In part, I suppose, for personal reasons. It would have been impossible for me to come to Princeton as a graduate student without generous fellowship support; and the education I received here has made an enormous difference in my life. It is for those of you who are graduating today to speak of the difference Princeton continues to make in the lives of individuals, but I shall be very surprised if a number of you in subsequent years do not provide testimony as eloquent as that of your predecessors. Just last week I saw the comment of a member of the Class of '77 whose education here was made possible through a series of scholarships. She wrote: "I am ready to give life and the world my very best efforts! Thank you, Princeton, for making so many of 'the positives' possible."

From an institutional perspective, this University has a clear interest in continuing to be open to the widest range of talent. The quality of both the undergraduate college and the Graduate School depend on our continuing to enroll the most outstanding individuals, whatever their circumstances. Otherwise, our commitment to excellence would be partial at best.

Moreover, we believe that the educational opportunities that Princeton offers are far richer for all because of the variety of students who are here. As one of our Trustees has said: "We do not learn very much, we do not grow significantly, when we are surrounded only by the likes of ourselves." Differences in background — and therefore in assumptions and in perspectives — can be disturbing and at times profoundly uncomfortable; but it is precisely such interactions that are often educational in the largest sense. The present-day diversity of the student body at Princeton is not something separate from the University's commitment to educational excellence; it is required by it.

I share the view of many that we are only at the beginnings of what it ought to be possible to achieve through personal associations and friendships in a university community that includes students from widely differing backgrounds. Do we do as well now, in these respects, as we should? Of course not. But how far we have come. And the path to further progress surely does not lie in constricting access to Princeton — or to other great universities.

In arguing for efforts — private and governmental — to sustain openness to individuals of talent, I am in no sense urging "handouts." As many here today know so well, at Princeton we expect each person, and each family, to sacrifice — to contribute up to (and some would say beyond) their own capacities before extending scholarship assistance. We do not give anything resembling "free rides." What we do is supplement personal and family contributions with additional resources so that all who qualify for admission are able to come. These institutional contributions accrue to all students, not only scholarship recipients, since even those who pay full tuition receive implicit scholarships equal to the substantial educational costs we incur in excess of the tuition rate. Far from being "handouts," investments in educational opportunity seem to me our best defense — or more properly our best offense — as we work to maintain in this country a belief that opportunity is real; that there is hope for our children, whatever the limitations under which we have lived.

Allow me a personal reminiscence. Some years ago, on the night before Commencement, I was talking with the mother of a senior. She was a woman who I knew had had no schooling beyond the seventh grade. She was surrounded that evening by family who had come from many places to be here for graduation, and in looking at all of those people she said: "You know, Mr. Bowen, my son thinks we are making too much of all this. But you must understand," she went on, "that I knew from an early age that there was a limit on what I could achieve because of my race and my education. I was determined that for my children there would be no limits."

Was her son's presence at Princeton — and his great success here — due in large measure to what she and other members of her family had given to him? Of course. But not even that family could have done it alone. It was — and is — up to all of us to help, not in a patronizing or condescending way, but with a sure sense that we are serving each other, that we are advancing common goals.

The future of this society depends, in my view, on our capacity to continue to call on the idealism of America as well as on the talents of our people. In his recent book, Theodore White has suggested that, in contrast to other, more homogeneous societies, "Americans are held together only by ideas . . . by a culture of hope." Many seem to believe that in America today the idea of opportunity is dead or dying. I don't agree. And I don't think that it will die as long as those fortunate enough to have attended universities such as this one are determined to give it long life.

Princeton is sometimes said, especially by our detractors, to be a place of privilege. In an important sense it is. So much has been given to us here: an idyllic setting, a rich history, substantial material and human resources. Yet I think we recognize that responsibility is the other side of privilege. Each of you graduating today will decide individually what use you are to make of your education. But whatever you do, I hope that you will find time in your own lives to help to build a society in which there are fewer limits on the aspirations of others — and to see that Princeton, in particular, remains a place of opportunity as well as a place of privilege.

To each of you, Godspeed.

Ernest L. Boyer

Ernest L. Boyer

"EDUCATION IN AMERICA"

I'm pleased to congratulate the Class of 1982:. I congratulate you for chosing Whittier College and for completing—with success—your academic program. I'd also like to congratulate the parents of the graduates, both for the encouragement and for the money you have given. And I know that now you hope the graduate will finally leave this fine campus and go out and get a job!

Many years ago I decided that commencement speeches are the least remembered utterances on earth. This fact was painfully driven home one day after I had delivered what I thought was a most effective speech. At the very end a graduate met me on the lawn and said my speech was so moving he had actually been inspired to write a poem. I was, of course, deeply touched until I read the poem. The young man had written:

> I love a finished speaker.
> I mean I really do.
> I don't mean one who's polished.
> I just mean one who's through.

I'd like to say to the graduates that—even if you're inspired—I'd be very pleased if no one wrote a poem.

Just 25 years ago Sputnik was projected into space. This nation was enormously distressed. Our confidence was shattered. Dwight David Eisenhower proposed something called the National Defense Education Act. In pushing this landmark legislation, the President said: "If the United States is to maintain its position of leadership and if we are further to enhance the quality of our society, we must see to it that today's young people are prepared to contribute the maximum to our future progress and strength and that we achieve the highest possible excellence."

Today the United States confronts a crisis far greater than a satellite in space. And yet, the national response is to reduce support for education. To pretend that this nation can be strong—without a vital network of public schools—is a massive miscalculation. The failure to adequately educate a new generation of Americans would be a shocking denial of their rights and a fatal undermining of the future of this nation. But how do we proceed?

The Carneqie Foundation for the Advancement of Teaching—with which I am affiliated—is conducting a study of the American high school. We still have 12 months to go, but already one issue is absolutely clear. The quality of education in this nation is inextricably linked to the quality of teaching. And if the teaching profession is diminished the nation's future is diminished too.

From the very first Americans have had an almost touching faith in education. In 1647—over 130 years before the Declaration of Independence— the Massachusetts Bay Colony passed a law requiring *every* town or village of 50 or more souls to provide at, public expense, a school master to teach the children to read and write. Literacy was too important to be left to chance and hiring a school master to serve all of the children was a public—not private—obligation.

And yet, while we have believed deeply in the process of education, Americans have been curiously ambivalent about teachers. Dan C. Lortie of the University of Chicago captured this ambivalence when he wrote: "Teaching in this country is—at once—honored and disdained, praised as dedicated service, lampooned as easy work . . . Teaching from its inception in America has occupied a special place . . . Real regard shown for those who taught has never matched professed regard."

This lack of "real regard" was colorfully described by a writer who talked about the Nebraska school he attended a century ago. He said the first teacher was run of town by a boy who used stones as weapons of assault. The second teacher met the same agony. But when he had "soundly thrashed" one boy, and the father of another, the reign of terror ended. At that time the writer said many considered the teacher "public enemy number one."

Today we don't stone our teachers, or openly run them out of town. But we do expect them to work miracles every day—and in response they get only silence from the students, pressure from the principal, occasional criticism from an irate parent, and lectures from the editorial page of the local press.

Teachers today are called upon not only to teach the "basics" but monitor the playground, police for drugs, reduce pregnancy, teach students how to drive, counsel the delinquents, and eliminate the graffiti. And when teachers fall short anywhere along the line we condemn them for not meeting our idealized expectations.

The harsh truth is that the profession of teaching in the nation is imperiled. In just eleven years—from 1969 to 1980—the number of parents who said they would like to have their child become a teacher dropped from 75 to 48 percent. Less than five percent of last year's college freshmen said teaching was their vocational preference—down almost 40 percent from ten years ago. Almost 50 percent of teachers in the public schools say they would not become a teacher if they could start again.

While teachers—nationwide—earned an average of $17,200 in 1980, sanitation workers earned $19,000, and football players signed million dollar contracts. A Texas study showed that over 20 percent of all teachers moonlight earning an annual supplement of $2,800. While moonlighting they mow lawns, baby-sit, wait on tables, and take other part-time work. The condition was captured in a recent cartoon that pictured two young people looking at a vendor on the street. The one said: "I think we should buy an apple for the teacher." The other said: "I have news for you. That is our teacher." If we continue to give greater status to standup comics than we do teachers then we will get what we deserve.

Especially disturbing is the fact that good teachers are not financially rewarded for their work. The good and bad drift along together. And to get ahead in teaching you must leave the classroom, become a counselor or principal or football coach. To achieve excellence in teaching, entrance standards must be raised, teacher preparation must improve, parents must support the schools, and state scholarships for attracting good teachers may be needed. But above all, outstanding teachers must be rewarded for their work.

Several weeks ago in *The Washington Post*, there was a poignant story of Ben Eichelberg who left teaching, he said, "because I had five classes and four preparations. During one week I had to collect tickets at the basketball game on three nights. I also had to beg for everything—even equipment for experiments—because I didn't have a science budget." He learned, he said, that the best way to satisfy the public is "to fix light fixtures and unplug kitchen sinks—not stretch the minds of children."

There is, of course, a happy side to all of this. Recently, I have been visiting high schools from coast to coast. And in every school, I find superb teachers who are doing a superb job. Several months ago I visited a junior high school in New Haven. In one classroom 25 students were huddled with their teacher reading and enthusiastically discussing Oliver Twist by Charles Dickens. This brilliant, young teacher had brought London to New Haven. These young students had identified completely with the little urban urchin as he struggled for survival. And they knew intimately every "good guy" and every 'bad guy" in the novel.

There are poor teachers to be sure. But I have talked to dozens of great teachers who enjoy their work and who take pride in what they do, and who's satisfactions come, not just from the pay check, but from the progress of their students and from recognition of a job well done. And yet, such recognition is often too little or far too late.

When I was United States Commissioner of Education, I called together 20 high school students from around the country. We spent the day talking about schools and how they should improve. Near the end, I asked the students to grade the teachers they had had—from A to F. When everyone had responded we ended with an above average grade—a solid "B" at least. And all the students said that they had at least one teacher who was "absolutely tops."

Then I asked the crucial question: "How many of you ever thanked a teacher?" Not one hand went up: As one student put it, "It's just not the thing to do." These high school students had been with dozens of teachers every day for four years and yet not once—even after an exciting session—did a student stop by the teacher's desk or drop a note to say "Thank you very much."

Several months ago, I was having dinner with Father Timothy Healy of Georgetown University and we got on this subject of teacher recognition. Father Healy said that about two years ago he called 15 students into his office. All were graduates of Bronx High School of Science and he asked who was the best high school teacher they had had. They did agree—quite quickly and Father Healy called the principal at Bronx High School to make sure the students weren't giving him a fictitious name. Sure enough, there was such a teacher who had been there for many years. "Yes," the principal said, "he is outstanding."

That spring at commencement time Father Healy said, "I would like to introduce a candidate for an honorary degree. He teaches at Bronx High School of Science. He is one of the great educators who has made Georgetown possible." The audience was deeply moved. And the university faculty was reminded that their success depends upon great teaching in the schools.

I am enormously pleased that many of you who graduate today are prospective teachers. You have chosen one of life's noblest professions. You bring credit to your alma mater. And you should teach with confidence and pride.

To those of you who have other plans, we are proud of you as well. I am confident you, too, will be successful in your chosen field. I do suggest, however, that in the days ahead you support the schools. And remember to say "thank you" to those who teach your children.

James Agee said on one occasion that "for every child who is born, under no matter what circumstance, the potential of the human race is born again." Those who teach our children are the potential of the human race. And, I believe, deserving of our recognition and support.

Lewis M. Branscomb

Lewis M. Branscomb

COMMENCEMENT ADDRESS
PACE UNIVERSITY
June 5, 1982

"BETTER MANAGEMENT
FOR AMERICAN ENTERPRISE"

I am very proud to become associated today with graduates from Pace University's Lubin Graduate School of Business, as a new degree holder from this fine institution.

The pride with which I accept the Honorary Degree conferred on me is amplified by the admiration I have for you who have earned yours through hard work and high dedication.

While I was preparing these remarks, someone reminded me that almost nobody listens to a commencement address except, perhaps, a few parents engaged in one last effort to get something for their money.

As a scientist invited to a business school commencement, my concern deepened when I recalled what happened a year ago when Virginia Tech's class of '81 gathered for their graduation ceremonies, and the exuberance of the occasion led to chants as the degrees were conferred.

First, graduates of the College of Engineering rose en masse, enthusiastically chanting, "We've got jobs! We've got jobs!"

To which the graduates of the College of Business cheerfully responded, "Working for us! Working for us!"

I'm glad you're laughing . . . because the message I have for you today is: If that continues to be the model of relationships between managements and professionals, we're all going to be out of work.

Pace students and graduates of all ages and backgrounds have a reputation for high motivation. Very few of you came to Pace to "find yourselves." You know where you are going.

And that's fortunate. Because if any of you would like to live a quiet, peaceful, uneventful life, you are not only living at the wrong time — you studied the wrong field.

Commencement speakers used to tell graduates that the future was theirs. If I were to say that today, you couldn't be sure if it was a promise, or a threat.

Never since World War II has the U.S. business community been so challenged, nor has it had such an opportunity to prove what it can do. The *challenge* comes no longer from down the street, but from around the world . . . in Japan, Europe, and elsewhere, where we face competitors with growing skills and, above all, higher productivity trends than we have.

To put the effect of that in an historical context, consider that all during the period from 1870 to 1950 the annual growth rate of U.S. productivity was only six-to-eight tenths of one percent higher than in the United Kingdom, West Germany, and Japan. That small difference, compounded over 80 years, was the decisive difference that made the United States the world's economic and political leader.

Now, remembering that in the last three years we have actually had a net decline in productivity, imagine what the world will be like in only another 10 years if we should continue to have negative productivity differences, not of point-six percent, but of three, four, and five full percentage points, compounded, versus the rest of the world.

What will we be by 1990, remembering, too, that productivity correlates almost perfectly with real income, so we are talking here about the American people's standard of living — not to mention our national security. Let's take a look at six things it will take to make America fully competitive again. For I am not a pessimist. I am persuaded that whatever Americans put their minds to, they can accomplish.

The first requirement is: *no complacency.*

Perhaps, we Americans believed what a worried Frenchman named Servan-Schreiber wrote 10 years ago about America's overwhelming industrial might — the power of U.S. management, technology, and skill to sweep all others off the board. Perhaps, we have been resting on our oars — not really making an effort ... while our competitors have been making tremendous efforts — working very hard.

If so, that would be going down a very slippery slope. For even my own industry, with its prodigious productivity record, is being challenged. The U.S. is still world leader in computers, but the Japanese have declared their determination to achieve technological parity, if not superiority — whatever the resources required, and however long it may take.

And given their success elsewhere, the U.S. computer industry has reason to take the challenge seriously.

Secondly, *no excuses.*

Government regulation, for example, is a problem, but it's not the reason American industry has productivity troubles. After all, where we are uncompetitive in our own markets, vis-a-vis, Japanese automobiles or televisions, our competitors have to satisfy U.S. regulatory requirements just as our own companies do.

Consider, too, how U.S. and Japanese companies typically responded to the laws on auto emissions and miles-per-gallon requirements: American manufacturers sent their lawyers to Washington to get the rules changed or delayed; the Japanese sent engineers to find out what the rules were, and to lay plans for satisfying them.

So, although the Government has been guilty of needlessly complex and bureaucratic regulation, let's not try to pin any *single* villain with the blame:

- Our nation's business executives for being insufficiently visionary;

- Labor for being too impatient or too reluctant to accept change;

- Banks for being too conservative;

- Or engineering and business schools for being too theoretical.

Yet, all these trends — and others — taken together, spell trouble.

Number three: *stay flexible.*

This continues to be an American strength. We almost make a religion out of change . . . out of being ready to change tactics — to roll with the punches. That's what it took to build a nation. It's consistent with our innovative spirit, and those capabilities are a strong by-product of the process of management we practice — a process that is, above all, pragmatic, looks at financial results, does not get confused by hopes and dreams, but faces realities. Thus, American companies find it relatively easy to reorganize themselves, to shift course, to change business direction.

In a world of rapid change, that's a big asset. In fact, it is that asset, I believe, that the Europeans most envied when they were examining the American system of management and comparing it with their own — which was very tradition-bound.

If you happen to find yourself fascinated with, and very adept at Pac-Man and other video games, you probably have the kind of skills that *Business Week* suggests a business leader needs in a rapidly changing world. The target constantly moves; new opponents zoom in from various vectors. Playing the game well requires heightened reflexes, plus the ability to anticipate changes and to make fast, rational decisions. As a matter of fact, I think American business executives are traditionally so much more flexible than their European, or even Japanese counterparts, that sometimes they are too flexible — too willing to accept defeat when they suffer a temporary reverse on a strategic path.

Point number four: *continue to lead in the technology of management.*

From the point of view of quantitative theories of management and management processes, the U.S. business community surely leads the world. And that accounts in no small measure for the spectacular success of our computer industry . . . because if it weren't for the success American business executives have had in using computers profitably to help them manage their businesses and achieve productivity, the computer industry would not have grown at anything like the rate it did.

Mastery of information systems support and management of the data, on the basis of which a business is run, are the key — not only to productivity, but also to control of a business and up-to-date knowledge of its status. That, of course, is a prerequisite to taking advantage of a propensity for flexibility . . . because if you don't know what's happening in your business on an up-to-date basis, then you really can't have the confidence to make the hard decisions quickly. To that end, I'm sure you recognize that tools of the management trade are knowledge-based tools. And these will become more and more essential to you throughout your professional life.

Fifth: *people skills.*

Nothing is more important in business or any other walk of life than how successfully you relate to other people. Your training has designed you to be a leader of people, and you have probably heard a lot more than you want to hear from people who think they can tell you how to do that. There's an enormous amount of free advice available to you on managing people. Most of it you will find doesn't fit your situation. Let me give you two examples:

The first is a superb little book by John Jay, called "Management According to Machiavelli."

It's a relatively recent book, in which the author derives lessons for modern corporate management from the descriptions in Machiavelli's "The Prince" of techniques for the seizure, plunder, and establishment of a colonial government in conquered provinces. From this, Jay draws lessons on how you should organize a takeover or a divestiture, and what to do with the management people you acquire.

The advice available to you ranges all the way from that amusing book to a 337-year-old book on Samurai sword strategy, called "A Book of Five Rings," which became a best seller when its American publisher put out the word that many Japanese businessmen use this book as a guide for business practice. I hear it's very popular in American business schools these days.

One thing I'm sure of is that wholesale imitation of Japanese customs, which are rooted in their culture and don't travel well, will not help here. What we can and should emulate, however, is their success in making people productive. Above all, the Japanese accord high value to education, to intelligent and dedicated hard work. I recently asked a Japanese colleague what was the greatest strength of his computer group.

"Our people are very innovative," he replied.

"What do you mean by 'innovative'?" I inquired.

He explained, "Each day, each engineer in this laboratory comes to work knowing precisely what the goal is for the day, and he doesn't go home until it is achieved. We are very *innovative*."

Well, as you know, that's not innovation; that's commitment, and commitment will take you a long way.

My sixth and final point is: *know more about your business than anybody else in the world.*

Earlier this week, at Rensselaer Polytechnic Institute, a senior executive of Cincinnati-Milicron and I were being interviewed by the press about the problems of modern American business management.

One reporter asked whether we believed the best system of management is one in which professional managers work in many different kinds of companies, as they move from one job to another of increasing responsibility — thus acquiring very broad management experience . . . or, did we believe more strongly in people learning a business from the bottom up, and in promoting management from within an enterprise?

My answer and that of my colleague were unequivocal: We both believe the latter path is the necessary way to acquire sufficient depth of expertise in a business to become an effective general manager. That's not to say there aren't lots of people in general management in this country who are smart enough that if they leave one business and go to another, they can't learn the second business in a hurry. Nor is it to suggest that the not-invented-here syndrome isn't a major hazard that threatens objectivity of judgment for those who spend a lifetime within a single business.

But if you truly believe you have the propensity to be flexible and to accept change . . . and you keep your eyes open to what's really going on in your business and around it . . . you'll find that the biggest difference between an American company and a Japanese company is the hundred-percent dedication of the Japanese company to basing their progress on knowledge and communication.

IBM founder, Thomas J. Watson, Sr., is said to have outlawed organization charts when he ran the company. It was his view that people drew organization charts primarily to avoid responsibility — to be able to say that a problem didn't fall within their box on the chart.

Another story told in IBM is about Mr. Watson's arrival at an IBM branch office in a small town. As he approached the front door, he saw a dirty hand-print on the glass, where someone had pushed the door open. Mr. Watson, it is said, reprimanded two individuals: the branch manager, who was responsible for the proper appearance of the office; and the last IBMer who walked through that door — and didn't do anything about the hand-print.

His view was, every IBMer should see the Corporation's interest as a whole; if he saw a problem that was not his personal responsibility, it nevertheless was his responsibility to call it to the attention of someone equipped to do something about it.

That sort of collective responsibility for the well-being of the enterprise is a cornerstone of Japanese attitude. And it's not a foreign attitude in the United States. Indeed, it's an old tradition in IBM.

You will observe from what you read about the Japanese consensus style of decision-making, that it is not the clumsy process of consultation it might appear. It is, in fact, a sophisticated process for gathering detailed information and understanding, about alternative decisions . . . so that when the final decision is made, everyone is not only committed to it, but understands it in detail.

A second problem is the importance of management's having *depth* knowledge of every aspect of the business.

Obviously, the professionals in a business have to have this expertise. But too often managements assume that it is unnecessary for them to share the depth of knowledge their professionals have . . . because they believe all they have to do is choose between recommendations made by the professionals.

When my son was five years old, a lady asked him, "Sonny-boy, what do you want to be when you grow up?"

And he answered, "I want to be a manufacturer of futuristic automobiles."

The lady, trying to be helpful, said, "Oh, that's wonderful! That means you'll have to study arithmetic and science and engineering."

He looked at her with disdain and said "No. If I need any of that I'll hire engineers to do it."

That, ladies and gentlemen, is one of the things that's wrong with American attitudes toward business.

I was recently in a discussion with a number of business leaders on the role of the chief executive in a modern corporation. One man made the point that a chief executive should consider every major segment of his business as potentially available for sale to another corporation. After all, such a segment might fit better into the structure of another company, and, therefore, be worth more for sale than its accounting value to the present owner.

That thought was picked up by Alan Greenspan who warmed to the point, saying, yes, the role of the chief executive is that of a portfolio manager who should view the segments of his business as elements to be managed as you would an investment portfolio — in a completely cold-eyed way with a view to financial return. I responded that I thought that point of view had contributed much to the weak performance of American businesses which found themselves in competition with Japanese corporations having a much more single-minded purpose in life.

In such an environment, it is essential that the chief executive view himself as the best leader in the world of a business dedicated to a specific purpose. He should view his principal responsibility as training and motivating a team of hundreds or thousands of people, who share with him that special dedication and commitment to understanding every detail of their business and of its competitive environment. Why? So they can be the best experts in the world on the substance of that enterprise.

If you approach your business careers from this point of view, you will stand out from the crowd, and your superiors will very quickly pick you out as someone who has a lot more to offer the business than simply a fine mastery of management techniques and a good attitude toward other people.

For that's what great business success is based on. That's what was behind the spectacular early growth of companies like IBM and Polaroid and Xerox ... where the top leadership created the business, in a sense, with their own two hands, and had a personal commitment to its success — not just the success of business in general — that took them over the hard spots and enabled them to invest for the long-term future.

A manager, it has been said, is a person who imagines the future . . . and persuades it to happen. French author, Andre Gide once wrote:

> "The possible and the future are one. All that is possible is striving to come into being; and all that can be . . . will be, if only man helps."

That will be your job as managers. To help what can be to be . . . to help the possible and the future become one.

Thank you . . . congratulations . . . and best of luck!

Urie Bronfenbrenner

Urie Bronfenbrenner

COMMENCEMENT ADDRESS
BRIGHAM YOUNG UNIVERSITY
August 20, 1982

"CONTINUITY OF VALUES
IN A CHANGING WORLD"

It is a special privilege, and a deeply moving experience, to stand before you in the shadow of these majestic mountains and to be honored by an academic institution representing a spiritual tradition that, from its very beginnings, has never ceased to accord the highest value to the concerns that have been at the center of my professional and personal life—the well-being of families and children. In such a context, it is an even greater privilege, and an awesome responsibility, to address a new generation in the presence of the old, and to honor both. For the achievement that we celebrate here today is, in a profound sense, the work of hands, hearts, and minds joined across time—the shared accomplishment of parents and their children, of teachers and their students, each giving from one to the other over the years and over the generations.

When I was a child, my father used to say to me, "Remember, little one, you are the people in your life." At the time, I did not understand what he meant. I took it as his funny, grown-up way of trying to tell me how important *I* was. It was not until I grew older, indeed not until I became a parent myself, that the meaning became clear to me, or so I thought. What he was saying, said I at 35, is that children become what they are through the care and attention of their parents. "Honor thy father and thy mother," said I to the children, forgetting to cite chapter and verse.

But then, as I grew older still, there came a sobering realization. It was not only the older generation that had given me such skills and talents as I had— for these skills and talents were still not wholly mine. To the extent that they were at my disposal, it was because they were being constantly sustained, shaped, and even further enhanced by those around me, by "the people in my life." First and foremost among these was my wife. As one of my European friends put it, not recognizing the double meaning, "Without her, you would be impossible." He is probably right, on both counts. But then a discovery even more difficult to accept. Gradually I began to realize that my children had been teaching me, not only recently as magically capable and congenial adult companions, but all the way along, from the very first moment of their lives.

Moreover, as teachers, they had been doing an expert job right from the beginning—always coming up with a more colorful way to present the lesson. The main problem was a common one in educational experience; I, the pupil, didn't always pay attention, especially at the beginning. I figured my wife would tell me all about it. Fortunately, she refused. She was, and is, a woman ahead of her time. She just kept after me to be a parent in my own right. So I didn't miss out learning what we all worry about these days—the basic skills—in this case, the fundamental knowledge and know-how that I would need for the rest of my life—not just as a parent, but—to no lesser degree—as a worker on the job, as a citizen, and as a human being. It is your parents who help you to develop as a child, but it is your children who teach you how to become a mature adult, if you are willing to learn.

What is all this about? Why am I saying these things to you who are graduating today? Let me explain. I am just trying to help you to get your degree. You didn't know it, but before you can receive your diploma from this great university, you still have one more requirement to complete. It is a crash course in the one subject that all of you need to master for success in your chosen field, whatever it may be. Whatever your specialty, your field will be drawing heavily on my field: human development and family studies. That holds for whatever work you will be doing, including that ominous option that nowadays too often becomes the only one—no work at all.

But let's not worry about that now. We still have the present to deal with and do not have much time left to complete the course, so that you can graduate. Actually, we have already finished the first part, which deals with the theory. Now we go on to part two,which is concerned with application and will take a bit longer. That's because, whenever you move from theory to practice, things get more complicated and more controversial. To make it easier for you, let me give you two working principles as a practical guide.

I see you have forgotten your notebooks, so you will have to use your minds instead. I hope you have brought those along because you will be needing them, especially after you leave here.

Here is the first working principle:

Principle 1: In the last few years, scientists have confirmed what some people believed even without the scientific facts to back them up. *The most efficient, humane, and by far the most economical system known for making and keeping human beings human is the family.* By "making human beings human" I mean producing people who are competent and compassionate members of their society. Any other methods for doing that—and there are some—just don't do the job as well. First, they are less efficient. By that I mean they take even longer, are much less reliable, and, alas, make more errors.

These other methods are also less humane—more likely to involve disregard of human feelings, and abuse not only of children but also of adult men and women of all ages. If you think that the abuse of children and adults is high and rising in families, which it is, you should look at the data on institutions, private as well as public. But above all, these other methods are less economical; they cost more money. And by that hard-nosed, contemporary criterion, the family is hard to beat. First of all, there are no labor costs. It is all done for free. Also, you don't have to pay for recruiting staff—training, workman's compensation or paid vacations. All those costs are met, would you believe?—by the employees themselves. It is like the good old days.

So there's our first working principle: families are the best and the cheapest. But there's a catch. (There's always a catch.) Families can only work their magic under certain conditions. And that brings us to our second working principle.

Principle 2: For a family to be able to develop children into competent and compassionate human beings requires public policies, practices, and systems of belief that insure opportunity, status, resources, encouragement, example, stability, and above all, time for parenthood, primarily by parents, but also by all other adults in the society. At this juncture, you may well ask how old are the children referred to in the preceding statement. The point is debatable, but I would suggest anyone under the age of, say, 89. For what we have been talking about is the human condition, and what we are saying is that, throughout all our lives, we need each other. We need each other at two related levels. There is a word for each of these levels in every language. In the tongue that you and I speak, those words are *family* and *community*. When uttered beneath these majestic mountains, these words have a special resonance, since here, for more than a century, they have been translated into action sustained on a daily basis to this very hour. "This is the place."

But though the values of family and community may continue to be honored and observed in this and in other areas of our country, this can hardly be said for the nation as a whole. As you know, in recent years the rate of divorce in our country has been skyrocketing. Today, as we meet here together, more than one fifth of the nation's children are living in single parent homes. If the family is such a wonderful system for making and keeping human beings human, why are so many human beings breaking up the families that they have? We are just beginning to understand the nature of these disruptive forces, and some of them are rather ominous. For example, family breakup tends to increase in periods of economic decline, especially if the father loses his job. Of course, the main reason why parents separate is because they can't get along with each other. But shouldn't they be thinking more about their children? It is here that, when one looks at the data, the issue becomes more complex. For example, several investigators have compared youngsters from divorced families with children whose parents decided to stay together despite high levels of marital dissatisfaction and conflict. The results of the study revealed that the latter situation might have even more detrimental effects on children than the former. But perhaps the most disconcerting data came from some recent research indicating that the degree of stress and frustration reported by an average group of married mothers was higher than that for a matched sample of single-parent women who had been divorced for several years. Such findings suggest that we may be creating a society in which it is easier to maintain the home and raise children in a split family than in one that stays together. The fault lies not with the family, but with the community and the society that has forgotten who and where they are. If raising children in a split family is easier, many parents may simply be discovering this reality and acting accordingly. A key question, of course, is what the long-range effects of these arrangements may be both for children and for parents. Here the evidence is not yet in, but even if it were, it would not constitute an adequate basis for decision. There are other and more important values than those of science.

But what of the second and even more sweeping change that has been taking place in American family life? As you know, with each succeeding year, more and more mothers are going to work outside the home. Just a few years ago, this pattern became the new American norm, with the majority of the nation's mothers in the labor force. The proportion today is close to 60 percent with the rate increasing most rapidly for mothers of preschoolers and infants.

If parenthood is so important, why are so many women leaving home to go to work? Are we creating a society in which mothers no longer care about their children? One of the problems with being a researcher is that the data can contradict some of your most strongly held personal beliefs. Like most parents of my generation, I believed, with considerable feeling, that children, especially when they are young, needed to have their mother's care fulltime. But the research data do not back me up, at least at the simple-minded level at which I was thinking about the issue. It turns out that, after one controls for other relevant factors, like parent's education and social status, children whose mothers are in the labor force don't look any different from those whose mothers work at home for free. I was so sure that they would that I did a study of my own, and I couldn't make it come out the way I wanted. Several studies, however, have broken the phenomenon down a bit further and found a group of youngsters who appear to be at something of an advantage—those whose mothers are working, but only part-time. On a variety of criteria these children look better than those whose mothers were either fully employed or not working outside the home. A possible explanation is suggested by the fact, in comparison with mothers working only part-time, the other two groups reported more stress and dissatisfaction in their lives, more loneliness, more lack of recognition of them as human beings. This was true both for those mothers who were employed in a fulltime job and for those who remained at home.

Finally, there is a small number of researches suggesting that, especially among middle-class families, mother's full-time employment may have a somewhat negative effect on boys, but a positive influence on girls. The sons of such mothers did not do quite as well in school, but the daughters were more highly motivated and had higher self-esteem. The differences were not very big, however, and were dwarfed by another factor; namely, whether the mother preferred to work, or to remain at home. If she could have her preference, whichever way it was, it turned out better for the children. Once again, a caution, I'm not saying that's the way things ought to be, but this is the way things are today in the kind of society we are creating.

But none of these developments were as important as the third major change that has been occurring in the lives of American families. Today, it is taking place even more rapidly than the other two and is even more powerful in its consequences. Yet, I wager that few in this great audience can identify what it is. It eludes identification, not because it is difficult to see, but because we do not wish to see it, for it contradicts one of the most cherished hopes and convictions of the American dream.

I refer to the growing gap between the poor families in our country and all the rest of us. Just this month, there appeared a report issued by our National Academy of Sciences. In it there is a graph showing how well the nation's families with young children have kept up with inflation between 1975 and 1980, the last year for which data were available. It turns out that two-parent families in the top four-fifths of the economic distribution were doing quite well, for their incomes were keeping up with the cost of living. The bottom fifth, however, was falling behind at an accelerating rate.

But these intact families were not the group most disadvantaged by the rising cost of living. Falling behind much faster and starting from a far lower base are all single-parent mothers in our country with children under six. They ended up in 1980 with a median income of $5,046. That means half of them had to get along on less. The facts I have been giving alert us to one of the principal reasons why more and more mothers, especially those who are single parents, are going to work; they need the money to sustain their families. That is the kind of society we are creating.

What is the net effect of these economic changes on American families? One answer to this question is revealed in the characteristically faceless facts and figures presented in the official census report on family income for 1980. It documents what it describes as "the largest decline in family income in the post-World War II period," resulting in the addition of 29.3 million persons below the poverty level, for a total of 13 percent of the U.S. population. As revealed in the accompanying tables, however, the poverty rates for children were even higher, especially for the very young. For example, the figures for family income in 1981 have just come out. They reveal that, as of March of last year, more than a fifth (22%) of all children in America under three years of age were living in families below the poverty line.

What happens to young children living in such circumstances? The immediate consequences are well known. They take their toll on both children and their parents in the form of illness, family strife, and child abuse, among other equally inhuman things. Indeed, the effects of the current economic trend have already begun to hit the headlines. Here is a recent Associated Press report of a well designed study carried out by a trio of researchers, one of whom, I am proud to say, is one of my former students. The group investigated the effects of inflation on 8,000 families in California. The lead of the article reads: "the toll of children battered, maimed, and slain by parents and other relatives is climbing, and experts say the economy—especially unemployment—appears to be the key factor."

There are also data showing longer-range effects. My colleague at Cornell, Glen Elder, followed the life course of two groups of children whose families were victims of the Great Depression during the 1930s. The first group were teenagers when their families experienced economic loss. Surprisingly, for these youngsters, economic deprivation appeared to have a positive effect on their subsequent development. They did better in school, were more likely to go to college, had happier marriages, and exhibited more successful work careers. Elder concludes that financial misfortune forced the family to mobilize its own human resources, including those of its teenagers; the youths had to take on new responsibilities to work toward the goal of getting and keeping the family on its feet. In the words of the banished duke, "Sweet are the uses of adversity" (W. Shakespeare, *As You Like It*, act 2, scene 1).

But adversity was not so sweet for the second group of children who were of school age when their families were hit by the Depression. By contrast, these youngsters subsequently did less well in school, showed less stable family and work histories, and exhibited more emotional and social difficulties, some still apparent now when they are in their late middle age.

Such findings give added significance to the growing number of children being cast into poverty in our own time. They also raise questions about the severe cuts being proposed and put in force affecting programs and resources made available to low-income families and their children in our country. There can be no question that as a nation we must learn to live within our means; to do otherwise is to court national disaster. It is also clear that some existing programs have been wasteful, ineffective, and severely criticized even by the very families they were supposed to help. But there are other programs that have been working and are now showing important long-range constructive effects. These successful approaches have two distinctive features. First, they provide concrete resources and services that are needed by family members, such as medical care, food, and education. Second, instead of labeling families as inadequate and making them dependent, these strategies treat their recipients as competent human beings who can and do take active responsibility for themselves and for their children. Such programs, like the well-known and successful project Head Start, are building family and community; yet, these programs too are being cut.

But even more destructive is our failure to recognize the importance of jobs for the survival of families, not only economically, but—what is even more important—psychologically. By tolerating growing unemployment now, we risk creating new generations of unemployable Americans in the years ahead. The most effective programs for strengthening our families and children are those that create jobs. Economize we must, but in doing so, we must not betray our distinctive values and strengths as a nation.

There are those who say that that is exactly what we are doing, that we Americans have ceased to care about each other. Such critics claim to see the rise of a new separatism across the land, a turning away from a concern with the problems of others to a preoccupation with maintaining and maximizing the status and power of one's own particular group. To be sure, such phenomena are occurring in some segments of our society, but I do not believe that they constitute the broader and deeper streams and strengths of our nation. They are merely filling a vacuum during a period of temporary inertia in the historical movement of our nation in pursuit of its ideals. At this moment, the best of America is conscience-stricken and confused. We are momentarily immobilized by the conflict between the distinctive values derived from our past and the dissonant realities created by the economic and social changes taking place not only in our country but around the Western world.

This brings me back to my opening theme. I had said that it was a special privilege and an awesome responsibility to deliver a commencement address at this particular place and at this particular time. For we are met here today at a critical period in the history of our nation. The vacuum created by our temporary inertia leaves the field open to destructive forces that can divide us as a people. Once again the Union is threatened, not the political union of the states, but the spiritual union of the basic parts of our pluralistic society—the diverse families, communities, generations, and religious and cultural groups that make the magic of America. To preserve that union, we must recognize and reconcile two seemingly conflicting truths. The first truth is one that this institution and the spiritual tradition from which it springs have steadfastly nourished here in these hills and in the world beyond. The truth affirms the unique power of family and community to create and sustain competent and compassionate human beings. To disregard that truth, as our nation is presently in danger of doing, is to undermine the greatest source of our strength as a people and our future as a republic. But there is a second truth equally fateful for our national survival and growth. American families and American communities are facing new economic and social realities that force our basic institutions to take new forms to adapt. What forms are best suited to these new realities we do not yet know, but two facts are sure: families must be their foundation; and families are wherever the children are. It is there that we must focus our resources and value commitments. As a nation, we are no longer as rich in resources as we once were, but we have neglected our value commitments even more. To renew our national strength, we must turn to those institutions in our society who have kept the faith, and challenge them to adapt that faith to a changing America and a changing world. It is a challenge to be met by the younger and the older generations together. As today's ceremony testifies, such institutions as this one are alive and well in America today. "This is the place," and this is the time. Thank you.

Art Buchwald

Art Buchwald

COMMENCEMENT REMARKS
COLLEGE OF WILLIAM AND MARY
May 11, 1980

My fellow Indians, it is a great honor for me to be here today to address the 1980 graduating class of William and Mary consisting of 776 men and 830 persons. Before I begin I think it only fair that since you gave your mothers such a rousing hand that you also applaud your fathers who coughed up the outrageous tuition for the last four years so let's hear it for your fathers. Now I think we should add for the faculty who had to put up with you while your mothers and fathers thought you were getting an education.

Now I don't want to be here under false pretenses. I don't have any use for education and I'll explain why. When I was sixteen years old World War II started and I was afraid it would be over before I got in. So I ran away from high school and joined the Marine Corps. While I was in the Marines I realized that if I ever hoped to get out, I'd better go to college. I was going to go to night high school and make up the credits and then go to college but I didn't know what I needed. So I went down to the University of Southern California and I got in line with 4,000 ex-G.I.s. It took about four hours to get up to the head of the line. I finally got up there and I said "I would like to" and the woman said, "Fill this out." I said, "Yes ma'am" and she said "What do you want to take?" and I said "I don't care." She said, "English," and I said "sounds good," and she said, "math," and I said "why not?." She said "French" and I said "O.K." She said "have it stamped over there." When I went to the next desk the man stamped it and I was in college. A year went by and they called me in and said "you don't have a high school diploma." I said, "I know." They said, "Then you're not supposed to be in college." I said, "I know. What do you want me to do now?" They said, "We'll make you a special student." I said, "What does that mean?" They said, "You can't work for a degree." I said, "Well, that's O.K., I don't have a high school diploma, there's no sense having a college degree." And I went for three years and had a ball, but I had my revenge, Last year the University of Southern California made me alumnus of the year. So all of you have been wasting your time.

I am not here today to bring you a message of doom. I have been studying the situation closely and have come to the conclusion that the class of 1980 is the luckiest class that ever graduated and possibly the last. Not long ago President Carter told you that we are running out of oil and gas and this will require all of you to change your lifestyles. The American Dream of owning the biggest car on the block has been shattered. I know many of you are bitter at our generation for using up all our oil reserves but I would like to remind you of one thing. It was our oil and our gas and we could do anything we wanted with it. Your generation has to find its own oil. I could help you find it because I know where it is but it would take all the fun out for you. You are the generation of Watergate and Three-Mile Island. You were raised on Star Wars and the Grateful Dead. Walter Cronkite is your godfather and Nixon was your President. You had swine flu shots and H.E.W. said you drank too much. But I don't feel sorry for you and I told President Carter just the other day after Bible class, we never promised you a Rose Garden.

The tendency in this country is to wring your hands and say that everything is rotten but I don't feel that way. I am basically an optimist. Otherwise, I would never fly Allegheny Airlines. I don't know if this is the best of times or the worst of times but I can assure you of this: it's the only time you've got. So you can either pick your expletive, or sit on your expletive deleted or go out and pick a daisy. We seem to be going through a period of nostalgia and everyone thinks that yesterday was better than today. I personally don't think it was and I would advise you not to wait ten years from now before admitting that today was great. If you are hung up on nostalgia pretend today is yesterday and just go out and have one hell of a time.

I know all of you are worried about jobs but I can assure you out of this class of 1,606 graduates that at least 130 of you are going to find work. I do happen to know who you are but I am not at liberty to tell you. I know in this class of 1980 you are all going in different directions. Some are going to become lawyers which is an honorable undertaking and the second oldest profession in the world. Some of you are going to become scientists and others of you are going to become doctors and those of you who go out for the money are probably going to become teachers. And, God forbid, maybe even some of you will decide to become journalists. The media has been under attack for some time in this country. In a recent survey people rated newspapermen even lower than garbage men in the public's esteem. Now I think this is unfair. I know many newspapermen who would make good garbage men, but I don't know one garbage man who would make a good newspaper man. Whatever you do you will face a credibility gap. If you choose to be President of the United States you will be regarded with suspicion. I know because I have travelled all over this land and everywhere I go people ask the same question: Why out of a country of 220 million people can't we find an outstanding person to run for President? Well, I'm going to explain it to you today.

There are 144 million people over the age of 18 who are eligible to vote.

But at the moment there are only 99 million registered voters. Out of this 99 million, 38 million are under 35 years of age and are therefore ineligible to run for the Presidency. Now 1 million were not born in this country so they can't run either. This still leaves us 60 million people to choose from. But about half this number are women and whether we like it or not this country is not ready for a woman president for at least six months. This leaves us roughly 29 million Presidential prospects. We have to take off 3 million because they are afraid to fly. Now you can't have a President of the United States who is afraid to fly so we are down to 26 million. We have to take off 2 million because their wives don't want to move to Washington. And there are 2 million more who are being audited by the IRS. And then there are 12 million who are mentioned in Elizabeth Ray's book. So we are down to 7 million. Surely, you say, we can find one outstanding person in 7 million. We could, except this country will never accept a President who has had a mental disorder or who has been treated by a psychiatrist. There have been 6,999,998 people in this country who have had psychiatric treatment. So last time this left us with a peanut farmer from Georgia and a guy who played football without a helmet.

There is a lot of discussion about students these days and whether they have it or not. Well, I have a lot of faith in students because I speak on college campuses and they have their heads together and they are thinking right. And I was talking to an English major just yesterday here on campus and we got to discussing Hamlet. And I said to him, "Suppose you were a prince of Denmark and you came back from school to discover your uncle had murdered your father and married your mother and you fell in love with a beautiful girl named Ophelia and mistakenly murdered her father. And then Ophelia went crazy and drowned in a brook. What would you do?" And he thought for a minute and he said, "I guess I'd go for my Master's degree."

I don't believe this class faces any problem once you graduate because we the older generation have given you a perfect world and we don't want you to louse it up. A few of you might ask how can one cope with life when every day we are given more and more bad news. And I have been searching for this answer for years and I finally found it lask week in, of all places, the Playboy Mansion in California. I asked Hugh Hefner, the publisher of *Playboy,* I said, "Hugh, I am talking to William and Mary next week, what do I tell them?" And Hefner said, "Tell them to stay in bed. If you never get out of bed nobody can hurt you." I said, "Is that all there is to it?" and he said, "sure. Just keep the covers over you and everything will be all right." I think there is a message in this for all of you. When things look the blackest, when everything seems to be going wrong, just go to bed and stay there. You'll be amazed how small your problems look compared to those people who are still walking around. As Rosie Ruiz said after the Boston Marathon, "It isn't whether you run the race or not, it's crossing the finishing line that count."

Though I live in Washington I am not a cynic and my final message to you today is that no matter what you read in the newspapers or see on television, I assure you that we are all going to make it. For two hundred and four years this country has muddled through one crisis after another and we have done it without changing our form of government and despite all its flaws it is a very interesting thing happening in the world today. Although there are no restrictions on anyone emigrating from the United States, no one seems to be leaving. It is just the opposite. All the boats and planes filled with political refugees are heading this way. America with all its imperfections is still the freest country on this planet and I am counting on every person in this graduating class to make sure you damn well keep it that way.

Now I could have said something very profound today but you would have forgotten it in twenty minutes. So I chose to give this kind of speech instead so that in twenty years from now when your children ask you what you did on graduation day, you can at least say, "I laughed."

Thank you.

Maurice C. Clifford

Maurice C. Clifford

COMMENCEMENT ADDRESS
HAMILTON COLLEGE
May 23, 1982

As I considered what I would say today, my mind went back to my undergraduate days, and I decided to tell you a story. It's a story from the past, from a long time ago, and it is a true story.

Once upon a time . . . a long time ago . . . a father drove onto this campus in a shiny, secondhand Ford roadster, an ancient wardrobe trunk standing up in the rumble seat. He was bringing his son, a boy just turned seventeen, to start his freshman year. The day before, they had journeyed up from Washington, and that night the boy had slept for the first time away from a family home. Now, in mid-morning, father and son found their way to North College, and unloaded the car.

In a little while, the father had to start the long drive back, and they parted . . . stiff upper lip. The boy went up to 7 North, where he was to live alone. Never had he stayed in such unfamiliar surroundings. He sat on the bed and gazed out over the lawn, his spirits sinking. Already he missed his father, and soon he found himself longing for his mother and his grandmother and his sister, and dreaming of the warmth and comfort of their family circle, and then came the tears.

He knew almost nothing about this school. He didn't know anyone who had ever seen Hamilton College. But sitting alone in his room that morning, he knew one thing for sure—he knew that he was a long, long, way from home.

All his life, until that first day here, he had lived under racial segregation. In his home city, the nation's capital, he had been barred, like all colored people—except foreigners—from sitting in a downtown movie theatre. He couldn't eat a hot dog in Woolworth's ten cent store, couldn't go into a barber shop downtown. In a department store, his mother wasn't permitted to try on a hat, and in some of the shops on F Street they'd be told, "We don't serve colored here." For their kind, there were separate water fountains, separate schools, separate wards in hospitals, separate graveyards.

In all his seventeen years, the boy had had but two contacts with youth of another race. One year, his parents rented a friend's vacation cottage in the country. All summer he played with the farm boy across the road, learning the lessons farm boys teach city boys—lessons like not to stand too close during the milking, unless you want to get warm milk in your eye—and how to tell a growing carrot by its top, and pull it up, knock off the dirt, and have a snack. Their friendship ended with the summer.

The other time, the boy was chosen to represent the colored high schools on a radio broadcast with three students from the white high schools. All spruced up for the occasion, the four of them sat in a silent, anxious circle, waiting to go on the air. Afterward, they chatted for a few moments before going their separate ways, back to their legally separated lives.

Except for those two experiences, the boy had lived all his life in a colored world. How he would have cried, that first day here, if he could have foreseen that during his entire four years—except for one semester—he would be the only colored youth in this College!

He got hungry around noon, but he skipped lunch, because he didn't want to go to Commons alone. Instead, he ate the cookies his mother had packed for him. The sad prospect of four years in this far away place gradually shrank in his mind, to the less unhappy span of six weeks—the six weeks until he'd go home for the Thanksgiving holiday. Eventually, he concluded that he could probably survive that long, and he thought he might as well go wash his face.

Heading down the hall, he was nearly bowled over by a red-headed fellow who came running around the corner in his undershirt. Instantly, the runner pulled up short, and demanded, "Do you play bridge?" Hardly waiting for the boy's reply, he strode off, calling over his shoulder, "Come on along, then; we need a fourth." That's how it happened that the boy found himself seated at a card table with three upperclassmen, playing bridge. Dinner time came, and when Reds Quimby gave the word, the four trooped together to Commons and sat together at dinner. The boy ate his first meal with persons not of color. The dinner was not very different, he found, from other dinners he had eaten, and his companions not very different from other boys he had known.

After dinner, it was back to the bridge table, and a late bedtime. The next day, more bridge. That bridge partnership was without doubt the key to his survival here, that first semester.

As time went on, the boy made friends among his fellow students, and was welcomed with encouragement and kindness by his teachers. But that first encounter inspires my message today—Reds Quimby's demonstration of spontaneous immediate acceptance of another human being, without regard to color.

James Elwin Quimby was graduated in 1939, the year my father died, and two years before my own graduation. Our paths have not crossed since then, but I understand he practices medicine in a small town in Alabama as an obstetrician and gynecologist—the same medical field as mine. This story—my word of thanks four decades later—will come as a surprise to him, I'm sure.

I don't know much about Reds beyond what I've told you. I don't know where he was born and reared, for example. But wherever it was—north or south, east or west—he didn't hesitate that day, didn't stop to ask himself the color question.

His instant acceptance of his new-found partner holds a message today for all of us. For just as he accepted that stranger into partnership forty-five years ago, your spontaneous acceptance—or mine—may do the same for another stranger today or tomorrow. And that's important. It's important because until somehow we find the partnership that brings us all together, the American dream of freedom and equality for all people can never come true.

That promise is still a distant dream for America's unassimilated minorities. Black youth unemployment approaches 80%. Urban Hispanics drop out of school—85% drop out. Native Americans die of tuberculosis at a rate 13 times the national average, and their infants die at triple the national rate. By every standard, whether it be health, housing, employment, education, income, or mortality, by every measure of human welfare—in comparison with the majority—minorities suffer a grievously inhumane differential.

And times are hard. In times like these, social progress bogs down. Sometimes, it seems to stop. But, young graduates, it must not stop. So I challenge you now to take up the struggle for a life of decency and dignity for every person. Defend the just causes of women, of children, of the aged, of minorities. Harness your youthful strength to the chariot of social progress, and move this great country on toward the day of freedom for all people, the day that Martin Luther King spoke of when he said: "This will be the day when all of God's children will be able to sing with new meaning, 'My country 'tis of thee, sweet land of liberty, of thee I sing. Land where my fathers died, land of the pilgrim's pride, from every mountainside, let freedom ring.'"

Charles W. Colson

Charles W. Colson

COMMENCEMENT ADDRESS
WHEATON COLLEGE
May, 1982

DARING TO BE CHRISTIAN

You have made me feel much at home today — which is not all that surprising, accustomed as I am to speaking to institutional audiences.

This is a special occasion for many reasons, not the least of which is the privilege of participating in this last commencement under the presidency of a great Christian scholar and leader, Hudson Armerding. Wheaton — and indeed the larger Christian community — is grateful for the extraordinary accomplishments of this man. And I am personally grateful for his friendship. His gentle spirit — his genuineness — have been a great blessing and encouragement.

One concern, however, is the fact that Dr. Armerding announced his resignation right after I agreed to be here today. Well, I'm accustomed to that; it seems to happen to presidents I associate with.

I am aware that my participation in your commencement has sparked some controversy. I'm accustomed to that as well. I have in mind the headline in the *Wheaton College Record*, "Ex-Con Colson Slated to Speak at Commencement" which prompted a spate of letters from friends, rising to my defense and apologizing for your editor's supposed insensibility.

The revered journalistic maxim — that dog biting man is not news but man biting dog is — clearly makes it news for an ex-convict to speak at the commencement of this most prestigious educational institution. So let me assure the editors of the *Record* that this is one of those very rare occasions when I can say that the press is absolutely fair.

In fact, my being here today is a testimony. Society is unforgiving of its offenders — at least that small percentage which it catches and prosecutes. Ex-convicts can't vote, most have a hard time getting jobs, and few ever escape the scarlet letter with which we are branded. But, in the Kingdom of God, it is different. Through the Cross of Christ, we are all pardoned.

What's more, while I am not proud of having gone to prison, I am profoundly grateful to God for that experience. I understand how, even after

57

10 years in a wretched Soviet gulag, Alexander Solzhenitsyn could write, "bless you, prison, for having been in my life."

Unthinkable, you say? Not at all. For Solzhenitsyn writes in his memoirs that in prison he learned "the meaning of earthly existence lies not, as we have grown used to thinking, in prospering, but in the development of the soul." It was prison that God used to restore the Nobel Laureate's Christian faith, and prison that shaped his prophetic words to western society.

As with Solzhenitsyn, it was prison God used to give real meaning to my life. I have visited perhaps 250 prisons in America and abroad. As I walk between the dreary cell-blocks on my way to the chapel or auditorium to speak, I am invariably struck by the same scene: rows of men clinging to bars, their dead eyes without hope, gray and listless, as if life itself had been sucked from them.

But when I walk into a Prison Fellowship meeting and look into the faces of the Christian inmates, I see not death but life — men and women with hope and joy, their dignity restored by the living God.

On those occasions I am always reminded of the great paradox of my life. It is not my accomplishments — the honors, awards, scholarships, arguing cases in the highest courts, sitting at the right hand of the President of the United States — that are the legacies of my life. Rather, it is the defeat I experienced, the only thing over which I had no control, that God in His sovereignty has chosen to use to touch the lives of thousands.

I've thought of that not only in prisons, but in palaces and Parliaments as well. Several months ago as I addressed the Senate House monthly prayer breakfast, I realized that I was there not because I was once Special Counsel to the President, but because I had fallen from political grace — only to be restored by God's grace.

This is what Jesus meant when He told His disciples, "Whoever wishes to save his life shall lose it, but whoever loses his life for My sake shall find it." This paradox is an impenetrable mystery for the secular mind — and a cardinal truth of the Christian faith.

As you celebrate your graduation from this great institution, be reminded that what will really count in your life, more than what *you* accomplish, will be *what God chooses to do through you.* Your singular challenge is to be unswervingly obedient to our risen Lord, at all costs. And that can be very difficult in a society which denies Him, the One, as C.S. Lewis wrote, "without whom Nothing is strong." Indeed, nothing *is* very strong in this culture which stumbles in its narcotic stupor, panders its every passion and exalts its material excesses.

The format for the august academic ritual we enact today has remained unchanged from time immemorial: neat rows of perspiring students in oddly shaped hats endure the somber words of an elder, similarly attired, presumably wise in the ways of the world. The elder expounds upon the perils and opportunities of the age, and exhorts the graduates to overcome the one and exploit the other.

So, being a traditionalist, I began my preparation by reflecting on the perils and opportunities of our day; being an amateur historian, I looked for precedents from previous eras. Only then did I realize how unusual these times are, for I could find no precedents.

Previous graduates have, for the most part, faced readily discernible challenges: economic depression in the '30s; war in the '40s; reconstruction in the '50s; the cold war of the '60s; and civil dissent in the early '70s. But the challenge of this age does not fit into any such tidy, clearly-defined category.

America is a nation in transition in the eye of a storm which pollster Daniel Yankelovich calls a "sweeping irreversible cultural revolution . . . transforming the rules that once guided American life." Powerful forces are shaking the very substructure of American life.

Like all revolutions, the most profound struggle is going on in us. We are desperately seeking certainty in the midst of confusion and hope in the face of disillusionment. Above all we are confounded by the maddening contradictions which plague us. Consider just these four illustrations:

- The boundless affluence considered to be the fulfillment of the American dream led to indifference and spiritually destructive materialism.

- The technology which promised to lead mankind to a new promised land now threatens to obliterate it in a giant mushroom cloud.

- The self-fulfillment spree of the '70s led not to the expected expansion of the human potential but to isolation, loneliness and the death of community.

- The lofty visions of freedom and democracy which enabled America's mission as a world power floundered in the rice paddies of a distant continent, raising unprecedented and unanswered moral questions.

Our dilemmas are compounded by a technology which dramatically telescopes history, accelerating the speed of cultural change. While it took early pioneers a full century on foot and hoof to hack their way across the wilderness of this continent, the jet age measures such distance in hours and seconds. So today's pilgrimage is that of a people being propelled through a wind tunnel tumbling and falling helplessly, unable to gain secure footing long enough to catch their breath.

Jacques Ellul, the French lawyer-theologian, wrote: "Day after day the wind blows away the pages of our calendars, our newspapers, and our political regime, and we glide along the stream of time without a judgment . . . If we are to live in this world . . . we need to rediscover the meanings of events and the spiritual framework which our contemporaries have lost." Precisely! We are a people wandering in a spiritual wilderness, searching frantically for our roots and crying out for an understanding of the context in which we live.

If you follow daily headlines you will quickly conclude that the dominant issues in American society are those of inflation and economic policy, or defense spending and social security, or conflicts between conservative and liberal political philosophies. But these are surface issues. The deeper issues are first, what values will we live by — absolute truth, the Holy Word of God, or the arbitrary, relative whims of the humanist elite; and, second, who will set the moral agenda — the church or the bureaucratic social planners and vested economic interests of secular society?

America's moral leadership is up for grabs — and that is where you and I come in. The outcome of today's revolution will be determined by how we respond to the cries of our people for moral direction and vision'

Recent government budget cutbacks put the challenge squarely before us. For fifty years, politicians have led us to believe that government could provide answers to all social ills. Their recipe was simple: enact a law, add at least one government agency; pour in money and stir continuously.

But the $100 billion deficit for 1982 and a stagnant national economy shatter that myth. We are learning that there are limits to what we once thought was the endless abundance of the American economy. So government deficits must be curbed, lest they continue to fuel morally indefensible, double-digit inflation.

But the cutbacks hurt those most dependent on government aid, that is, the poor. If inflation is a moral issue, so too is society's concern for its disadvantaged and oppressed. We Christians know from the Old Testament prophets that a people who would sell the poor for a pair of shoes stand in fearsome judgment of Almighty God.

So the government's budget crisis raises a moral dilemma for our society, and a spiritual issue for the church. How we respond will say much for the kind of people we are and hope to be; that's why I consider the budget crunch Round One in the battle for America's moral leadership.

The church faced its first test in New York City. Last Christmas 36,000 homeless men and women were wandering the city's streets at night. Mayor Koch appealed to religious leaders for help: if each one of New York's 3,500 churches would care for just 10 homeless people, a desperate human problem could be quickly solved, and without huge government expense.

The *New York Times* reported the religious leaders' response. One Protestant representative was concerned about protocol: "The mayor never mentioned this to me . . . nobody in his office called to apprise me of this" A Catholic spokesman sidestepped. A Jewish leader explained that many of the synagogues would not have money for increased heating bills.

The *Times* summed it up: the church leaders would need more time to study the mayor's proposal. There was a disturbing silence from evangelicals.

One can almost imagine how it might sound on that day promised in Matthew 25 when our Lord says, "I was a stranger and you did not invite Me in." And the religious leaders will respond, "But, Lord, You didn't give us time to study the proposal."

I don't mean to belittle our brothers in New York; the issue is complicated and government cannot immediately transfer to the church full responsibility for the needy. But their sorry response should make us ask ourselves some tough questions. Have we become so caught up in doing our own thing, putting on massive television extravaganzas and organizing vast publishing and parachurch empires that we have lost sight of our biblical mission?

Church bureaucracies can become as bogged down as government bureaucracies, so wrapped up in writing pious statements of faith and issuing press releases that they forget their reason for existence: to proclaim the Good News and obey the clear commands of the Scriptures. Of course, the Bible requires justice and righteousness from government, but it also demands that *we* care about our neighbors, clothe the naked, feed the hungry and visit the sick and those in prison. That's *us* our Lord is talking to, and we don't discharge that obligation by paying our taxes or dropping dimes in charity boxes. We discharge it by *doing* the Word of God.

Amazing things happen when we do exercise our biblical duty. A few months ago we took six convicts out of the federal prison in Florida and brought them to Atlanta, where each one was assigned to the home of a Prison Fellowship volunteer. Each morning the six convened for several hours of Bible study, then converged on the homes of two widows in a deteriorating section of the city. For two weeks they insulated, weatherstripped, caulked, sealed and painted.

It was all part of a model project demonstrating that nonviolent criminals can do something better than vegetating in a prison cell at a cost to taxpayers of $17,000 per year. Without red tape and delays a project valued at $21,000 was completed at no cost to the public. So it proved, too, that people getting busy helping other people can do the job faster and cheaper than cumbersome bureaucracies.

But Atlanta also gave us lessons of far greater significance. I visited one of the widows, Roxie Vaughn, 83 years old and blind. When we first told Roxie that her home was to be restored, she was elated. When we told her six convicts were going to do it and Roxie turned ashen. You see, she had some personal experience with crime — her house had been broken into four times in the prior two years. She had lived in constant fear.

Well, by the third day those prisoners worked around Roxie's home, she had them in for cookies and milk; the next afternoon television cameras caught a picture of Roxie sitting at her organ playing "Amazing Grace" with those six convicts around her singing.

I spoke at the service at the end of the project. The widows were there. So were the volunteers who had hosted the inmates, and their children. None of them wanted to see their guests leave. The children were hugging the convicts, the volunteers were hugging the widows. That dark, musty old inner city sanctuary that hadn't been filled in forty years was jammed full of Christians from all over Atlanta — black and white, rich and poor — in the most exciting and joyous worship imaginable. What we were witnessing was the incredible power of the Gospel to heal prejudices, to deliver people from fear and to reconcile us to one another.

Our twentieth century technology has brought clinical impersonalization: machines solve all problems; television reduces us all to spectators as real life appears in a condensed version from six to seven each evening, in living color. And the by-product of modern technocracy is the loss of our sense of caring and awareness of one another. But, if we Christians get out of our pews, seek justice, do the Word of God, and lift Christ up, we will see that sense of community restored.

Think what this can mean for evangelism. The world perceives us as pious and self-centered in our protected sanctuaries and multi-million dollar church complexes — but that is simply not where most of the sick, hurting and hungry people are, so they never hear our message. But imagine what would happen if the poor and needy could see us where *they* live, as we meet them at their point of need.

And, if we heed that call, we will be reasserting a proud heritage of the evangelical church. In the 19th century, evangelicals were at the forefront of the most significant social reforms in western society: enacting child labor laws, ending abuses in the coal mines; establishing public education and public hospitals; and abolishing slavery. This great institution you graduate from today was born out of a passion not only for Christian education but for social reform and abolition as well.

Round One in the contest for America's moral leadership is still going on: whether the church is willing and able to step up to its biblical responsibility is still to be decided. It may be the greatest question we face. For if we fail even the simple test of responding to human needs in our own community, what possible claim will we have to assume a role of genuine moral leadership in society? We dare not fail.

Today you graduates join in that battle, caught up in the swirling currents and cross currents of the cultural revolution under way in America. Do not falter; wade boldly into the rushing waters. Dare to be Christian — and to live out your faith, for you have an opportunity to respond to the deepest yearnings of a people weary of the bankrupt ways of the world.

But, you are asking yourself, how can you make a difference? The strategy and policies of the church, after all, are determined by elders. Well, the key to change and renewal is not through the deliberations of its so-called leaders — I haven't seen much change from the meetings I've sat through. No, the key is faithful and holy Christian living by God's people.

So, let me leave you with some concluding thoughts about faithful Christian living.

First, take your stand on the solid foundation of the holy, inerrant word of God — and submit yourselves wholeheartedly to its authority. That means you take the whole word of God, absorb it, cling to it, and live by it.

Then, study the classical doctrines of the Christian church; read the great Christian scholars. Our bookshelves today are crammed full of puffy testimonies all with the same happy victorious endings; while they are written in Gospel language, their goal is to sell big to a self-centered, success-oriented culture — and their sales are phenomenal. But they are whipped cream concoctions of cheap grace and false Gospel. We need meat, such as the works of Augustine, Calvin, Luther, Edwards and modern-day greats like C.S. Lewis, whose continuing ministry Wheaton has done so much to enhance.

Second, beware of glib cliches and easy answers. We impatient Americans expect to get answers to complex problems like our order at the fast food counter: "One double burger, shake, an order of fries." And we are faddists. Just look at the rash of new diets dominating our best-seller lists, or the mind-boggling sales of Pac-Man and his computerized brothers.

Now, that "quick fix" mentality has invaded the Christian church. We want to reduce our faith to score cards by which we can instantly rate our politicians, or painless steps to salvation and material Prosperity. Well, formulas don't convert people; slick slogans and cute phrases are no substitute for hard spiritual truths. You must challenge these tendencies, and be discerning, not only of society but of the evangelical subculture also.

Third, jealously guard the integrity of your witness. Much of the world associates Christianity, especially the evangelical wing, with hucksterism. When TV preachers tell folks to send in checks and God will give them back multiplied, when Rev. Al promises that his "health, happiness and prosperity plan" will bring "new homes, better jobs, and new cars," then we get a black eye, and, what's more, we deserve it. Believers ought to root such fraud out of our ranks as fast as we can.

Money is the most obvious area in which our witness can be sullied, but there is a more subtle peril: compromise of the very Gospel we proclaim. Sometimes Christians make the Gospel sound easy and unthreatening, a painless answer to all life's ills, that God is love and forgives all, asking nothing in return.

My friends, that is heresy, and it abounds in America today. Dorothy Sayers put it well when she said, "Surely it is not the business of the Church to adapt Christ to men, but men to Christ. It is the dogma that is the drama — not beautiful phrases, nor comforting sentiments, nor vague aspirations to loving kindness and uplift, nor the promise of something nice after death — but the terrifying assertion that the same God who made the world lived in the world and passed through the grave and the gate of death."

The Gospel of Jesus Christ is a two-edged sword, calling us to repentance as well as belief. And that means we must want to leave the old ways behind, to die to ourselves and to live for Christ. Before it can be the good news of redemption, the Gospel of Jesus Christ must be the bad news of the conviction of sin. Let the world know that we follow Christ, not because it's the easy way, but because He is Truth.

Fourth, hunger and thirst after righteousness. Our God is a Holy God. He is pure, compassionate, just, righteous, perfect. And, because He has chosen to live and dwell in our midst, He demands that we be holy as well.

The Christian world has established its own cultural standards for holiness: We don't smoke, drink, in some places we don't dance, go to the movies or play cards. Obviously, we must be concerned with our witness, but do not be confused. These things involve our piety. You must never, never confuse piety with righteousness.

When God speaks of righteousness, He is speaking of justice, caring for the widows, the orphans, the oppressed. "Hate evil, love good and establish justice in your courts," demands the prophet Amos. "Let justice roll down like waters and righteousness like an ever-flowing stream" When you come before our Lord for an accounting, I doubt that His first question will be how often you played cards, but I can assure you He'll want to know when you fed the hungry, visited the sick and cared for the least of these, His brethren.

Fifth, remember that you are called not just to holy living yourself but also to be part of a Holy Nation. Becoming a Christian is more than being separated from our sin; it also means being joined to a holy people. Conversion may be personal but it can't be private; corporate caring is the essence of our covenantal relationships with God and one another. To a society obsessed with looking out for #1, bearing one another's burdens and laying down our lives for our brothers and sisters are foreign concepts — but they are precisely what we are called to do.

Sixth, seek first the kingdom of God. We've had a tradition in America of equating God and country, Old Glory and the Old Rugged Cross; it's a popular notion that we Americans, so richly blessed by God, are His chosen people. This is a dangerous heresy. Never make the Gospel of Jesus Christ hostage to the political fortunes of any man, party or kingdom. Never confuse the will of the majority with the will of God. They may be, and frequently are, very different.

Remember the wise counsel of Augustine. In A.D. 410, when the news reached him that his beloved Rome had been sacked, he spoke calmly: "All earthly cities are vulnerable. Men build them and men destroy them. At the same time, there is the city of God which men did not build and cannot destroy and which is everlasting."

Seventh, be prepared as a Christian to take your stand against the world if need be. Nearly two centuries ago a young recently converted member of Parliament rose on the floor of the House of Commons to denounce the slave trade, then a chief source of revenue to the British Empire. He was booed, mocked, slandered. For 20 years his Christian conscience drove him on, though it cost him a chance to become Prime Minister. But it was William Wilberforce's determined campaign that resulted in an epic victory in 1807, when a majority of votes were cast to abolish the barbaric slave trade. It was a victory for the Gospel over the world.

You may never have the chance to be part of such a great crusade, but I guarantee you will have many chances in matters small and large, to take your stand. (If you don't, you need to question your commitment.) It is not easy to buck the cultural virtue of conformity, but I beseech you: *Dare to be different. Dare to be Christian.*

Eighth, and finally, take Jesus as your model — reach out to identify with the most unlovable, those hurting inside, many sick and despairing in ghettos, in prisons. These are the people who have never come into our churches. And without your going to them, they never will.

Next to the bodily Resurrection, the most convincing evidence for me of Christ's deity is the supernatural capacity He demonstrated to relate to every human being He came in contact with. He didn't say, "Wash up, put on your best clothes, and let Me take you to the temple." If they were in the gutter, He was in the gutter with them. If they were suffering, He was suffering. And that is why He touched everyone He dealt with, except for the hard-hearted religious people of His day.

The greatest blessing awaits us when we follow our Lord's example. It is a spiritual mystery that sharing in the suffering of others draws us closer to our Christ Who suffered for us. The must meaningful communions I have had with my Lord have not been in the great cathedrals of the world I've been privileged to preach in nor in the Parliaments where I have spoken, nor in the most influential gatherings of Christian leaders. No, they have been on my knees on the grimy, concrete floor of a rotten prison cell with my hand on the shoulder of a tough, burly convict who sobs with joy as we meet Another who was in prison, executed and rose for us — His name is Jesus.

My congratulations to each of you. May you lose your life for Christ and His kingdom — and serve Him gloriously all the days of your lives.

© Prison Fellowship.

Marian Wright Edelman

Marian Wright Edelman

COMMENCEMENT ADDRESS
BRYN MAWR COLLEGE
May 15, 1982

I am deeply honored to participate in your Commencement. It comes at a point when our nation and world teeter on the brink of moral bankruptcy. An escalating arms race and nuclear proliferation hold hostage not only the future we adults hold in trust for our children, but also the present that is, for many millions of our young and old in America and throughout the world, one of relentless poverty and deprivation.

Hunger is the enemy faced daily by hundreds of millions of people throughout the world. Children are the major victims. Six diseases — measles, polio, tuberculosis, diptheria, whooping cough, and tetanus — are also child killers. The World Health Organization (WHO) estimates that every minute 10 children may die as a result of these diseases. Although vaccines have existed for decades, only 10% of the 80 million children born yearly in the developing world are immunized, although the cost of immunization is a mere $3 per child.* Something is badly awry in a world that spends an estimated $550 billion a year on arms but does not allocate the relative pittance needed to immunize and educate its children. Our nation, first in military power, cannot manage to ensure immunization for thousands of its own neediest children. More than 40 percent of poor Black Children, 5 to 9 years old, living in inner cities, are not immunized. Our nation's capital still suffers a Black infant mortality rate that exceeds that of Jamaica, East Germany, Bulgaria, Czechoslovakia, Hungary, and Poland.

In 1953 Dwight David Eisenhower warned:

> "Every gun that is made, every warship launched, every rocket fired signifies ... a theft from those who hunger and are not fed, those who are cold and are not clothed. "This world in arms is not spending money alone. It is spending the sweat of its laborers, the genius of its scientists, the hopes of its children."**

---

* These figures are from Ruth Sivard's *1981 World Social Expenditures*. She estimates that $4 billion would enable us to take direct action to meet current food needs of the world's children and undertake some long-term programs to combat poverty and develop food growing areas.

**Address, "The Chance for Peace" delivered before the American Society of Newspaper Editors, April 16, 1953.

And how blatant was this theft in the budget decisions of Fiscal Year 1982 when more than $10 billion was taken from needy, abused, homeless, and handicapped children while military expenditures were increased by $32 billion and even nonessential ones, unrelated to national defense, went untouched. Another $8 billion in cuts from poor, homeless, abused, and handicapped children is proposed for Fiscal Year 1983, while the Administration still proposes $44 billion in additional defense expenditures.

One point six trillion dollars in defense expenditures is being proposed by this administration for use in the next five years. If we had spent one million dollars every day since Christ was born, we would have spent less than half of what President Reagan wants us to believe the Department of Defense can spend efficiently.

The budget battle in 1982 confronts us with basic moral decisions as a nation. It is a battle for a fair and decent America. It is a battle about whether we will continue to invest federal dollars in the young, in families, in the needy, and in working men and women, or whether we will invest in the rich and in more and more arms. It is a battle about whether we invest in human capital—new generations of healthy, well-educated, productive citizens—or whether we choose short-term profit and easy political fixes. It is a battle about who and what we Americans are as a people and as a nation.

We spend about $100 million on 100 separate military bands which is almost equivalent to the additional amount of money needed to implement the Adoption Assistance and Child Welfare Reform Act designed to help thousands of homeless children gain permanent families. President Reagan is proposing to repeal the Act and cut child welfare funding by almost 23 percent.

President Reagan proposed a $3 million cut in the childhood immunization program for Fiscal Year 1982 which would eliminate immunizations for 75,000 children at risk. In Fiscal Year 1983 he plans to cut $2 million more. The Defense Department spends $1.4 million on shots and other veterinary services for the pets of military personnel. Additional millions are spent on the transportation of military pets when personel are transferred. If the veterinary benefits for military pets were eliminated, at least 35,000 low income children could be immunized instead.

For Fiscal Year 1981 and Fiscal Year 1982, President Reagan rescinded and proposed cutting a total of $23.9 million from the Preschool Incentive Grants for handicapped children which serves more than a quarter of a million handicapped 3 to 6 year olds. In Fiscal Year 1983 he is proposing to effectively eliminate the program through a block grant and further cuts. These children are given early instruction in learning and communication skills so that they will be able to benefit from later schooling. The General Accounting Office has estimated that almost half of all messages sent over Defense department teletype nets are routine non-priority messages better sent by mail at a savings which would total $20 million a year. The excess teletype machines could be donated to programs for deaf children, thus further increasing savings.

President Reagan eliminated the Child Nutrition Equipment Assistance program that helped child care centers and schools in low-income areas buy the kitchen equipment needed to serve hot lunches and breakfasts to eligible low-income children and saved $15 million. The Army plans to spend $58 million to give away industrial machines, most of them new (e.g. five 2,000 ton capacity, four-stage mechanical forging presses, 166 power lathes, etc.), to defense contractors free. The $58 million is for the Army to pay to move and install the equipment. If it sold the equipment instead on the open market, and returned the proceeds to the Treasury, perhaps the $58 million dollars and more could be put back into the school lunch program which about 2000 schools have eliminated because of budget cuts.

The State of Virginia has fewer than 160 full time homemaking aides serving more than 2,500 aged, blind, disabled persons and families with handicapped children at home. The Pentagon has 300 personal servants tending to fewer than 300 senior officers, none of whom reports himself seriously disabled. Virginia's program costs about $1 million a year. The Pentagon's program costs over $5 million a year. President Reagan cut Virginia's program by more than a third; he increased the Pentagon's program by 15 percent.

This year's decisions on military, tax, and social program spending will dictate the nation's choices, indeed shape the national character, for decades to come. They are far too important to leave to the politicians or the experts.

I urge each American therefore to confront and think hard about what we can and must do about the twin but related plagues of growing militarism and poverty.

I want to do a case study of one children's issue — the lack of child health and dental services — to illustrate how needed, how possible, yet how hard and frustrating social change is. I worry about the persuasive unrealism in our nation about what it takes to solve problems and bring about needed change. I worry equally about those who take the easy road of opting out of often discouraging political, bureaucratic, and community processes or who refuse to take one needed step because the world stairway is not revealed. I agree with Albert Einstein that ". . . the world is in greater peril from those who tolerate evil than from those that commit it."

I have chosen child health because, unlike so many other areas of social policy, there is a wide consensus about the health services children and expectant mothers need and how these services can be best organized and provided. The solutions are neither mysterious nor expensive. The majority of unmet needs can be filled through modest expenditures with little new money, if new funds are used to harness and leverage the billions currently spent on health care for children.

Yet our attempts as a Children's Defense Fund to meet those needs over the past five years is a study of frustration and of hope. Let's look briefly at the problem; the barriers to solving the problem; and briefly the process for doing something about it. The steps and process are not atypical, I think, of what is required to make a difference on most problems.

Many battles are bigger — many smaller — but most are hard, take time and patience, a lot of work and persistence. But they must be fought. And I hope young people like you will be willing to fight them.

A few weeks before Christmas in 1978, Isidro and Rachel Aguinagas' 11-month-old baby became seriously ill. They rushed the child to a community clinic in Dimmett, Texas. The doctor there told them to take the child immediately across the street to (The Plains) Hospital. He called to notify hospital emergency personnel that the parents, migrant workers of Hispanic descent, would arrive with their desperately ill child and that intensive care services should be readied. When the family arrived the hospital administrator demanded a pre-admission cash deposit of $450. The parents did not have such a vast amount of ready cash and left after repeated entreaties that the baby be admitted. They drove 45 miles through a storm to another county to try to get their baby into a public hospital. They were told at that hospital, however, that since they were not residents of the county, and since "the baby was going to die anyway," the infant would not be admitted. The baby died in the parking lot as the parents arrived back in Dimmett to plead again their child's case for admission to Plains Hospital. The administrator was subsequently indicted for a misdemeanor in the baby's death.

This child is one among many children, pregnant mothers, and families that are daily refused access to hospital care when they need it. It is still routine for many hospitals, even ones built with federal Hill-Burton funds, to refuse patients who cannot show ability to pay. Mrs. C. of Texarkana, Texas, arrived at the hospital in labor, was turned away because of her inability to pay a preadmission deposit, and suffered a miscarriage upon reaching a second hospital. When Mrs. D. arrived in labor at St. Elizabeth's Hospital in Beaumont, Texas, she was also refused entrance because she had no preadmission deposit. She was given a bus ticket to go to a public hospital in

Galveston — 60 to 70 miles away — where she ultimately delivered her baby. These practices are growing as hospitals fear poor high-risk mothers will deliver babies that may require expensive and long-term intensive care which may exceed the period of Medicaid reimbursement. Medicaid suffered a $1 billion cut last year and faces an additional $1.5 billion in proposed cuts in Fiscal Year 1983.

Many of these mothers have not had any prenatal care at all or not until the last trimester. Over one in every eleven of all Black mothers receive no prenatal care until the final trimester. Seventeen states do not cover maternity care during a woman's first pregnancy even though the absence of such care is associated with low birth weights, increased numbers of birth defects, and high infant mortality rates. Up to 220,000 pregnant mothers are delivering babies each year with little or no prenatal care. Their numbers will grow with the 36 percent cut in maternal and child health funds.

Other patients are denied *de facto* access to health care, even in emergencies, when hospitals in poor and minority neighborhoods are closed. There are few or no community clinics to replace them, and they lack transportation as well as money to get to care when they need it.

In Eastern Tennessee, poor children graduating from 8th grade often receive "clackers" as a graduation gift. "Clackers" are the children's nickname for false teeth which are a necessity by the end of adolescence for the many children who have never seen a dentist and have lost most or all of their permanent teeth. They are among the 1 in 3 American children who have never seen a dentist.

Eight-year-old Archie Douglas has already failed the first grade twice. His problem is a hearing loss which developed as a result of an ear infection he suffered when he was two. Archie would have been spared much of his suffering had he received basic primary health care. The hearing loss could have been identified much earlier before it seriously affected his language skills. Once his problem was identified, Archie could have gotten a hearing aid and services in school suited to his special needs. But he did not. The consequences to his young life are already considerable. He is one of 10 million American children (one in seven) who have no access to regular health care. He and millions of other children who are poor in our midst lack what you and I who are more affluent take for granted. And we are losing ground in our fight against poverty. More than 3 1/4 million more Americans have recently fallen into poverty, including 1 million children.

Archie and the Tennessee children are eligible for demonstrably cost-effective health and dental services under a Medicaid preventive health care program for children. But there are few dentists in eastern Tennessee and fewer still who accept Medicaid patients because of that state's low reimbursement rates. Although the state was required to provide these children transportation to get to the nearest participating dentist, it did not. As a result, these children lose their teeth because there are simply no available dental services for them to purchase. Archie's mother was never informed of the program as required by law and he is handicapped for life as a result. He loses. All Americans lose in costly remediation and decreased productivity.

What Can Be Done?

While many people will take up the cause of an individual poor child or family unfairly treated or denied access to health care whom they know about, should we change a system that excludes millions of children and families from a basic human service and how do we go about doing so?

The first step I have learned is to break down big problems into smaller, manageable pieces for action and to go step by systematic step. It is so easy to be overwhelmed and discouraged by all that needs to be done or to tell yourself it's okay to bow out because you can't make a difference anyway or it's too big for an individual or a few people or groups to tackle.

Pick a problem or a piece of the problem that you can solve while trying to see how your piece fits into the broader social change puzzle. Tailor your remedies to the specific needs identified and that you can do something about and build from there.

Although all the examples I have described share a common denial of health services, each involves a different target population and requires a different set of remedies and strategies. Denial of emergency treatment was a problem we could try to do something about, at least in hospitals constructed by federal Hill-Burton funds through seeking a federal regulation change explicitly prohibiting such hospitals from turning away emergency patients because of poverty. And while it is not going to keep some callous hospital administrators from continuing to do it, it is a handle with which to begin to discourage such practices and to inform legal services and religious groups working with poor communities around the country that they should begin to check out and challenge such denial of services. Since the migrant child died of an illness and not an accident and since only a little digging made clear that migrant children as a group were excluded from Medicaid and other critical benefits by states on grounds they are not residents, a second remedy — to cut down on the number of migrant children who get seriously ill because of delayed medical attention — was to seek another regulation change and get other groups to join in persuading HEW to ensure that the thousands of children in migrant streams are not barred from health and other services because of residency requirements.

Simultaneously we tried to put into place an information sharing, technical assistance and monitoring network of groups working in poor communities. This monitoring process can never stop. Getting change is not a guarantee of keeping change. Individuals and groups who care must fight to translate laws and rights into the daily lives of poor or handicapped children families, the elderly, and the homeless. There have been too many Santa Clauses and not enough elves to put the pieces together to make the services for children and families in communities throughout the country.

The other examples involving the lack of routine dental and medical services required a broader range of approaches and a continuum of remedies for different groups of children and mothers in different places and of different backgrounds who faced a variety of barriers. What existing public programs/handles were available? What could be done immediately for some or all of the groups of children, using our available community and religious groups resources? What more substantial long-range changes could be made to serve all the children who now have no care? This required a second step which is an essential ingredient of most effective change: *thorough homework*. Good facts coupled with good analysis are needed if good remedies are to follow and if an effective case is to be made for a particular cause. Too many good intentions and causes are wrecked, and victims left unhelped on the shoals of sloppy investigation, hipshooting rhetoric, political grandstanding, fiery sermons, and simplistic remedies that sometimes create more problems than they solve.

A detailed two-year study of the Medicaid program for children led to corrective action in states like Tennessee that refused transportation and provoked the administering federal agency to pay a little more attention to how the law they were responsible for was actually working. As usual, agencies always say they don't have enough staff and everybody denies responsibility for any particular problem, so you have to work your way through the agency until you cover everybody who has any relationship to the problem.

Which gets us to step three in the change process which is *follow-up*. Most institutions, public or private, are seldom self-policing. Competing interest groups seeking their ear coupled with natural inertia almost assures that a one-shot effort to correct a problem will be agreeably ignored. Being a change agent for the disenfranchised means being a good pest; wearing down those you want to do something. And you always have a better chance of getting something done if you are specific: address one problem at a time; outline what the person responsible can and should do; have thought through why it is in their self-interest to do it; don't mind doing the work for them; and make sure they can take the credit for getting it done. All of these steps paid off over several years in clearer and more precise regulations (which the Reagan Administration is now undermining) protecting children and defining what states had to do and even with substantial additional dollars to ensure dental treatment. But that still left millions of children unserved and that required larger and longer range action.

This led to lesson four, which is: *touching all your bases — trying everything and never putting your eggs in one basket.* There is no one right way to do things.

All the agency and community improvements, however important, could not lead to health coverage for the hundreds of thousands of poor mothers and millions of poor children who were not eligible for health care by law. Therefore we sought, unsuccessfully for four years, to help pass a major child health bill. Every year we and other advocates struggled to keep the child health bill alive in the budget and pull it through committee, badgering HEW and White House help at critical points. Every year for four years we almost made it but not quite in the last minute crush of Congressional business when everybody who was for poor children was never for them quite enough. But there was a positive side to all these losses.

Every year we got a little better at our job and a little tougher. Every year more and more Representatives and Senators became informed about child health and were hearing from more and more constituents. Last year when the Reagan Administration sought to undermine the already inadequate existing health protections for poor children and mothers, we were able, for the most part, to prevent this. However, the same battle to hold on to what we now have and to resist new cuts in health programs for the neediest young and old citizens, until we can move ahead again, will have to be won again this year, and the next year, and the next.

Which leads to my last two lessons for all of us who would help the disenfranchised: *Do not give up, or ever cease believing that each of us — as individuals — can make a critical difference* if we simply care enough, and bring to that caring skill, targeted action, and persistence. We must not mind losing for things that matter although we can also win some important battles this year. Caring and good intentions are not enough. Engaging in a one-shot protest is not enough. Personal action, while important, is also not enough if we stand by while *our* government — that represents us — makes domestic policy, budget policy, military, and foreign policy decisions which can either lead us forward on the path of national decency and reconciliation, or backwards to a polarized society between black and white, rich and poor, military and civilian.

I hope you will leave this college not content to be bystander critics but citizens who will recognize that the real world is always a place of imperfect choices and who will work with what you have to make it into what you need and desire over time even when you doubt that you can. I hope that you will know that caring and good intentions are not enough; that knowing is not enough; that talking and dabbling in good causes or engaging in a oneshot protest are not enough. I hope you will ferret out and respond to the pressing human needs that our society still neglects; will examine carefully the options and strategies for meeting these needs; the probable consequences of those options and then fight to make them real in small ways that can add up with others to big ways. In short, I hope you will be the leaders of the next generation who are not afraid to lose for things that matter; who will understand that nonparticipation in the outside world or total devotion to one's job or children is in the long run not in one's own or the nation's self-interest. I hope you will know and act upon the fact that individuals can make a difference if they care enough and bring to that caring skill, persistence and targeted action.

Sojourner Truth, a slave woman who could neither read nor write, pointed the way for us. She never gave up talking or fighting against slavery. Once a heckler told Sojourner that he cared no more for her anti-slavery talk "than for a fleabite." "Maybe not," was her answer, "but the Lord willing, I'll keep you scratching." The Lord willing today, we should keep those who would turn their backs on the social "outcasts" of our society scratching. Enough fleas, biting strategically, can make even the biggest dog — biggest community institutions of government — mighty uncomfortable. If they flick some of us off and others of us keep coming back, we will begin to get the basic human needs heard and attended to and oil the creaks of our institutions that many say no longer work.

Carlos Fuentes

Carlos Fuentes

COMMENCEMENT ADDRESS
WESLEYAN UNIVERSITY
1982

"AFTER THE MALVINAS"

It is a great honor for me to speak at the Commencement ceremonies marking the 150th anniversary of Wesleyan University.

All of you young men and women who are physically leaving this great center of learning today are certainly aware of the privilege you have enjoyed. Let me join with you in the celebration of this space for the meeting of all minds, where no ideas are foreign and no civilizations strange. As a writer, I deeply believe in the urgent need to introduce ideas and civilizations to one another.

You know that in the University all the faces of mankind see and recognize each other instead of hiding in fear from one another. You know, thanks to the University, that there exists a time when the past is present and the future an actuality enshrined in the instant.

We have but our present to remember our past and imagine our future. Let us preserve the glory of the mind and the body present in the fullness of life from the menace of nuclear extinction.

You know that in the University the universality of presence, the unity of body and mind, of science and humanities, of politics and imagination, are the keys to the universe, not the false universalities offered by the modern world: violence and celebrity; sometimes celebrity only at the cost of violence. You know, having studied at Wesleyan, that there is a place of teaching and learning where information, knowledge, imagination, and wisdom are not divided from one another, so that knowledge truly is power, as Francis Bacon said, but also defies power, as Shelley desired, when power seems omnipotent.

For you also know that on leaving this campus you will enter a world where information is usually severed from wisdom and power divorced from knowledge and sundered from imagination, a world of armed and arrogant ignorance; and your formidable task shall be to seek, against terrible odds, this reunion of the great faculties of the human mind without which human actions are perishable and, often, cruel.

Wesleyan has a greater track record than most in assuring just this continuity of the lucid, generous, and unified universality of the University in a world of suspicion, hatred, and extermination of what we do not understand, dedication to brutality and silly diversion in the bubbles of entertainment, commercial fetishism, and mad hunger for instant recognition.

Let this middle-aged party tell you that youth is never lost. It is won at the end of a long effort. Believing otherwise, I fear, is but a way of precipitating ourselves into a faceless destiny where we become useless before we become old. Planned obsolesence is not only for machines.

Well, if you are aware of all that I have just said, then the generation that has taught you has not failed. Yet, as you graduate today, you will be facing new challenges, uniquely yours, wedded to your own time and sensibility: What you have learned here will now be tested, and your responses will not be those of your parents and teachers. You will be faithful to them the same way that they proved faithful to their teachers and parents: by testing the lessons of the universal mind, the respect for the other, and the sacrality of life in the present, against conditions of rapid and often confusing change.

Few things are changing more rapidly these days than relations in the Western Hemisphere. This is our common home, our heavy Utopia, the site of our memory and of our imagination: the Americas, North, Central and South. We cannot turn our backs on their history or their destiny, especially today.

The time for re-evaluation has come. What can be done, after this deep crisis we are living through, in favor of good relations among the countries of this hemisphere?

Let me answer, first, from a personal point of view. I grew up in the United States in the 1930s, more or less between the inauguration of Citizen Roosevelt and the interdiction of Citizen Kane. Following my father in his diplomatic journeys, I traveled to Chile in the 1940s and witnessed the profound transformations wrought there by the leftwing Popular Front government. The Roosevelt administration in Washington did not seek to destabilize the Chilean radicals, communists, and socialists democratically elected to power there.

I also went to school in Argentina during the rise of Juan and Eva Peron. I love that country profoundly and feel deeply hurt by its constant inability to find a degree of synchronization between the bounty of its natural and human resources and the poverty of its political institutions.

And I am, above all, a citizen of Mexico and grew up convinced that my country and yours could live in mutual respect: the respect that President

Franklin Delano Roosevelt showed toward President Lazaro Cardenas of Mexico when my country, in 1938, nationalized its oil resources in what is now recognized as the first act of economic emancipation in the Third World. (We were then called, in the North, "the backward countries.")

President Roosevelt resisted tremendous pressures to apply sanctions and even invade Mexico by force. He resisted them from principle: Mexico was entitled to recover and administer its own wealth. He also resisted for pragmatic reasons. He wanted an ally, not an enemy, on the 2,000 kilometer-long southern border of the United States for the fight against the Axis.

Franklin Roosevelt—whose centennial we are celebrating this year, and I say "we" because he belongs to us all—taught us to believe in the United States as a nation capable of living up to its ideals. This is your true greatness, not material wealth, not arrogant power misused against weaker peoples, not ignorant ethnocentrism burning itself out in its contempt for others.

As a young Mexican growing up in the United States, my primary impression of your country was that of energy, imagination, and the will to confront and solve the great social issues of the times without blinking or looking for scapegoats. It was the impression of a country identified with its own highest principles: political democracy, economic well-being, and faith in its human resources, especially in that most precious of all capitals, the renewable wealth of education and research.

Franklin Roosevelt restored America's self-respect in this essential way, not by macho posturing. And because the American people respected themselves and their values, they respected the values of others—as proven by the Good Neighbor Policy in Latin America—and defended them—as proven by the decisive participation of the United States in World War II.

The Good Neighbor Policy was not a moralistic crusade. President Roosevelt had no need to be born more than once. His policy simply consisted of practicing the enlightened diplomacy of nonintervention.

Roosevelt did not overthrow governments in Chile or Guatemala, he did not blockade or invade any islands; he coexisted with sundry Caribbean dictators, with the corporate state of Getulio Vargas in Brazil, and with the welfare state in Uruguay.

He could be a cynical pragmatist. He could say: "Somoza is an s.o.b., but he's our s.o.b." But I could add that the unsung heroes of the agrarian reform in Mexico, of social security in Uruguay, of collective bargaining in Chile, and of popular education in Guatemala, were also his heroes, your heroes, con-temporanes to your own decisive action during the years of the New Deal and the World War. Problems can be solved, people can solve them, if left to their historical experience, their own native genius, their trials and errors.

The result was that at the end of the war, the majority of Latin America had been able, with the immense help of good example and discreet diplomacy from the United States, to muddle through toward democratic forms of government.

In 1945 there were only three military dictatorships on the South American land mass—Bolivia, Argentina, and Paraguay—and the Somoza and Trujillo dynasties in the Caribbean basin. And for the first time in this century, Guatemala had a democratically elected government, also born, along with Roosevelt's policies, in 1944, and a program of social reform that only came to a brutal halt in 1954, when the Central Intelligence Agency overthrew the elected government in Guatemala City, installed a military junta, canceled all social reforms, and precipitated the bloody Central American crisis whose consequences are today painfully evident to us all.

After 1954 we saw that the Good Neighbor Policy had only been an interlude of goodwill, an intelligent blend of principle and pragmatism that precluded the crude policies of Manifest Destiny and Gunboat Diplomacy. No equivalent policy, not even the short-lived spark of John Kennedy's Alliance for Progress, has been able to replace it.

So now is a good time to think about the future of hemispheric relations, accept new realities, limit losses, and look toward the future.

A few hard things have to be understood clearly. First, that our great dispute with post-Rooseveltian America is that you have universalized the values of modernity, freedom, economic development, and political democracy—but that when we move, in our own way, according to our own cultural tradition, to achieve them, your governments scream "Communist!," side with the military protectors of a status quo dating from the Spanish Conquest, attribute the dynamics of change to a Soviet conspiracy, and end up with one or two undesirable solutions: either the self-fulfilling prophecy of revolutionary governments dependent on the Soviet Union because the United States has left them with no other plank on which to float; or the vain attempt to legitimize brutal right-wing caretakers of petrified injustice, veritable murderers who see it as their quasi-divine mission to kill as many oppositions as possible in the hope that the problems will die with them.

Today, 18 months of hard-nosed "realism" from the administration in Washington, favoring alliances with right-wing dictatorships in order to build an anti-Communist consensus in the hemisphere and then impose it by force of arms in Central America and the Caribbean, have sunk in the icy waters of the South Atlantic, along with larger historical policies such as the Monroe Doctrine and Panamericanism.

Latin American governments of all stripes—right and left, democracies and dictatorships—have supported the nationalistic claims of the Argentinian junta. Everyone has forgotten the criminal nature of the junta in Buenos Aires in the name of nationalism. This means that if the issue of nationalism is not clearly addressed, then nothing else can be understood about Latin America. And this issue is riddled with contradictions.

Nationalism cannot be socialism, which is internationalism. But nationalism can be an anachronism: The fight for the Malvinas can be seen as one more chapter in the protracted war between the English and the Spanish Empires, between Protestants and Catholics, between thrifty capitalist colonial administrators and baroque, cruel, and spendthrift Hispanic *hidalgos.*

You can be a nationalist and a conservative in Latin America. Perhaps the United States will finally come to recognize this, since Latin nationalism is often and mistakenly equated with leftist insurgency in this country.

Indeed, the historical origins of Latin American nationalism in the 1820s are part of the conservative doctrine of maintaining colonial privileges in a Latin America isolated from capitalism and the democratic philosophy, consequently, from the territorial ambitions of the United States.

It was the liberal left that originally supported the democratic and revolutionary influence of the United States. That was long ago.

This leads me to consider the other side of the coin, and that is that Marxist movements in Latin America are often "Marxist" in name only, because they permit us to be conservative, essentially Augustinian, hierarchical, and religiously dogmatic nationalists, while paying lip service to the modern Goddess of Progress. The anti-American element in Latin American nationalism is heightened by the awareness that the brand name "Marxism" frightens the United States to jittery incoherence. If it did not provoke such unholy reactions, believe me, it would soon be dropped in favor of the current spook that most frightens Washington: If need be, we would call ourselves Mahayana Buddhists.

Yet, having said all this, let me also remind you that nationalism represents not only a contradiction, but a profound value for Latin Americans simply because of the fact that our nationhood is still in question. In New York, Paris, or London, no one loses sleep asking himself whether the nation exists. In Latin America, you can wake up and find that the nation is no longer there, usurped by a military junta, a multinational corporation, or an American ambassador surrounded by a bevy of technical advisers.

Nationalism has been the constant channel for popular demands in Latin America. It is intimately associated with the cry for land and freedom and work, but also with the organization of viable modern states with efficient public sectors representing what John Kenneth Galbraith calls the "counter-vailing power" to gigantic foreign pressures against minimal economic autonomy.

That the junta in Buenos Aires, acting under the impression that it had been given the green light by the administration in Washington in exchange for mercenary services in the destabilization of Nicaragua, should have so perverted the sense of nationalism in Latin America is a sorry fact. But it permits us to ask more seriously than ever during the past 28 years: What is Latin America's way out, and what should be the rational U.S. response to it?

The fact today is that the immense loss of faith between the United States and Latin America will lead us in three possible directions:

First, the more irate will seek closer cooperation with the Soviet Union. This is a blind policy, not only because of the tyrannical nature of the Soviet regime, but because of the internal and external crisis it is going through: Discredited in its economic performance, bankrupt in its political appeal, resented by its neighbors and its minorities, it cannot establish far-flung outposts in Argentina or El Salvador, and even in Cuba it wants to reduce its profile and cut its losses.

Second, the more equanimous and pragmatical will make a bid for greater political, economic, and technological support from Japan and Western Europe. This will be a good thing. Because they do not wish to drive our countries into the Soviet embrace by blocking the revolutionary movements in Latin America, leaders in France, Scandinavia, and West Germany are in a better position than the United States to further policies of economic development with human rights.

This is essential to our national growth because, let me say it with the greatest conviction, we shall never be full-fledged nations if we do not face up to the challenge that we cannot have true, useful, and permanent economic development without human rights and political freedoms. The Latin American concept of human rights must indeed be wide and demanding. It means that basic freedoms can no longer be sacrificed to capital accumulation parading as revolutionary socialism. It also means that economic justice cannot be sacrificed any longer to purely formal representations of democracy by the entrenched oligarchy.

Beware, in this context, of a new and, again, ill-advised policy unveiled by the American administration before the British parliament: a program for developing democracy in the Third World through open U.S. financing of political parties, labor unions, and newspapers. Let me tell you that no greater stumbling block for democracy in Latin America has ever been so unwittingly devised. Let me tell you that these organizations will be immediately tainted and rendered totally ineffective: Democracy cannot be imported into Latin America; we must be ourselves, not a cartoon replica of you; we must find our own paths toward democracy, and it seems incredible that Washington should come up with this political Frankenstein precisely when the South Atlantic crisis has shown that nationalism, not Marxism, not faith in "the magic of the marketplace," is the driving force in Latin America.

And third, the more prophetic souls will find in the present crisis an occasion to further the structuring of a multipolar world, where several centers of power will coexist beyond the present two-power domination. Latin America sees itself as one of these new centers of power, along with China, Japan, India, Islam, Black Africa, Western Europe and, eventually, hopefully, a united Europe, East and West.

The United States administration has paid the price of its mistaken policies by having to choose publicly between two major alliances, NATO and the Rio Treaty. This is a dramatic and embarrassing thing to happen to a major world power.

Nevertheless, I, for one, applaud the U.S. decision to come down on the side of Britain. This clears the air immensely. It confirms that, as should be, the United States prefers its cultural and political bonds in the Anglo-Saxon community and that, in effect, its most important economic, political, and security arrangements lie in the Atlantic Alliance, not in the Gulf of Fonseca or the River Plate.

This actually opens the happy possibility for the United States of having a more modest presence in the hemisphere—to avoid, as my friend William D. Rogers says, becoming intoxicated with crisis, and to be but one more factor, not the only one, although always an extremely important one, in Latin America's relations with the world.

But what I am suggesting is not, once more, a policy of benign neglect as a pendulum reaction to busybody adventurism. No. After the war in the Malvinas, the United States has the extraordinary opportunity of rebuilding relations and demonstrating its good faith toward Latin America in an active way and in two immensely important areas: political negotiations in Central America and global negotiations for North-South economic development.

First, Central America. The rebellion of the poor and oppressed people of the region against situations dating from the arrival of Columbus in the New

World cannot be attributed to Cuba—they would persist even if Cuba sank into the sea—and they cannot be solved by foreign armed intervention. The greatest advantage that the United States could give the Soviet Union would be a policy certifying that the problems of Central America can only be solved by foreign intervention.

The time for political instead of military operations is here. The problems of Central America and the Caribbean can be negotiated: non-aggression pacts, border patrols, reduction of armies, strict non-interference, and mutual concessions are all possible if willed through effective diplomatic means. Again, the United States should not be alone in this process but, rather, become part of a quadrilateral negotiating team that might include citizens from Mexico, Venezuela, and France.

A greater equilibrium would then exist, and irrational fears might be allayed. What Helmut Schmidt, Margaret Thatcher, or David Rockefeller have said of the Marxist regimes of Black Africa is also true of present or eventual Marxist regimes in Latin America: If you can coexist with them, if you can do good business with them, the face of national interests will finally break through the mask of ideological dogmas. This is true of Angola; it can be true of El Salvador. If you can coexist with 800 million Chinese, you can surely coexist with 10 million Cubans. Relations with Nicaragua can be as pragmatic as relations with Zimbabwe.

This is a challenge. For once, outwit the Soviets by respecting revolutionary change. You are, after all, the fountainhead of revolution in this hemisphere.

The second opportunity the United States now has to renew hemispheric ties at a new level of seriousness has to do with North-South relations or, as President Francois Mitterand of France appropriately calls it, with co-development.

It must be clearly understood that the developing nations are not acting as supplicants in this matter. The solution of these problems is vital to both developed and developing countries. You are suffering from inflation with unemployment and slow growth, shrinking services, declining standards of living, and exacerbations of social tolerance. We are suffering from extreme dependency on exports, lack of public capital for infrastructure, and an incapacity to buy what you produce, therefore impoverishing both ourselves and you.

We believe — as the America of the New Deal knew and proved—that through rational cooperation, the economic community can reawaken if social and economic conditions are created for elevating demand in the developing nations. This is what is needed to guarantee greater use of labor and equipment in the industrialized world, therefore reducing costs and prices, but at the same time reducing the terrible gulf between potential and real demand in the Third World.

So you see, we are not the Indian tribe shooting arrows at your covered wagons; we are with you on the same stagecoach, defending ourselves, like you, against the slings and arrows of outrageous fortune.

Instead of supplying arms to torturers, instead of proving machismo by slapping around undernourished 7-year-olds, instead of drawing the line on Soviet expansionism where it does not exist—El Salvador—and where it wishes to withdraw—Cuba—and condoning it where it is all too flagrant—Poland and Afghanistan—instead of making love to good authoritarians who turn out to be the worst enemies of what your country stands for, instead of these failed policies, I propose today the policies of modesty, discretion, and coexistence in Latin America: coexistence with autonomous political change and coexistence in economic co-development.

The New World created the Modern World. Let not its destiny be to kill it as well.

*   *   *   *   *

I would like to finish, then, by saying that for me, the modern world was founded by the two greatest men of genius of our respective languages, English and Spanish.

Shakespeare, the tragedian of the human will, reminded us that there are always more things in heaven and earth than are dreamt of in any philosophy: The scope of life is always vaster than any possible theory on life.

And Cervantes, the comedian of the human imagination, sent Don Quixote forward from the shelter of his books and his village, forward from the enclosed and secure *civitas* of the Middle Ages to the open roads of the Brave New World of the Renaissance, there to discover that the world, painfully and joyfully, had changed, and that his larger charge was to accept the diversity and mutation of the world, while retaining the mind's power for analogy and unity, so that this changing world would not become meaningless.

Today we know better than ever that the alternative to political imagination and diplomatic negotiations is not power, or glory—it is death. Joseph Conrad understood this as he steamed up the big black river into the heart of darkness, there to discover that power over nothing does not lead to glory, but only to madness and destruction.

I know that sooner or later, your generation will be facing, courageously and decisively, the human needs in this country: democracy not only in the voting booth, but in the working place; decentralization, reindustrialization, the stamping out of crime, better schools, thorough racial integration and sexual equality, the great technological breakthroughs that can only be achieved through the quality of higher education and investment in research, all of this inseparable from compassion and legislation favoring the poor, the elderly, the handicapped.

At the same time, let Latin America catch up with you by leaving Latin America to muddle peacefully through its explosions and to find its own models of development. Leave us to overcome our contradictions, achieve our national identity, affirm our cultural heritage, and solve our family quarrels in our own ways. Be with us, not against us.

I know that you are, each one of you, a force for life, for imagination, for the true power and the true glory of existence on this earth.

A. Bartlett Giamatti

A. Bartlett Giamatti

BACCALAUREATE ADDRESS
YALE UNIVERSITY
May 23, 1982

"IN THE MIDDLE DISTANCE"

On September 5, 1978 we began our voyage together, and I am delighted to see so many of your company gathered here again. I can report that much of me has returned as well. In the interim, I have merely decayed, albeit with an insouciant grace, but you have, impressively and almost without effort, matured. You are now, in the view of the faculty and the trustees, ready for the greater voyage and it is my pleasant duty to be your pilot to the harbor's mouth. There you will set full sail and I, somewhat like Vergil' s Palinurus, will be washed head-long overboard, to float ashore on our island in the autumn, barnacled in wisdom, there to guide the next group of impressed young mariners to the point of embarkation. You will be well away by that time, we all devoutly trust.

Over time, these sea changes suffered annually by your pilot do not necessarily produce a figure rich and strange. Rather they tend to rot with motion the pilot's firmness of vision and steadiness of bearing. It is a matter of great consequence to me, and should be to you, for you will also be pilots henceforth, how to keep a clear eye and a moral compass pointing true.

How to keep one's bearings in the tempest ahead, given all the flux and fury of the past and the present, is therefore my theme today. You will, to extend the figure, sail into very savage seas in your voyage. We live in a world where the human race must decide, soon, how not to use the capacity to destroy itself through nuclear weapons that it has exactingly, lovingly crafted. We live in a time when, in the name of nationalist necessity, someone is killed every day. We see resources, human and natural, squandered or jealously sequestered; their consequent maldistribution gives rise to understandable yearnings and tremendous, dangerous tensions. We find in our own country an apparent incapacity to cope with the rhythms and dynamics of our freely-chosen economic system. And in the sphere I primarily inhabit, the world of education, we sense that the public loses faith in education and that a sense of failure mounts. Is that eroding faith, that sense of failure, justified? Is it only another form of apocalyptic wailing to ask how we will educate better or if we educate well at all? Or are there legitimate issues concerning education and our moral bearings which reasonable people must attend to?

I know this is a happy occasion, meant to gather family and friend in a moment of celebration. And I have no wish to dampen the atmosphere. But before any of us, my shipmates, indulges in self-congratulation on how well the University has served you, permit me a few remarks on some of the apprehensions I have. They are apprehensions about the process of education and, because I see education as central to the country's well-being, about the well-being of our culture and its political bearings. My thoughts will have at the outset a personal caste, which I trust you will indulge, because they spring from a recent experience of mine which forced me as I have been forced never before to face up to the consequences of a failure to educate people to think humanely and historically for the benefit of others. I realized how essential to our human freedom and dignity an education rooted in reality, ideas connected to circumstances, must be. But I anticipate.

Briefly stated, this March, on a gray and windy day I went to a place in Jerusalem called Yad Vashem. Yad Vashem is a monument to the heroes and martyrs of the Holocaust and a memorial to the six million Jews systematically murdered by the Nazis. To descend beneath the stark, concrete plaza to the underground museum is to descend into Hell at one remove. It is to go into mass moral chaos and yet it is only a representation, in photograph, artifact and text, of the horror of the camps and the monstrosity of the events and the minds that made them. To be immersed in our human capacity to be inhuman was for me to be flayed. I will not recount the reasons for that sense of being stripped of all customary assumptions and reactions because I do not intend to exploit that horror or the memories of those who died. I do intend, however, to assure you that one may have, as I had, one's certainties challenged and one's faith shaken in a radical way by confronting a reality that is now part of the inheritance of the human species.

Coming up from underground, I was forced to face the consequences of ideology. I had seen close up, even if at a remove, what can result when human beings ignore circumstances; that is, ignore our common moorings in our accumulated, common humanity. I use the word "circumstances" as Edmund Burke used it in his *Reflections on the Revolution in France* when he said that "Circumstances . . . give in reality to every political principle its distinguishing color and discriminating effect. The circumstances are what render every civil and political scheme beneficial or noxious to mankind." At Yad Vashem one sees the logical extension of abstraction without circumstances, of System without history, of ideology — moralistic, legalistic, internally complete — in the hands of the true believer: insanity can result and people can die. When timeless dogmas are allowed to run unconnected to time, that is, to the accumulated experience and contending currents of humanity, an ideology can encourage people to murder as easily as it can encourage them to claim nobility. Not every bloodless abstraction will necessarily spill someone else's blood, but every bloodless abstraction, of Left or Right, will necessarily swell toward authoritarianism, and from the urge to control to the self-righteous justification to kill is but a short step.

Why does any ideology tend to be authoritarian? Because any system of ideas that consciously purifies itself of previous condition or prior context —Burke's circumstances — and claims to contain all value must logically also wish to exert complete control. Any scheme for regulating life that systematically asserts it is internally and systematically complete, a law and a morality and a context of value and a machine for living unto itself, must logically will to exercise its power completely, or its claims for itself are invalid. The self-righteousness of all ideologies is a function of their self-perceived completeness; each element reflects the alleged correctness of every other. These closed systems are attractive because they are simple and are simple because they are such masterly evasions of contradictory, gray, complex reality. Those who manipulate such systems are compelling because they are never in doubt. Burke is clear in warning us against what he calls "the delusive plausibility of moral politicians." It is a warning one ignores only at great risk to one's freedom.

Yad Vashem raised for me those thoughts, among others, and I raise them here, now, because I explicitly and fervently hope your education has taught you what an education must teach — to fashion principles and purposes in context and to treat ideas in reality. I hope your education has taught you to think circumstantially and thus to transcend ideology. It is when I think of how education must be the means to develop resistance to ideology, must be the process for you and your children and theirs to test values and to keep the mind open, connected and growing, that I think of the burdens public education in America bears and how it is periodically asked to bear burdens of an ideological kind. You and I and our children will see again and again the urge to use the schools for ends other than the commencement of the lifelong process of education. And the most recent version of this ideological thrust is the desire of certain "moral politicians" to pass a constitutional amendment allowing voluntary prayer in public schools.

At first glance, this may seem remote from you. But it is not.

I happen to accept the need for prayer and to believe in prayer's efficacy. I believe we Americans are a believing people, though as individuals we do not, and we must not be forced to, believe in the same way, nor should we be forced to believe at all. Such are the circumstances of a pluralistic culture, of diverse peoples and religious traditions, and of the protections of the Bill of Rights. I believe it is the federal government's obligation to protect the right to worship or not to worship. I do not believe it is the government's obligation, and it should not become it, to encourage through the Constitution in the public schools organized religious expression.

The public school is not the arena to teach children how to pray or what or whom to pray to. The church or synagogue or house of worship is the place for that teaching and practice. The family is the forum for that teaching and practice. A public school is not a family or a house of worship. Any American government concerned with the integrity of the family and the viability of places of worship must recognize that its obligation is to keep some things separate, like Church and State, and that it has no role sustaining particular religious values. Its role is to preserve and protect a pluralistic environment in which religious practice, in the family and church, can flourish.

We have heard the argument that no child was historically harmed by praying in public school. That argument carries the very accent of the ideologue. It ignores reality — the circumstances of a pluralistic culture, of the protections of the Constitution, of the separation of Church and State, of the proper role of family and organized religious life; and it ignores the actual history of those children who in fact were coerced and made to feel exiles from their fellows and their circumstances by organized school prayer. It self-righteously assumes that whatever someone finds completely agreeable on moral and legal and abstract grounds must necessarily be agreeable to everyone else also. Such an argument reveals the tendency to authoritarian control of any ideology in the assumption that if people are not all the same, they should be treated as if they were for their own good.

Why do I bring up this issue? Certainly not because I believe all theologies are ideologies (which they are not); not because I enjoy being told I am a dangerous secularist (which I am not), or that I am a symbol of the decline of the West (which I could not be even if I did not hold, with Burke, to the relevance of our historical values and inheritance). I raise it because we as Americans, whatever our differences, face a serious set of problems in our schools, problems you will have to live with and try to solve, that will worsen if the schools and the means of education are used as staging areas for particular ideological goals.

When schooling takes second place to ideologically based policymaking, the very process for teaching all of us to think — to accumulate wisdom, to imbed information in values and experience — suffers, and society suffers as a consequence. I fear that the eighties will continue to witness what we see already, a politicizing of the schools for radical goals, cloaked in the rhetoric of morality and equity, in the same way the universities were politicized from the other end of the political spectrum in the sixties and early seventies. Beyond the example of the desire to amend the Constitution to allow prayer in schools, "voluntarily" or not, a larger pattern emerges, as it always emerges. And that is ideologue calling out to ideologue, and opposites turning out to be twins.

My larger point is that in the choosing between ideologues of the Right and of the Left, I choose to eschew both because they are finally, in their desire to control and exclude, not different. If you believe they are, if you believe that an ideologue of the Left is less authoritarian in impulses and acts than one of the Right, look again. I do not believe it.

Let me close, as I opened, on a more personal note. In urging you beyond ideology, in urging you through education to a civic circumstantiality, in urging you to care for the schools and those processes of education which are one of America's main defenses against authoritarian control from within and without, I offer the view of one person, one who is clearly middle-aged, middle-class, middle of the road; a view of one not given to extremes but to the middle. My middle view is the view of the centrist, who would also, as Alexander Bickel from whom I have learned so much — so eloquently put it, fix "our eyes on that middle distance, where values are provisionally held, are tested, and evolve within the legal order — derived from the morality of process, which is the morality of consent. . . ." To set one's course by such a centrist view, my shipmates, is to leave oneself open to the charges, hurled by the completely faithful of some extreme, of being relativistic, opportunistically flexible, secular, passive, passionless, lacking in timeless principle and of possessing characteristics and qualities even less elegant. Be of good cheer, for if the source of these charges is someone selling a System, you can always, with me, find your bearings with Burke, specifically in his sense of the need to embrace the contingent and the circumstantial, the real world of history and competing values and complex solutions, those "opposed and conflicting interests . . ." which produce "*temperaments*" (his italics), the tempering, cautionary, staying considerations that finally render "all the headlong exertions of arbitrary power, in the few or in the many, forever impracticable." To act according to an open and principled pragmatism, to believe in the power of process, is in fact to work for the good. I do not simply urge a long night of watching against the ideologue's delusive plausibility. I urge the positive, balanced, continuous operation of the mind and spirit that surges to do the work of civilization from the center without simplistic zealotry.

Ladies and Gentlemen of the Class of 1982:

A commitment to believing in process, either of education or law, in no way means one does not hold dear beliefs in equality, in social justice, in the reward of merit, in freedom to speak and worship and assemble. One must have convictions, but one must be willing to submit them to the testing and tumult of the middle distance. What binds us together as free women and men and as Americans is a shared faith in those processes by which we evolve and test our several beliefs and traditions. Fear as Hell the self-inflicted blindness of self-righteousness, where all perspective is foreshortened and all doubt is denied, and keep your eyes on the middle distance, where means and process live.

Note: The two texts from which I have derived much in composing this meditation are Edmund Burke's Reflections on the Revolution in France and Alexander Bickel's The Morality of Consent.

Leonard H. Goldenson

Leonard H. Goldenson

COMMENCEMENT ADDRESS
EMERSON COLLEGE
May 31, 1981

Doctor Baker, President Koenig fellow honorees, members of the graduating class of 1981, families and friends:

I have spent most of my life in the world of communications and entertainment, so I'm particularly pleased to be with you here today. You, the graduating class, have chosen to attend a college that is distinguished in those two fields. Now you've completed the course and won your degrees, and as I look at you, I hope that many of you are planning to carve out careers for yourselves in these same areas.

The 1980s are going to be a decade of enormous change for all of us who are involved in any aspect of communications — but then, change is a characteristic of the communications industry. The difference today is that the changes are of such magnitude, and they are coming so fast, that the industry is facing a new concept of communications.

This change indicates we cannot rely just on our intelligence and our mastery of traditional skills. As communicators, as performers, as creators —and as citizens — it necessitates a new kind of literacy. It will be a visual literacy, an electronic literacy, and it will be as much of an advance over the literacy of the written word we know today, as that was over the purely oral tradition of man's early history.

"Roots" was the story of Alex Haley's search for his African ancestry and heritage. In both the book and the television mini-series, there is a minor character who made that search successful — the "griot," or village historian of a tiny Gambian village. He could neither read nor write. But he had memorized every name and event in his village's history for hundreds of years. Alex Haley had to travel thousands of miles to ask the griot a single question. He had to listen to hours of recitation to get his answer. And an everyday accident could easily have prevented his getting the answer at all.

The "griot" was the communications system of a time long gone. But he helps us to understand that the growth of civilization has been in part made possible by the growth of communications — the solutions to the basic problem of how to gather, store and transmit information. When I speak of information, I am speaking not just of facts and data, but of a much broader spectrum — of opinion and analysis and interpretation, on one level — and, on another level, of entertainment and performance and participation in events. For just as scholarship adds to our knowledge, our cultural activities illuminate our values and explore solutions to our problems.

Despite this growth in capabilities, communications is still a field with very clear limits. Some of them are technical — there's a limit to the number of broadcast signals that can be put into the air before they begin to interfere with each other — and others are economic. But none of these limits is insurmountable. We are approaching a time when we can conceive of access to all available information, in the form, time and place of our choice.

Not very long ago, you were putting the finishing touches on your last college term paper, with footnotes on each page and a long bibliography at the end. Those additions to your text were your way of telling your professor that you had used the available communications media intelligently. But both you and the professor were also acknowledging that somewhere in this world, there might exist an information source far more useful than anything you were able to dig up — even by using the advanced data banks of Emerson library's "Dialogue" system. Imagine, then, a telephone-and-computer-based system that would instantaneously have given you every reference having anything to do with your topic. Research would have become a routine electronic function; what would have mattered to your professor would have been only this: Did you ask the right questions? And how well did you use the answers you got?

The computer, is of course, only one of the many technological advances that are making the communications revolution possible. I think you know the names of the other principal elements as well. There is cable television, with the ability to multiply greatly the number of electronic channels entering and leaving the home or office or classroom. There is fiber optics, with still greater channel capacity. There are satellites, able to carry signals to and from any place on the globe. There are video tapes and discs, with their temporary or permanent storage capability. There is electronic journalism, with its data banks. And there are still more developments beyond these.

The point, though, is not what these things can do in and of themselves. It is what else they will make possible. Each time we open up a new channel of communication, the existence of that channel is far more important than any one piece of information we put through the channel. By way of analogy, the elevator at 100 Beacon Street is a simple device that moves people and things up and down. What it makes possible is a building far taller than would otherwise be usable. And what it means is a concentration of human activity far greater than could have been dreamed of a century ago.

We are creating an era of total communications — an era in which any piece of information can be created and stored and used by any person in any situation he chooses. That will be true whether the information is a scholarly essay, a piano recital, a surgical technique, a commercial transaction, a cooking recipe or an invitation to dinner. Like the elevator, but on a greater scale, total communications is going to change the way we live.

Just how they will change is something we do not completely know. The computer people say that "hardware creates its own software." We build machines for one purpose, and then find that they evolve to serve another and perhaps greater purpose. In my own business of television, we began by imitating every form of information or entertainment we could adapt to our medium. Those that worked, we kept. With time and experimentation, what gradually evolved was a service clearly different from that provided by any other communications medium. The same can be said for any other major communications advance.

People take time to adapt themselves to change, and change in communications is a very fundamental change indeed. Television is now a third of a century old, and we are learning new lessons every day about the role that it plays in the lives of its audience.

It is here that we will need what I have called the New Literacy — The literacy of electronics and visual communications. It will be partly a matter of knowing, technically, how to use the new communications media, and being comfortable using them. But it is not just a matter of knowing how to employ cameras and cassettes and computers. It is also a matter of knowing when to use them, and why.

Thus, we will need a generation of people who do not fear and do not dissipate their energies fighting the communications revolution, as the Luddites opposed the Industrial Revolution. And we will need a generation of people who will not embrace and abuse the new media in the manner of a child turned loose in a candy store. It has been fashionable to say that the liberal education is obsolete today; my own view is that the balance and perspective it provides will be ever more important as the events of the next decade unfold.

Beyond the New Literacy, there will be one commodity in great demand in the fields of communications, in information and entertainment alike. That commodity is creativity.

Just in the world of entertainment, the demands for creative talent today are enormous. One television network alone presents some 2,000 hours of original entertainment in a year, in addition to the many informational and other programs it airs.

So the demand for creative talent is already immense, and it can only become greater as the new media become more prominent. But the need is greater than sheer volume. When communications services were limited in number, for technical or economic reasons, the professional communicator needed only to offer a service that was better than the small number of alternatives.

But when the number of alternatives is very large, that approach no longer works. It's necessary to provide a service that's desirable in comparison with everything else that's available. And that means identifying very clearly what the consumer of communications wants, and concentrating on those things that you can do better than anyone else. At ABC, we've been giving a great deal of thought to this kind of analysis, and I'm sure everyone else with a future in communications is doing the same thing.

For those of you who are planning to enter the media, let me point out that the need for this type of strategic analysis is not new. In my experience, it comes with the territory.

For example, with the advent of commercial radio in the 1920s, the recording industry was fearful that consumers would stop buying records — because records could be heard free of charge on the radio. At first the recording industry was adversely affected, but today records are a multibillion-dollar business — because people in that business used radio, their competitive enemy, in a creative manner to sell records.

In the early 1950s, when television became a commercial reality, the motion picture and radio industries thought they, in turn, would be forced out of business. As a matter of fact, when my Company acquired ABC at that time, we were the largest motion picture theatre operators, and people in the motion picture industry called us traitors.

Our answer, then and now, was that if one could place advertisements for new films in every American home, it would make the movie business greater than ever. For a period of time, that industry was adversely affected. But before television, there were few pictures grossing more than $5 million. Today, using commercials on television, the average picture is grossing over $15 million, and a number of releases have reached over $100 million.

The radio industry initially was worried by the challenge of television, too. The amazing vitality with which radio survived is reflected at ABC. We pioneered the expansion of the network concept, creating four separate radio networks, each directed to a specific audience. This creative change has proven successful — and far from witnessing the end of radio, we are now considering the launching of two more networks.

With the onslaught of the new technologies, some people are once again prophesizing doom for the established media, especially the three commercial networks. But they are correct only in assuming that things will change. There will be some dilution of the network audience at first — but what is more important, the three networks will continue to be the mass medium sought by advertisers and the public. During the 1980s, the number of television homes will grow from 80 million to over 100 million, and we expect the networks will be serving more homes than we do today.

Broadcasters won't be able to reach that larger audience by programming as we do today. It won't be "business as usual." Broadcasting in the future will require continued ingenuity and creativity, bringing unique programs to the American public, different from what they receive from pay cable and satellites.

On a personal note, I've always been excited by challenges of this type in the communications business. For those of you entering the field, in whatever form, the problems will constantly be changing as technology evolves. I think what we've seen in the growth of communications until now is only a taste of what we can look forward to in the very near future. I find the business increasingly exciting today, and I am confident you will find that feeling contagious if you join in the communications profession.

Thank you and good luck to you all.

Dr. Donald Grunewald

Dr. Donald Grunewald

COMMENCEMENT ADDRESS
MEDAILLE COLLEGE
Thursday, May 26, 1983

Members of the Class of 1983, ladies and gentlemen.

When President Downey asked me to speak at your Commencement, I was happy to accept for two reasons. First of all, Medaille College is an exciting place and it is a privilege to be able to become associated with it and with you through paticipating in this Commencement. Secondly, as a long time professor and academic, it is a great opportunity for me to give you your last undergraduate lecture. Relax, it will not be for the standard fifty minute academic hour. I have only four basic points to make and they will not take very long. Besides, when I asked President Downey what I should speak about, he said, "About 15 minutes". Then too, unlike your other college lectures there will be no examinations afterwards — whether you pay attention to what I have to say or not, you will still have completed this Commencement and you will be *bona fide* graduates of Medaille College in a few minutes.

Point one, you didn't do it all yourself. You were aided by others and you must in turn help others. I congratulate each one of you on your accomplishments in completing your undergraduate education at Medaille. Again you didn't do it all yourself. All through your life, you had help from many persons. Some of those who helped you develop your potential are here today and I think we should acknowledge their help.

First of all, we should thank your parents, spouses, and members of your families. Would the parents, spouses, and relatives of the graduates who are here today please stand up? Thank you for what you have done for the graduates.

Secondly, the faculty and administration of this college have done much to help you wend you way through both the high points and the difficulties of a college education. Would the members of the faculty and administration who are here today please rise, to be acknowledge? Thank you for a job well done.

Your college education would not have been possible without the benefactors who paid for much of your education. Tuition at a first rate college like Medaille covers only a part of the cost of your education. The Founders of the college, the Sisters of St. Joseph, have done much to help the college. So have the Board of Trustees and the Alumni. The taxpayers have also provided a very modest subsidy to the cost of your education — a much smaller amount per student than they provide to government operated institutions like the state university or the community college. Would the members of the Sisters of St. Joseph who are here today, the members of the Board of Trustees, and the alumni who are here today please rise to be acknowledged? Thank you for making a quality education possible for so many at a reasonable cost.

There are many others who may not be here today who have helped you. I know each of you will take the opportunity to thank them whenever possible.

There is one person here today who should be especially acknowledged. He has had the challenge of leading his college — of raising money, of providing educational leadership and of providing leadership to all the diverse areas of the college. He is one of the outstanding educational leaders in our state. President Leo Downey, will you please rise to be acknowledged? Thank you for what you are doing for all of higher education and for what you are doing for Medaille College.

We have acknowledged some of those who have helped you to get here today. Now it is time to acknowledge you. Will all the graduates rise to be acknowledged? Thank you. Remember all those others who have been acknowledged today for helping you. It will now be your turn after you leave here today to go and do likewise for others who will follow you at Medaille College. Each of you can help them get the same high quality education you received by making a gift each year to the alumni fund. You can help in other ways by your example in the kind of lives you lead and what you do for your country and for yourself.

Point two, plan ahead for your future and use role models to help you. Think what you would like to do in five years. Start now with some kind of a job that can be built upon or with graduate school. Look to the careers of others for inspiration. Read biographies and autobiographies to learn what others have done. Talk to many people in all walks of life. Pick role models and learn what they have done to achieve their goals. For example, if you desire to become a lawyer, study the career of a Supreme Court justice like Sandra Day O'Connor or a famous trial attorney like Clarence Darrow. If you desire to become a professor, you have many good models to pick from at Medaille. Careers of friends and relatives also can provide inspiration. Even college presidents have their heroes such as Eliphalet Nott who served more than sixty years as president of his college or the Presidents of Princeton and Columbia, Wilson and Eisenhower, who went on to well known careers in government after being college presidents. My own hero has been Benjamin Franklin whose autobiography has provided me with much inspiration over the years. Heroes and role models can help.

Point three, prepare for a lifetime of continued education. We call this ceremony today a Commencement — it is a beginning. You will need to continue learning for the rest of your life. Half of what you have studied at Medaille will become obsolete or you will forget it within five years. With the great changes in technology, developments in social sciences, and in other fields — the knowledge explosion — you can't stop learning now. Whether you continue in school in the future or you learn on your own in the future is your decision. But you must continue to learn if you are to keep up with a rapidly changing world.

Point four, strive for excellence in whatever you do. America will only continue to be a success if we strive continuously for excellence in whatever we do. When I take my car to be repaired, I want an excellent auto mechanic who will do the best possible job. When I go to the hospital for an operation, I want an excellent surgeon who will do his or her best. If we all do our best, in everything we do — whether it is collecting garbage or piloting a rocket to the moon — we will have a first rate society. The old grammar school motto says it best, "Never rest until you have made the good, better, and the better, best."

These four points will, I believe be of help to you. To summarize your last undergraduate lecture, recognize that you didn't do it all yourself. Turn around and acknowledge this help by helping others. Plan ahead for life and use good role models to help. Remember that you must continue to learn throughout life and do everything you do with excellence. Although you will receive no hour exam today you will be tested throughout life every day in many ways. I am confident you will pass these tests as you have passed your tests at Medaille.

It is a pleasure to share this graduation with you. Congratulations and every best wish to each of you.

Theodore M. Hesburgh

Theodore M. Hesburgh

COMMENCEMENT ADDRESS
RENSSELAER POLYTECHNIC INSTITUTE
May 16, 1980

One of the most perceptive tourists ever to visit America made his trip to our shores about 150 years ago, in 1831. His name was Alexis De Tocqueville, and on his return to France, he wrote two books, with a five-year interval between them, although both books bear the same title, *Democracy in America*. De Tocqueville had many acute observations about our country. A century and a half since he wrote those books, the central reality that he describes has become even more important in the life of our nation. I can't think of any reality more important in our nation's life today.

First, let me give you De Tocqueville's words: "Americans of all ages, all conditions, and all dispositions constantly form associations. They not only have commercial and manufacturing companies in which everyone takes part, but associations of a thousand other kinds—religious, moral, serious or futile, general or restricted, autonomous or limited, enormous or diminutive. The Americans make associations to give entertainment, to found seminaries, to build inns, to construct churches, to diffuse books, even to send missionaries to the antipodes. And in this manner they found hospitals, and prisons, and schools. If it is proposed to inculcate some truth or to foster some feeling by encouragement of a great example, Americans form a society. Wherever at the head of some new undertaking you see the government in France or a man of rank in England, in the United States you will be sure to find a voluntary association."

What De Tocqueville was describing, we call voluntarism. I doubt that even he could have imagined how voluntarism helped the building of America, as we know it, in the last century and a half. All of the early institutions of higher education, including this one, are the results of voluntary action. All of our churches, most of our hospitals. all of our businesses, our labor unions, our newspapers, radio and television stations. all of our clubs, our professional associations, our political parties, all of our operas, symphonies and ballet companies, all of our entertainment. all of our athletic teams—professional and amateur—all of our transport systems, our artistic endeavors ... in a word, almost the whole total fabric of our society was initiated, developed and is today maintained by voluntary activity of the private sector.

Volunteer support in gifts last year alone exceeded $39 billion. That is $7 billion more than the year before. And no one could possibly calculate the monetary value of all of the voluntary services involved in all of these organizations, including your own Board of Trustees. If you would wish to see how unique this makes America, visit a communist or a socialist society—Russia or China or Czechoslovakia, for example. There the society is gray, monochromatic, not multi-colored. If you read a paper, it is government-issued. So is radio and television. If you do business, you do it with a government entity. Olympic athletes are government employees and so are all transport services. If you join a club, it is a government-sponsored and supported club. All higher education—admissions, curriculum, professional and administrative appointments—all are made by the government. We take voluntarism so much for granted in America that its importance is not really appreciated until we compare our way of life to that of countries where everything is "of-the-state," "by-the-state," and "for-the-state."

I may perhaps make the point more forcefully if I put to you an interesting question. Suppose that tomorrow morning the most expensive multi-billion dollar endeavor in our land, namely the federal government, were suddenly to be inactivated. What would be the effect? The impact on your personal life? I would suspect that it would be enormously less of an impact than if all voluntary associations were suddenly disengaged tomorrow morning. May I make myself a guinea pig for the moment to test this hypothesis?

I was born in a private hospital, and grew up with private medical care, in a private home and not a government apartment. I was supported by money earned by my father who worked for a private concern, the Pittsburgh Plate Glass Company in Syracuse, New York. I attended private schools—parochial, elementary and high schools—and three private universities here and abroad. I was a Boy Scout. I swam during the icy Syracuse winters at the YMCA. For spending money, I had my own private enterprise—mowing lawns in the summer and shoveling ashes from furnaces in the winter. I went to a church, founded and supported voluntarily. I joined a private religious order, was ordained a priest, and taught and administered in a private university. Because I took the vow of poverty, all of my income goes to private causes, one-fourth to the Order and three-fourths to the university. I have served the government in a multiplicity of roles—from commissioner to chaplain to ambassador and, at the moment, chairman of the Select Commission on Immigration and Refugee Policy.

All of these tasks I do without pay because it seems more fitting in our country to volunteer one's services. Take the volunteer associations and activities out of just one life and there is practically nothing left. De Tocqueviile was right when he said, "What political power could ever carry on the vast multitude of lesser undertakings which American citizens perform for themselves every day?"

All our lives as we presently live them are impossible without the enormous involvement of voluntary associations, voluntary gifts that make them possible, and voluntary services that carry them out. If you agree with me that all of this voluntarism is good for America and for us Americans, may I suggest to you that in our day we are facing the beginning of a counter-movement that strikes at the very heart of what has made America great and unique among the nations of the world.

"Despite our history of voluntarism . . . I sense that today, there is a tendency to say 'Let the government do it.' And I say to you . . . that when the government does it, the doing is almost always more costly . . . less free . . . more complicated, and generally less productive and effective."

To the extent that we say, "Let the government do it," we are bartering away our human freedom. This may seem overstated; allow me to be more explicit. Before World War II, the government's involvement in higher education was minimal—less than $50 million a year. After the war, when we were tripling in three decades what we had achieved in three centuries of higher education in America, the federal government became our largest benefactor. In general, this seemed to all of us to be a good development. We needed government loans for academic buildings. We needed large research grants in science and technology. We needed scholarship help for the ever-growing number of students who otherwise would be unable financially to attend our universities. We needed medical grants and library subsidies.

When all of this had grown to over $80 billion a year, suddenly a wide variety of authorities with very special interests began to descend upon our campuses. They were not members of the three branches of government—the judicial, the executive, or the legislative. They were a new breed called regulators. They were regulating health, environment, women's rights, minority rights, OSHA, ORESA, employment beyond the age of 65, Title IX applied to athletics, IRS looking for unrelated income, and a whole spate of generally good causes. But they were single-minded in their concern with a particular issue, and unrelated to the common good of the whole institution.

It has been said jokingly that the three biggest lies in American life today are: "I'll call you back tomorrow," "I gave at the office," or thirdly, "I'm from the government and I'm here to help you."

A few weeks ago we had an officers' meeting at our university. It was long and difficult and complicated. And after it was over, it occurred to me that two-thirds of our time had been taken up with problems involved with federal intervention into the academic life of the institution. We hadn't spent those hours making a better university or planning for better higher education. We had spent them fending off what we looked upon as interference in what we were doing. The question arises, "How did we get ourselves involved in such a tangle?" Does it say anything to us about, perhaps, our lack of total enthusiasm about voluntarism, and our voluntary associations? I suspect that the real problem most fundamentally has to do with freedom and the conduct of those most important institutions freedom has founded and maintained and cherished in our land, such as this university.

One can understand how we accepted the beneficence of the federal government when we needed it to fulfill our mission in the 1950s and 60s and 70s. But we did so without very much serious thought about maintaining that freedom which makes our institutions so very important and central, especially our education institutions in the "Land of the Free."

I believe that at this point we must reassess our situation. It may be that we cannot accept the largesse of the federal government if it means the end of those free institutions that are at the very heart of what makes America great and unique among all the nations of the world. Or if the help is really essential, possibly regulation—this fourth form of government today, not established by the constitution, free-ranging, practically responsible to no one, not even the President—perhaps this new form of government regulation should be reined in by the other three forms of government that are established by the Constitution, and that are themselves mutually checked and balanced.

I would not want you to get the impression that I am completely and irrevocably opposed to any kind of regulation whatever. I am not. In a society as complicated as ours, we do need some regulation, because it is necessary to achieve the common good. That is the purpose of all government and of all law. It is needed in such things as essential food and drug regulations, in highway and airport safety, or in factors bearing on equality of opportunity for all of our citizens. It is only when regulations are blind to all except the single issue involved in being regulated, it is only when they are blind to the common good, and it is only when regulations proliferate to Orwellian dimensions— then I begin to sense disaster and to send up danger signals as I am now doing.

Regulations are fundamentally related to the achievement of laws, and one of the four essentials for just law—according to Aquinas—is that it promote the common good. Any regulation that is not concerned with the common good, with the kinds of checks and balances, tradeoffs that guarantee the common good in a democracy, any regulation that goes blindly toward one goal unrelated to the common good, is a bad regulation, and it is not part of what I would call rational law. Even in the present confused situation, let us not underestimate the continuing and the deep value of voluntary activity. Let me give you a quick case study of something that happened in the past several months that I think is a classic example of the private and the public sectors of our country cooperating for the common good, both national and international. In this case, the mutual roles of public and private are synergistic, not destructive of one another.

Last October it suddenly became apparent that almost one half of the Cambodian population—the educated and the professional half—had been brutally exterminated by the Khmer Rouge, the Pol Pot regime, and that the other half was in proximate danger of dying from starvation, disease, and the other ravages of war. Secretary General Kurt Waldheim was about to announce a relief plan. Phnom Penh was about to open up a bit for relief, and thousands of refugees were crossing over the western border to Thailand. Contrary to a previous order of the Thai government, these later refugees were to be helped, not driven back this time, as 40,000 had been to sure death and destruction.

At this time, there were more than 30 voluntary associations, both religious and secular, plus several national and international public organizations, that were interested in staving off this new holocaust of the Cambodian people. We (and I speak now as the Chairman of the Overseas Development Council) summoned all of these organizations to the board room of ODC on October 25th of last year In two hours we all agreed to act as one. We approved a letter to President Carter and to Secretary Waldheim, then we all went over to the White House and we met the President in the Cabinet Room. We made seven requests to our government, which had said ten days previously that there were only 2,800 tons of food for all of Cambodia next year, despite the fact that we were selling 25 million tons at that time to the Russians. President Carter listened very carefully, because we told him we represented 150 million Americans who believed in something. He granted our seven requests immediately.

A few days later, representing all of these agencies, I went to the United Nations with the then Secretary of State Cyrus Vance and we met with Secretary Waldheim and, together with a few dozen other nations of the world, we pledged a total of more than $200 million to activate our efforts. Part of this $200 million was $110 million from our country that the President had promised us when he made this agreement.

Then Mrs. Carter went to visit the refugee camps on the Thai-Cambodia border, and on her return we had another all-day meeting at the White House. It was opened up by the President and it was continued with a report from the First Lady on her visit. On this November the 13th meeting, two weeks after the first one, we formalized all of our commitments. We established a crisis center in Washington to coordinate all of the fund-raising and information gathering. We put a representative in the headquarters of UNICEF, the International Red Cross, and another in the offices of our Ambassador-at-Large to coordinate all national refugee and relief efforts. This gave us an hourly coordination among everyone working in the field. At the end of January we had one last meeting at the White House where we set up a national committee. And that committee in a matter of four months raised, privately, $45 million for Cambodian relief.

I tell you this because I think young people today feel a kind of hopelessness. The problems are so massive, so global, that you feel you really can't do anything. But here was a case where a group of private citizens really turned around a very bad situation. Much remains to be done. But the impending disaster, the threat of holocaust, was averted. Our path ahead to keep on averting it was clarified, and we established realistic goals and are meeting those goals.

All of this was done in the best American tradition of voluntary leadership and cooperation between the public and the private sector, between national and international organizations. I truly believe that with the absence of voluntary effort in the private sector, much of what happened in the public sector simply would not have been possible. There was no unseemly rivalry in all of this. There was no reaching for publicity or acclaim. There was just generous and wholehearted cooperation in what was a good and a just cause.

No matter that the victims were mostly Buddhists and that those who were helping them were mainly Christian and Jewish. No matter that the victims were governed by communist factions, the USSR and North Vietnam. We were looking at suffering people—dying human beings— and they desperately needed help. This case study, I believe, is a true paradigm of the kind of beneficent, creative, and voluntary activity that De Tocqueville had in mind when he described the building of the nation of America. It reached, as he put it, to the antipodes, beyond our shores . . . half way around the world.

Here, ladies and gentlemen, is a spirit that needs to be rediscovered, cleansed of over-regulation, and re-invigorated in modern America. All of you have to be a part of it. This spirit is the antithesis of "Let the government do it." This spirit transcends the meddling of excessive and irrational federal regulation, and nitpicking bureaucrats who pile up mountains of meaningless reports. This spirit surmounts the selfish, single-issue zealots who are unmindful of the common good of this nation. This spirit springs from free citizens who prize and who use their freedom to touch humanity and its basic needs and anguishes. They touch it by dedicated service, freely given.

Voluntarism in its many, many faceted manifestations in our land is, I believe, America uniquely at its best.

Dear graduates, in conclusion I'd like to give you a quick picture of a person who is a great volunteer, because I think one picture is worth a thousand words. This is a picture of one of my heroes who I suggest might also be one of yours, Dr. Albert Schweitzer. When Dr. Schweitzer was your age he had three brilliant careers open to him. He was a concert organist; he was a great budding Protestant theologian, one of the best in Europe; and he was, as well, a brilliant young doctor.

He gave up all that and left Europe, his homeland, and went to a little place on a turgid river in French Equatorial Africa called Lambarene. There he spent the rest of his life bringing medical care to an area that hadn't seen a doctor, ever. He was gentle and good with his people, and a great adversary to all the diseases that beset that part of the world. He still played the organ at night. He brought a little organ encased in tin with him, and even though the various insects of that part of the world made his organ less good, he kept on playing it. That brought him consolation in the evenings. He also spent hours at the end of the day writing long sheets of theology. It was less excellent because he was out of touch with the great libraries and the great developments of the world. But at the same time he was more in touch with his career of medicine, because he was in touch with the people where they ached and pained and where they died sudden and precipitous deaths. He cared for them. He cared for every living thing. And he cared for that little village of Lambarene and all the villages surrounding it. He became a symbol of what it is to give one's life for others less fortunate.

One day, Dr. Schweitzer was called back to Europe to talk to a graduating class like this, and he said to them something that sank into their souls, as I hope it sinks into yours.

He said, "My dear young men and women, you are enormously blessed with a great education, with competence, and you have the title of a great university after your name. I don't know where you're going to go in life. I don't know what you're going to do. But I must tell you one thing on which I would stake my life. Wherever you go, whatever you do, unless you block out at least a small part of your life to give to others less fortunate than yourselves, you will not really be happy."

My greatest wish and prayer for you this morning is that all of the members of this class may have happy lives. God bless and keep you!

Charles J. Hitch

Charles J. Hitch

COMMENCEMENT ADDRESS
COLORADO SCHOOL OF MINES
May 11, 1979

"RESOURCES IN OUR FUTURE"

We live in an era of limits, say the vanguard politicians. The intelligentsia agree that small is beautiful; that economic growth must be restrained, if not abandoned altogether; that present and potential shortages of resources will constrain society even if we do curb our greedy impulses; and that, in short, this generation of earthlings — and most especially this generation of Americans — has pretty well completed the job of squandering the rich legacy of resources bestowed on us at the Creation, however you view that event.

These views, or at least their essential core, have trickled down from the intellectual establishment into the people at large, so that the idea that we are running out of resources now represents majority opinion in this country. The Roper Organization conducted a survey last year in which a random sampling of persons were asked about a list of thirteen possible trends, most of them negative to most eyes.[1] These included such things as "deterioration of family life," "increasing population," "overcrowding in cities," and "declines in religion" and in "quality of education." At the.top of the list, heading the pack with 58 percent of the respondents indicating that they thought it likely to happen, was "rapid depletion of natural resources." How the public reconciles this view with another; namely, that there is no energy crisis but just shortages contrived by the oil companies, Roper does not attempt to explain.

Moreover, when the survey participants were asked to go back over the list and say which trends were serious threats to society, again "rapid depletion of natural resources" topped the list, with 44 percent.

Jane Yarn, the newest member of the President's Council of Environmental Quality, said in a recent interview that ". . . the big issue (of the 1980s) will be the scarcity of finite resources . . ."[2] I think she is right, not so much because of actual scarcity, for I do not think that will be the case, but because so many people believe in the threat of scarcity.

There are several strands of thought woven into this apparent new consensus. Among others, it's part Club of Rome, part the environmental reawakening of about ten years ago, part higher energy prices, and part the intuitive gut-knowledge that, after all, nothing on earth is infinite. Together they form a powerful expression of the theme first articulated by Malthus in 1798. Malthus, you may recall, wrote that:

> Population, when unchecked, increases in a geometrical ratio. Subsistence increases only in an arithmetical ratio. A slight acquaintance with numbers will show the immensity of the first power as compared with the second."[3]

Malthus' gloomy prognosis has enjoyed swings of popularity during the succeeding 180 years. Indeed, it was not very long ago that his *Essay on the Principle of Population* was looked on as a quaint relic of an outmoded age.

Of course, there is another school of thought which waxes as Malthusianism wanes, a view sometimes called technological optimism. Briefly, proponents of this approach hold that the concept of scarcity, while true enough as an abstraction and in eventual absolute terms, is almost irrelevant in the light of the abundance of most natural resources, and that the market place through the price system acts to conserve those resources that are most scarce. That is, prices for a scarce material rise to the point where demand falls off to a level consistent with supply. When prices go too high, or in the unlikely event of near or absolute depletion, research and technology are stimulated to develop an adequate substitute (which may even be cheaper, or more efficient).

By and large, the system of market allocation of resources buttressed by technological innovation seems to have worked well since Malthus' time. Thus, coal and petroleum transformed the energy-deficient 19th Century; more abundant aluminum is replacing more scarce copper in several applications; copper ore itself now can be mined economically in concentrations of .5 percent vs. 5 percent a century ago; and, in the industrialized countries, more food is being produced on fewer acres by a vastly reduced labor force. Despite the fact that world population has grown roughly four-and-a-half-times[4] since Malthus' day, people today are living better in real terms than they ever have before, and that—despite the relative severity of their position—includes those in most of the developing countries.

Almost twenty years ago, RFF's Neal Potter and Francis T. Christy, Jr., began the work that led to the publication in 1962 of *Trends In Natural Resource Commodities.* In a pioneering effort, they put the statistics for more than 100 resource products on a uniform basis for the years 1870 to 1957. Previously there had been so many gaps and inconsistencies in the figures that it was all but impossible to compare the statistics for one period with those for another.

Last year, Robert Manthy of Michigan State University brought the Potter and Christy work up to 1973, thus providing in one volume more than a century of statistics. These comprehensive and consistent data are essential for research on basic natural resources problems, but they also allow inferences to be drawn about the suggestion that many minerals and other raw materials are growing more scarce and perhaps even disappearing. If this is so, then it ought to be reflected in rising relative prices for the scarce commodities. Potter and Christy found no such trend in 1957, and Manthy discovered no major changes during the next sixteen years. Indeed he writes that:

"Historical trends in both the employment aggregates and deflated prices suggest that environmentalist and conservationist concern about the adequacy of natural resources is founded on a premise that the future will be radically different from the past. Both data series show resource abundance rather than scarcity."[5]

Leaving aside popular works—for as I have suggested they have had enormous influence—the single most important and influential appraisal of the adequacy of natural resources has been another RFF book, *Scarcity and Growth,* by Harold Barnett and Chandler Morse. Using the Potter and Christy data just mentioned, Barnett and Morse in 1963 found no evidence of growing resource scarcity and argued instead that the problem of natural resources is best viewed "... as one of continual adjustment to an ever changing economic resource quality spectrum. The physical properties of the natural resource base impose a series of initial constraints on the growth and progress of mankind, but the resources spectrum undergoes kaleidoscopic change through time. Continual enlargement of the scope of substitutability—the result of man's technological ingenuity and organizational wisdom—offers those who are nimble a multitude of opportunities for escape."[6]

More recently, Weinberg and Goeller similarly have suggested that, given enough energy—a big "given"—the interlocking systems that are the planet earth can be made productive almost without end. They propose, in what they call "the Principle of 'Infinite Substitutability'" that:

"with two notable exceptions—phosphorous and energy-producing fossil fuels... —the society can subsist with relatively little loss of living standards on infinite or near infinite minerals. Such a civilization would be based largely on glass, plastic, wood, cement, iron, aluminum, and magnesium: whether it will be anything like our present society will depend upon how much of the ultimate raw material, energy, we can produce—and how much energy will cost, both economically and environmentally"[7]

Demonstrations of human ingenuity are not convincing to the pessimists, however. Indeed, they say, growing affluence and consumption for growing numbers of people only accelerate the rate at which natural resources are being used up, only bring closer the day of reckoning. Far from refuting the Malthusian thesis, they maintain, the optimists are rushing pell mell to prove it. The pie of natural resources is only so large, and it is being consumed at an ever-increasing pace.

Where does the truth lie? In a cornucopia of future plenty? Unprecedented catastrophe? Somewhere in-between? If anybody could predict the future with any degree of certainty, there would be no controversy: the very heat generated by the topic attests to its insolubility. Nobody knows, for the future is full of imponderables and veiled by our incapacity to imagine a world startingly different from what we have known. Could Malthus fathom a world of automobiles, trips to the moon, and birth control pills? Did our grandparents plan on jet planes or television, on computers or high-yield grain varieties, on any of the myriad innovations that have become part of our routine experience? I think it is clear that we have not come to the end of new ideas and ways of doing things, that the future will have its own configuration now impossible to predict.

I am strongly persuaded that human inventiveness and adaptability can work to make our future secure, that most resources are sufficient for a very long time, and that effective substitutes can be found for those few which are vital and rapidly becoming less accessible. But if I find no basis for believing that doomsday is imminent, a philosophy of "onward and upward forever" has even less to recommend it as a strategy for the future. Clearly, there are limits to growth, despite the several flaws in the Club of Rome's report of that name. There are eventual limits, such as space for population, and probably waste heat accumulation. There are exceedingly difficult obstacles, such as the development of an abundant, clean energy source with a reasonable price tag. There are problems of food production and distribution that will sorely test our humanity. And the whole is shot through with risk, with none greater than that of nuclear war.

When all is said and done, I definitely come down on the positive side of the ledger, but with a keen awareness that many of today's trends cannot be continued. And there are two areas in which we must make a great deal of progress fairly rapidly. One, as I have suggested earlier, is energy. The other— safe guarding the environment—is closely related, for nothing pollutes quite as thoroughly as the extraction, transportation, processing, and use of fuel minerals. Let me take these topics up in order.

For the short term, the era of cheap energy is over, but to say that energy will cost more is not the same thing as saying that we are in imminent danger of running out of it. Its sources may change and it will cost more—because production costs are higher, because associated environmental costs are beginning to be charged directly to energy users (as they should be), because of international political and trade considerations—but it won't disappear, at least not soon and certainly not suddenly. Contrary to the popular "running-out" thesis, even without further technological breakthroughs, world fossil fuel reserves appear adequate for at least the next half century, and this estimate doesn't even count such things as oil shale and tar sands. We simply are not going to fall off an energy cliff in 1985 or 2010, as long as the true costs of extracting energy are recognized and paid.

Thus cost, not scarcity, is the most important short-term problem. This presents certain problems, but they are not nearly as serious as would be an actual shortage of world energy resources. To give you an idea of the magnitudes we are talking about, my research leads me to believe that, in the United States, we could tolerate fairly well a doubling of the real costs of energy during the next three decades, that is, to about $30 per barrel of oil (in 1979 prices) compared to about $15 (at the margin) now. But is a "mere" doubling of real energy costs all that we need to adjust to in the long run? Probably.

A likely cost ceiling is provided by our enormous reserves of coal and our uncertain but highly stretchable reserves of uranium: We will encounter some increasing costs as we expand coal production, but I can't see them more than doubling, even if the costs of controlling effluents rise substantially, and we are now controlling them so inefficiently that they could well fall if we adopt more cost-effective regulatory methods. Similarly, costs of uranium could rise as we deplete the richest reserves. But the cost of uranium is such a small portion of nuclear power costs (now about 10% at the bus bar), even *much* higher costs would fall far short of doubling the cost of electricity. And if there is real concern about "running out" there are all sorts of ways of stretching the supply, including advanced converter reactors, breeders, and the use of thorium.

Well, that takes care of electricity, I hear you saying, but what about our needs for liquids and gases, and in particular, for liquids for transportation? Here again I think coal provides a ceiling. The next-generation technologies producing synthetic liquids and gases from coal promise to get the costs down to around $25 to $30 per barrel (constant dollars). And there are all sorts of other possibilities for getting liquids and gases at the same or even lower prices—as yet undiscovered new fields (witness Mexico); tertiary recovery from old fields; unconventional sources of natural gas; heavy oils; shales and tar sands, to mention a few, all with very large resource bases. And quite probably, within 30 years, some $30 per barrel equivalent solar and biomass sources will come on line.

Of course, all this isn't quite certain. Post-Harrisburg fears may sharply limit the nuclear options. And carbon dioxide, with its potentially disastrous climatic effects, could conceivably, eventually, do the same for all the fossil fuels. If both occur, we could be in deep trouble indeed. At the very least, we'd have to look seriously at still higher prices, perhaps even a second doubling, to accommodate to solar biomass.

But probably, for some time, one doubling will be enough. This is important to know, and has highly significant policy implications. The foremost is that we place a high premium—far higher than we have in the past—on security of supply. Mere higher costs, at least up to a doubling and allowing time for adjustment, are not a serious threat to our prosperity, but sudden deprivations are. Present policies barely recognize this fact. The case is overwhelming for getting domestic oil prices up to world prices, and and getting rid of the cumbersome "entitlements" program which subsidizes oil imports. So is the case for building up a large reserve stockpile of oil. The case is strong, if not overwhelming, for going further and taxing oil imports.

A second policy implication is that we at least develop those nuclear, synthetics from coal, oil-from-shale, and other technologies which promise to provide a long-run ceiling for energy costs at about double present prices. We may not need some (or any) of them, and so may never fully deploy them. Fusion, solar, hot rock geothermal, unconventional sources of natural gas, or something else may come along and bail us out. But we'd better have them ready to deploy if necessary. This means carrying development through commercial size plants.

A third policy implication is we get on with conservation to damp down the amount of energy we need to supply in the long run, and thereby the residual quantities of insecure oil we have to import. In the main this should be cost effective conservation induced by prices, but there are some cases (e.g., more efficient motor cars) where a regulatory assist makes sense.

We frequently hear the argument that because we subsidize imported oil and, in various ways, nuclear power and, in effect by our regulatory mode, electricity and gas, we should—in fairness— subsidize solar and biomass and geothermal, etc. Because of the importance of conservation this solution won't do. It is indeed desirable to get the ratio of price to incremental cost the same for all energy sources—for reasons of efficiency, not equity—but the way to do that is by getting rid of the subsidies which now distort energy supply and use, not by adding still more. Getting all energy prices up to, or at least a lot nearer, incremental costs, will be of immense help in achieving long-term, secure, affordable sources of supply. High energy prices are not the problem, as so many people think, both in and out of Congress. They are the solution, or at least the unavoidable first step to a whole family of possible solutions.

The problems posed by energy price and supply are difficult, but those associated with environmental quality may be ever harder. We are learning that the large-scale production and use of energy—particularly from such dirty sources as coal—threaten to impinge on a different and more restrictive set of limits. When I spoke earlier of the measurements of relative price movements which indicated resource abundance rather than scarcity, I was talking about the costs and prices of private property resources, that is, industrial raw materials, capital, and labor which are traded on markets. I have no doubt that scarcity measured by such costs can be avoided nearly indefinitely, that Malthus' day of reckoning can be pushed far into the future.

There also are *common* property resources, however, things that nobody owns and, in a sense, everybody owns—the air, the oceans, aspects of fresh waters and land, even outer space, all those things that together provide the services which support life. Common property resources do not trade on markets and have no commonly understood money costs or prices, so economists have had no way to measure their relative abundance or scarcity. It is apparent, though, that we have been using these resources especially heavily over the last few decades and that, in some respects in some areas, we are in danger of overwhelming the life-support services of our environment. In greatly expanding our use of energy in particular and in so doing using common property environmental resources as both raw materials and as garbage dumps for wastes and by-products, we have been substituting unpriced and unmeasured resources for those which are priced and measured. In short, we may be guilty of overstating technological progress and understating the total costs of resources used to achieve that progress.

There is much about natural ecosystems which we do not understand, for which we have no predictive models. Yet we do know that we can and have disrupted and overloaded natural chemical and biological cycles, and that by continuing this course we are endangering climate, food production, and health. The need for greater knowledge and better monitoring is obvious, but so is the need for backing off, for releasing the pressure on the world system. In the past, society has travelled on narrow courses, focused on short-term goals. It is time now to widen and lengthen our perspective, both in safeguarding the environment and in choosing among energy options, for we can run out of environmental resources long before we are confronted with material scarcity.

This, of course, is where you members of the graduating class come in, for you soon will be helping to forge the future. As I hope I have made clear, I am among those who believe in the efficacy of technology intelligently applied. I also believe humankind to be immensely resourceful and creative. I think there will be plenty of resources in our future and that we can survive and prosper, all of us the world around.

But what if I am wrong? What if the environmental imperatives close down our most obvious energy options? My charge to you is to make your professional plans contingent not on some ideaiized picture of what might be, but on the whole range of future possibilities, including the threats. If you are able to cope with the worst, then there will be plenty of time left for creative break-throughs and good works. We dare not gamble on the fate of the world, and the dice soon will be in your hands.

1. *Survey by the Roper Organization (Roper Reports, 78-4)*, March 18-25, 1978, reprinted in *Public Opinion*, January-February 1979, p. 25.
2. Quoted in *Outdoor America*, March-April 1979, p. 9.
3. Thomas Robert Malthus, *An Essay on the Principle of Population*, 1798.
4. While impressive, the four-and-one-half times growth in world population falls far short of Malthus' "unchecked" rate and of biological potential. Since 1798, the year of Malthus' *Essay*, the annual growth rate has been on the order of 0.85.
5. Robert S. Manthy, *Natural Resources Commodities: A Century of Statistics-Prices, Output, Consumption, Foreign Trade, and Employment in the United States 1870-1873*, Baltimore: Johns Hopkins University Press for Resources for the Future, 1978, p. 9.
6. Harold J. Barnett and Chandler Morse, *Scarcity and Growth: The Economics of Natural Resource Availability*, Baltimore: Johns Hopkins University Press for Resources for the Future, 1963, p. 24.
7. Alvin M. Weinberg, and H.E. Goeller, "The Age of Substitutability," and address to the Fifth International Symposium of the U.S. Science Policy Foundation, Eindhoven, The Netherlands, September 18, 1975, p. 10.
   Interestingly, work done at RFF suggests that, as a practical matter, phosphorous may be omitted from Weinberg's and Goeller's short list of exceptions. See Frederick J. Wells, *The Long-Run Availability of Phosphorous: A Case Study in Mineral Resource Analysis;* Baltimore: Johns Hopkins University Press for Resources for the Future, 1975.
8. Allen V. Kneese, "The Faustian Bargain," *Resources*, September 1973, Washington, D.C.: Resources for the Future, p. 4.

Arthur Laffer

Arthur Laffer

COMMENCEMENT ADDRESS
HARVY MUDD COLLEGE
May 15, 1983

"IN THE QUEST OF EXCELLENCE"

Thank you very much. Mr. Baker, friends and associates of Harvey Mudd College, ladies and gentlemen, but most importantly to the graduating Class of 1983. It is truly a pleasure being here today. In fact, I tried to ponder the real reason why I was invited to give the commencement address here and I figure someone must have thought I needed the experience in coming out to Claremont. Having lived in Palos Verdes for many years, I really hadn't come out here on a hot day and I realized as I came out here, I noticed something in the air. Something they call smog, is that it? And I was commenting on the degree of smog when my mother-in-law, in great disbelief, pointed in her backyard in Ontario and said it's not that bad, look at that bluejay in the backyard. And upon closer scrutiny I realized it was a cardinal holding its breath. In fact, I understand weightwatchers is moving its headquarters out here because supposedly every breath is eight calories. Is that right? But none the less, I heard the mayor of Anaheim speak a while ago and his only comment that really stuck in my mind was that he didn't trust air he couldn't see.

But, my message today is terribly simple and it's straight forward. The point I'm making In the Quest of Excellence is that excellence literally starts at the top. If the top does not permit excellence then excellence does not have a chance to thrive and survive in this system. If you look at what's going on now in the United States, from my perception, excellence is not being encouraged from the very top of our political process. With the precepts of incentives, excellence is taxed and the failure to achieve excellence is being rewarded. If you look at it, nothing is more basic in economics than the very basic precept that in general when you tax something you get less of it and when you subsidize something you get more of it. Taxes reduce the equalibrium quantity of a commodity and subsidies increase the equalibrium quantity of a commodity.

If you see what we've been doing throughout our political process in the United States today is we've been taxing excellence, success, and prosperity. And we've been rewarding failure, leisure and non-work in the system. It should come as no shock, going back to the basic premises of economics, that when you do that you get less success, prosperity, and excellence and you get more failure, non-work and lack of success in the system. Basically, these incentives have been put into place and the political process, as it now stands, in my view at least, is faltering under the weight of its failure to provide correct incentives for excellence.

The future, however, I think is great. There's a major change coming in the political process. That change, noted by John Naisbitt in his "Megatrends," is coming in the form that it once again allows direct representation in that those people who bear the consequences of action once again have the rights and abilities to make those decisions. I think a lot of changes are coming throughout the representative system of initiative propositions in the United States.

We're moving in that direction, but much, much more is needed than we currently have. In fact, over the years the once bright future of American society — in truth the future of Western society in its entirety — has been covered by dark clouds of a persistent and pervasive decline in the highest echelons of intellectual achievement. Precise semantics has been transfigured into dissembling rhetoric as the skills of individuals have unrelentingly been shuffled away from technical knowledge toward shrill politicising.

If you just look at it today, the SAT scores of our graduating seniors from high school have been declining year-in and year-out. In fact, over the past 20 some years they've declined each and every year except with the minor exception of this year. This year was the first time in 20 some years that there's been a slight uptake, which gives this year the unique privilege of the first time in over 20 years it wasn't the worst in all history. It was only the second worst recording in history. The realization that excellence has been demoted in favor of ephemeral objectives barely comprehended by those who profess to be their proponents is self-evident.

Nothing could illustrate the depths to which we have sunk more than the recent mayoral contest in the city of Chicago. In the continuing comic tragedy unfolding in that city — by the way, one of our nation's greatest cities — the personal, moral and intellectual character exemplified by those candidates in that city's sequence of elections and post-election shenanigans would be more suited to screen testing for a film like "Animal House" than it would be for the city's highest elected officials. The shock is that Chicago's vainality does not stand alone. The entire governance of America is fraught with incompetence and vulgarity, thus deprecating literally everything with which it comes in contact.

A colleague of mine is reputed to have asked his class the following question. He asked the question, "How many of you really wish and intend to rear your children so that they can aspire to be a congressman?" Well, giggles went through the class. It was followed by another question, really more to the point, which really sent reams of laughter through the class. The professor asked the class to conjure up an image of a great president of the United States; think of them, Franklin Delano Roosevelt, Thomas Jefferson, Jack Kennedy, George Washington, Jimmy Carter — and again laughter went through the class. What it does is to point out quite simply that our institutional structure and those of other nations of the West have created an environment where excellence and success are to be exploited, thus providing the elicit contraband for a group whose sole attribute is that they occupy seats generated by gerrymandered districts resulting from a politically corrupt process.

Representative democracy, as it once was known, no longer serves or, more accurately, makes servile the population to whose authority the ultimate appeal is made. There is no room for excellence in a society where our nation's leaders not only don't understand but literally don't read the bills they pass; where courts and petty bureaucrats make minor and major decisions without the benefit of guiding principles and often do so in response to ugly vendettas and dark prejudices. Politics, in the fullest sense of the most recent meaning of the word, strikes a cord of the arbitrary exercise of unlimited power. What is at one moment fully acceptable and even admirable may in short order and retroactively be deemed illegal and reprehensible.

Even within the structure of the law, that which at this very moment is deemed legally desirable is often morally repugnant. Likewise, that which is morally admirable is often illegal. In the area of taxation, the distinction between legal and illegal has almost no bearing on what we all feel is moral and immoral. The moral force behind the tax codes has been eroded to the point where tax evasion is carried out in epidemic proportions. People no longer pay taxes because they should, people now pay taxes only to avoid punishment. In Congress, the tapestry of the big lie is being woven with threads of partial truths and illusions.

Does anyone here today honestly believe that the progressive tax system of the United States benefits the more modest in income at the expense of the super rich? Clearly the super rich are able to hire better lawyers and accountants than the government can. And if they can't hire better lawyers and accountants than the government they often can hire better congressmen and senators than the government can. In looking at it in this way, they don't pay the taxes, they're usually devoid of all those taxes. But when you take a middle income or low income person who doesn't have the ability, the financial backing, or the sophistication to get advanced accounting and advanced legal help, what they do is they pay taxes after taxes after taxes, and they never get the rightful rewards they so justly deserve.

When you look at other things on yet another vein, what I want to stress a little bit today is there's a tragedy of immense proportions that is continuing to unfold in our inner cities, in the barrios and ghettos of America. Targeted areas where America's dream and reality of prosperity has never been absorbed. The recent tightening of eligibility requirements so fostered by pseudo-humanitarians were in the garb of crypto-realists defended and justified on grounds of parsimony and equity has turned the safety net of a moral society into the labyrinth of needs and income tests that uses poverty to literally entrap the poor. Let me give you an illustration of the most recent data today on the poverty traps of the inner cities of America here in Los Angeles. In fact, as of 1983, what we did is we took a family of four — two adults and two children. We assumed that one of the adults was either disabled or unemployed and couldn't work and thereby had no earnings whatsoever. The other adult could or could not work as he or she saw fit. Then what we assumed is this family did not avail itself of any unemployment compensation.

The first question we asked is let's imagine that that one adult who can work decides not to work. What is the maximum legally available social welfare benefits that this family can acquire with no earnings whatsoever. We took the bonus value food stamps, California rent subsidies, Medi-Cal, etc. in this hypothetical model, and at zero earnings the family's total spending power per month came to $1,125.

We then asked the next question, which is let's imagine that that one adult who can work decides to work and goes out and earns $100 gross per month. We then took that $100 gross income we took out the employer's payroll tax, the employees payroll tax, any income taxes — which at this level, by the way, there were no income taxes — and we got the net after-tax earnings from that individual. We then recalculated the maximum legally available social welfare benefits at that level, of earnings — and of course you all know the more you make the less you get, the less you make the more you get. So the welfare benefits were cut down and we got the total spending power at $100 earnings.

Do all of you follow what I'm doing here? We did $100, $200, $300 on up to $1,300 per month earnings for this family of four in the city of Los Angeles right as of today. Guess with me for a moment. What do you think the increase in spending power is for this family of four going from zero earnings per month to $1,300 per month, including the loss in income due to taxes and the loss in welfare benefits due to needs tests, means tests, and income tests. Well going from zero dollars a month earnings to $1,300 a month the family's total spending power declines by $47. That corresponds to an average tax on inner city dwellers of only 103 percent of all earnings. How much would you work if you face a tax rate of 103 percent? In fact, if you went to the extreme, if I made tax rates really high enough so that every time you went to the office instead of giving you a check you got a bill, how long would you work?

Well you can see what's happening between, and just think of these numbers, between $900 a month and $1,100 a month earnings. The family's spending power goes from $1,305 down to $987. That's a decline in purchasing power of $318, from $900 in gross income to $1,100 gross income. That corresponds in that range to an average tax of only 255 percent of inner city dwellers earnings. Is it any wonder that inner city employment rates have fallen sharply relative to other employment rates, why non-white employment rates declined sharply. Participation rates of blacks and other non-whites have fallen sharply, much more so than whites. When you look at this the total spending on these programs has increased enormously. What has happened, is we have created enormous disincentive traps in our inner cities.

There are other major effects, too, from our current programs that eminate out of Washington because of a total disregard for incentives in the system. Disruption of the basic family unit is the direct consequence of other aspects of welfare desincentives. Welfare, for example, is directed towards families. If the family has two adults, one must work or at least attempt to work. If however, there is a single adult parent, head-of-household and the children are of school age, then there are no work requirements in order to receive welfare. Rewards for family division are most pressing when one member of that family is fully employed. The family loses all of its welfare benefits, thus elegibility requirements make family desertion a parental duty, not an act of cowardice.

Incentives are played throughout the entire system, destroying much of our entire basic underlying family structure. The real issue today is the issue of direct democracy and appropriate representation. Ironically, the root of direct democracy through referenda, initiatives, and propositions is the only way of achieving appropriate representation. The electorate, time and again, has told Sacramento that its redistricting legislation is tragically flawed. But the Legislature has not and can not respond because of its self-serving nature.

Only now is our chance to take power back into our own hands coming on the scene. The Sebastiani initiative today will soon qualify and be on the California ballot. The screams from legislators of both parties will be as shrill as they are anti-democratic. Fortunately we have the power to form government as we see it. The Sebastiani initiative will do much to rectify the evils bestowed upon us by our state Legislature and signed into law by our former governor. People deserve the governments they have.

Class of 1983, the power is in your hands. Use it wisely and use it often. In the last 10 years, the winds of change are strong and warm. We're on the right track, back to where our founding fathers envisioned we would be. To reiterate the words of my own class commencement, the last one I've been to since today, our guest speaker at that time — when I graduated we had the fortune of having the president of the United States be our guest speaker, President Jack Kennedy — pushed much of the same line. In the words of Jack Kennedy, at that time — which I think are as appropriate today as they were then — "The most urgent task facing our nation at home today is to end the tragic waste of unemployment and unused resources, to step up the growth and the vigor of our national economy, to increase job and investment opportunities, to improve our productivity and thereby strengthen our nation's ability to meet its worldwide commitments for the defense and the growth of freedom. " Thank you very much.

Sol M. Linowitz

Sol M. Linowitz

COMMENCEMENT ADDRESS
THE UNIVERSITY OF PENNSYLVANIA
May 17, 1982

President Hackney, Distinguished Honorees, Members of Board of Trustees, Members of Faculty, Members of Graduating Class, Ladies & Gentlemen.

I am very pleased and honored to be here with you today. It was just two years ago that I stood here and was honored by a degree from this distinguished University a fact which made the invitation to be your speaker at your Commencement today even more gratifying.

I must admit that I stand here with mixed feelings. For not only is it Commencement for you who are graduating today, but for some of the rest of us it is also a solemn — even painful — reminder of how many years it has been since we attended our own College or University Commencement.

I remember—vaguely—that when I was in college, I regarded with wonder the notion that anyone who has been out as long as I have could still remain vertical. At a recent Board of Trustees meeting of my alma mater, Hamilton College, one of the students asked me how it felt to be out of college 47 years. I replied in the words Clement Atlee used when someone asked him how it felt to be 80: "Considering the alternatives," said Lord Atlee, "it feels great."

Commencement time is, of course, open season on college and university graduates in this country. All over the nation those who, like you, have survived prescribed academic rigors, must now endure their final collective agony — the Commencement speaker.

Selected citizens — ripe in years if not necessarily in wisdom — will take the occasion to stand up and sound off on how the emerging generation can make a bright future out of the rather dismal present usually ignoring the fact that this dismal present was once their own bright future. In their prognostications, they will prove once again the wisdom of the sage who said.: "Forecasting is difficult — especially about the future."

Most speakers will persist in offering their own avuncular prescriptions, but few will have the forthrightness of a man named Leslie Townes — better known to you as Bob Hope — who spoke at a Commencement at Georgetown University some years ago. He summed up what he had to say in a few words:

"To those of you who are about to go out into the world and want my advice, here it is:. *Don't go!"*

As I stand here, it is inevitable that I recall my own Commencement speaker: He was successful; he was confident; he was a man of distinction. The year was 1935 and he spoke to us with sincerity and conviction; yet he never mentioned a man in Germany named Hitler or another in Italy named Mussolini. While I cannot recall his subject, I shall never forget what he talked *about:* It was *about* an hour and ten minutes.

I want to do what my Commencement speaker did *not* do — consider with you briefly some of the problems of our world and times, because at a moment such as this, we cannot talk sense to one another except in terms of all that is going on about us — and I respect you too much to do otherwise.

As you well know, we are at a time that has been called both the Age of Anxiety and the Age of Science and Technology. Both are accurate, for indeed one feeds upon the other. As our scientific and technological competence increases, so do our fears and anxieties. It is a time of paradox when we seem to have learned how to achieve most and to fear most — when we (as the Falklands make all too clear) seem to know more about how to make war than how to make peace, indeed more about killing than we do about living.

No one needs to remind us that this moment may be the most fateful in all the long history of mankind. And that our fate will depend on whether the human intellect, which has invented such instruments of total destruction as nuclear weapons, can now develop ways of peace that will keep any man, no matter what his ideology, his race or his nation, from pushing the fatal button.

In the past men have warred over frontiers; they have come into conflict over ideologies; they have fought to better their daily lives. But today each struggle overlaps the other in a vast human upheaval that touches upon every phase of our existence — national and international, religious and racial.

Part of that upheaval is as old as hunger. Part is as new as a walk in lunar space. The overriding fact is that today, we are all part of a global society in which peace and prosperity have become truly indivisible. And the fact is that, whether we like it or not, either we will all survive together or none of us will. Either we will all share the world's bounty, or none of us will.

At such a time, millions upon millions of our fellow human beings are no longer thousands of miles away from us, but just down the runway. And who are they? Here they are: During the next 60 seconds, about 230 human beings will be born on this earth. Two-thirds of them will be colored — black, brown, yellow or red. Of these 230 babies now being born, about 25 will be dead before they are a year old. Another dozen will never reach school age.

Those who survive, like their fathers and mothers before them, will till the soil and work for landlords, living in tents or mud huts. They will have an age expectancy of about 45 years. Most will never learn to read or write. Most will be poor and tired and hungry most of their lives. Like their fathers and their mothers, most will lie under the open skies of Asia, Africa and Latin America watching, waiting, hoping. These are our brothers and sisters on this earth.

What kind of a tomorrow is offered these people of this earth? Two diametrically opposed philosophies are placed before them. One is called Communism — the other Democracy. Each asks acceptance of a basic idea; each offers a larger slice of bread.

Make common cause with us, say the Communists, and accept three basic premises: First, *dialectic materialism* — all that matters is matter itself. Second, *godlessness* — accept the notion that there is no spiritual being who determines your destiny, that man has no inner life, no soul. Third, accept the idea that the *State is supreme* and will prevail over the will of the individual.

Accept and believe these things, say the Communists, and we promise you more food in your stomachs, more clothes on your backs, a firmer roof over your heads.

And what about Democracy? Because Democracy rejects absolutes, it also resists precise definition. But basically when we talk of "Democracy" as a political system we mean one dedicated to the preservation of the *integrity*, the *dignity* and the *decency* of the individual.

We speak of all men being created equal, but what we really believe is that all men are created with an *equal* right to become *unequal* — to achieve the glorious inequality of their individual talent, their individual capacity, their individual genius. In a Democracy we don't talk of the common man because we don't believe man is common. Rather that every person possesses a common right to become uncommon — to think uncommon thoughts, to believe uncommon beliefs, to become an uncommon person.

We like to say that in a Democracy such as ours every person has a right to life, a right to a decent life, which comes not from government, not from our fellow citizens, but from God. We say that it is the individual who matters; and because we count by ones and not by masses or by mobs, each human being, regardless of race, creed, color, has the right to stand erect as a child of God.

That is the basic principle to which we are committed as a nation and as a people. That is the foundation on which our system rests. That is what has made us the kind of nation we are.

In recent months, however, we have seen things happen in our society which risk sapping this basic source of our strength and call into question who we are and what we are about. We have seen widespread disrespect of law and disregard for the rights of others. We have heard the angry rumblings of hostility and the shrill outcries of violence. We have watched some Americans arrogate to themselves, both morality and majority and assert their right to judge who is a patriotic American and who is not, who is a child of God and who is not. We have witnessed the growth of the kind of factionalism in this country which our Founding Fathers feared was the danger most apt to bring this nation down. In many ways we have seen extremism grow and have tolerated it and even condoned it.

Let's face it: The bullet that struck down President John F. Kennedy almost 19 years ago — during your infancy — also struck something within all who believe in the sanctity and dignity of life and the individual. It did more too. It shook our confidence in ourselves. For no great nation seems quite so great or quite so able when it is marred by violence. Our national confidence was severely shaken again with the murder of Dr. Martin Luther King, Jr., and the assassination of Senator Robert F. Kennedy, and the subsequent nightmare of shootings and killings we have had to endure, culminating in the recent attempted assassination of President Reagan.

And now, at long last, we must finally begin to understand that we simply have to find an antidote to the poisons of hostility, tension and conflict which plague our nation. And if one thing is clear, it is that the answer will not be found in evasion.

For a long time we prided ourselves in the belief that extremism was not the way we did things in America. Yet these things have happened and we have allowed them to happen — in a society that well knows that extremism of any kind creates an atmosphere in which acts against humanity itself become possible, in which an assassin can find an excuse to trigger a demented or hate-filled mind.

We should know by now that there is no such thing as a little bit of extremism; and that we cannot condone any part of it in our pursuit of the ideals we cherish any more than when pursued by those who would slay those ideals. We have seen what that kind of extremism can do, and we must stop it at all costs, no matter where or how it occurs.

Ours is the charge to halt the knownothings, the preachers of hate, the fearful ones — wherever they are and whoever they are — who would try to stop the world and get off. They despoil the true spirit of America and blaspheme its heritage. They are no part of a citizenry trying to break the molds of the past and create a better life and a brighter future for ourselves and all mankind.

And that is where you come in — for this is a challenge to you and your generation even more than to me and mine. As I stand here I remember the strong currents of indignation and protest which ran through our college and university campuses in the 1960's. I then served as the Chairman of the Committee on Campus Tensions of the American Council of Education. At that time, students and faculty, deeply anguished about a misbegotten war, deeply agonized by the problems of our society, raised their voices in protest and indignation.

For many reasons, yours have been quiet years at our universities. For some period of time our campuses appeared casually indifferent to the issues of the day. It seemed that you were more concerned with your own individual security than with your country's; more with your personal dilemmas, than with the great human dilemmas facing our society today.

In recent months, however, there seems to have been an awakening on our campuses. Some of you have registered your protest and concern on an issue close to you — that of student aid. A number of you have also spoken out about the need for better answers than military conflict and many of you have joined the tide of protest against the everspiraling nuclear race.

I suggest that the time has come for you to raise your voices as committed, responsible citizens on a wide range of other issues that threaten the fabric of our society and challenge our leadership in the world.

As President Reagan said in his Commencement Address at Eureka College last week: "You are no longer observers. You will be called upon to express your views on global events because these events will affect your life."

The time has come for you — all of you — to make known what kind of a society and what kind of world you want, because it is *your* country, *your* world. It is time for you to respond to the bigots, the prophets of doom, the demagogues, the breast-beaters. It is time for you to assert your faith in reason rather than dogma, in rationality rather than inevitability, in the free rather than the shuttered mind.

So I ask you to raise your voices and state your protests, and make your own commitment on behalf of your own future.

I ask you to protest against intolerance and hatred and discrimination and prejudice in all their forms — against those who seek to set group against group and individual against individual in this country thereby damaging our mutual trust and respect.

I ask you to protest against the failure of our society to rid us of hunger and disease and illiteracy that still plague millions of our fellow citizens.

I ask you to protest against the lack of opportunity and hope facing too many here at home and the millions upon millions on this earth.

I ask you to protest against the malnutrition slowly starving at least one fourth of humanity; against the hovels in which millions of human beings on this earth are compelled to live.

I ask you to protest against all those who would risk co-extinction through nuclear war because they fear co-existence and the problems of peace.

I ask you to protest against all those who seek answers through desperate acts, no matter how noble their cause.

I ask you to protest against life as usual in the face of unspeakable human tragedy.

For your protest to be effective, it will not be enough to carry a banner of chant a slogan. It will mean becoming involved, making your commitment real, and your determination to play an active part in our society unflagging.

It will mean becoming a vital part of your world and as individuals — each in your own way — making your own contribution toward a better world for all people.

And that is the charge I would place upon you.

This year we observed the 100th Anniversary of the birth of President Franklin D. Roosevelt, a President who taught our nation to face the future without fear. I shall never forget his death and his funeral, thirty-seven years ago as one of the most devastating wars in history continued to rage. On a mild, drizzly April day in 1945, we stood — all 100,000 of us — on Pennsylvania Avenue in Washington, silent and watching and waiting. Then they came; the sounds of horses — seven white horses — and behind them a caisson. And on the caisson, a flagdraped coffin. And in the coffin, lay the body of an American President.

I was then an officer in the Navy; and as the funeral procession turned into the White House, I vividly recalled words I had just read at the Navy Department — words from Franklin D. Roosevelt's last address, which he did not live to deliver: *"The only limit to our realization of tomorrow will be our doubt of today."*

Thurgood Marshall

Thurgood Marshall

COMMENCEMENT ADDRESS
UNIVERSITY OF VIRGINIA
May 21, 1978

It is customary on giving speeches to say how honored and pleased the speaker is at being invited to stand before the invariably august body that is present. Sometimes this is a mere convention, and the speaker would rather be in any of a hundred other places. For several reasons, however, I am truly honored and pleased to be here today.

The University of Virginia is of course one of the outstanding universities of this country. It was conceived in grandeur, and has, more than most other institutions, fulfilled the ambitions and ideals of its founder, Thomas Jefferson. Jefferson started planning this great University over twenty years before it was chartered in 1819. His conception was, at the time, revolutionary — as befitted the man. He believed that a university should be an "academical village," a small democracy in action; it should consist of different schools devoted to different disciplines, with a curriculum that expressed the most modern ideas in scentific and liberal thought. He scandalized some of his contemporaries by proposing to omit instruction in "religous divinity"; in his view was such instruction at a state institution was inconsistent with the great constitutional principles of religous freedom and separation of church and state. And Jefferson insisted on getting only the best in their fields as instructors, even if that meant going to European colleges and, to use a modern word, "raiding" their faculties.

Thomas Jefferson, in short, conceived and executed in the early 19th century a plan for a very modern university. This university today stands as a testament to the enduring nature of what some at the time thought was a wild vision. His road to this achievement was no easy one — it took twenty years of planning, perseverance and vision. It also took a willingness to engage in the inevitible compromises of politics, for it was quite a battle to get the state legislature of the time to authorize the funds for this suspicious experiment. But Jefferson did not disdain the hurly burly of political negotiation, compromise and argument; he thrived on it.

Jefferson believed as deeply as anything that an educated citizenry could make rational and responsible decisions on almost any matter. Indeed, this belief in the intelligence and wisdom of a well-educated people not only drove

151

him to promote public education, at the primary as well as higher levels, but it also informs many of his most eloquent political passages.

I don't know how many of you graduating from the College of Arts and Sciences studied politics and government in your four years at this University. I do know that one innovation that Jefferson favored strongly was that of 'electives.' A favorite grandson of his had groaned under the rigidities of a set curriculum at another college of the day, and Jefferson was convinced that permitting students to choose their areas of study would improve the quality of their educational experience. There are educators in this country who believe this trend has gone too far, that students are not trained in the core aspects of what an educated person should know. The way the world looks to me, it seems awfully difficult to say what 'core' knowledge should be; and it may be that the last person in this country who could really claim to have mastered the whole of human knowledge was Jefferson himself.

But there are certain core values, embodied in Thomas Jefferson's handiwork in the Declaration of Independence and the Constitution, as well as in setting up this University, of which I hope you are all aware — those of you graduating with advanced degrees as well as the undergraduates. And these core values, tried and trite as they may appear, are in my judgment worthy of continued reflection, so that they may be better realized in this country, just as your university so well realized the values of its founder.

I can best introduce them by telling you of a brief incident. At one argument in a United States District Court, an attorney representing a City was arguing in support of an ordinance challenged as being unconstitutional. The details of the case are unimportant, but at one point in his argument, this attorney told the Court that there was 'something higher than the Constitution of the United States.' I asked him what he could be thinking of; and the poor man had no answer.

My first reaction, and probably that of many other listeners, was that his failure to answer illustrated that his assertion was wrong, and in a way it was; but in another, equally important way, the lawyer simply failed to come up with the right answer.

His assertion is wrong because our system is perhaps uniquely characterized by adherence to the proposition that this is a government of laws, and not merely of men and women — and the United States Constitution is the Supreme law of the land. The Constitution is binding on federal judges and municipal courts, on Governors of the States and on Presidents of the United States — in short, on all governmental decisionmakers in the state and federal systems. There simply is no 'higher law' in this country.

The democractizing aspects of the Constitution cannot be overstated. For me, its cardinal principlc is that all persons stand in a position of equality before the law. The Constitution gives to each and every one of you an equal right to your own opinions and to participate in the process of your own governance. These are precious rights that we must continually strive to preserve, and whose promise we must seek to attain. There are still far too many persons in this country who cannot participate as equals in the processes of Government — persons too poor, too ignorant, persons discriminated against by other people for no good reason. But our ideal, the ideal of our Constitution, is to eliminate these barriers to the aspirations of all Americans to participate fully in our government and society. We have realized it far better than most countries, but we still have a long way to travel and we must continue to strive in that direction.

This brings me to my second point about my poor lawyer's assertion. As I said a moment ago, his statement was profoundly true in a way, for there *is* something 'higher' than the Constitution — that is, quite simply, the people. I do not mean that 'the people' are not bound to live under our system of laws — any other proposition could lead to violence and from there to anarchy. But what I do mean is what Thomas Jefferson said in the Declaration of our Independence — that just governments derive their authority from the consent of the governed. And because of this, you have not only a right but a responsibility to the government of this country.

Let me elaborate. Governments derive their *power* from many sources — the military or police are instruments of power and may in the short run enforce the government's directives against an unwilling people. But *authority* is a different question — and no government can govern long, or well, without the authority that comes from a shared consensus among the governed. They must believe that theirs is a rightful, and lawful, and just government.

But in order to preserve this power in the people — the power of defining and limiting the authority of their government — it is first and foremost essential that the people be well informed. Jefferson's commitment to this University was only part of a larger commitment to the value of public education. That vision accounts for the primacy of public schools in the American community, for it was Jefferson's guiding hand that helped draft the Northwest Ordinance, which resulted in public lands being dedicated across the new territories for public schools. Today, however, just as in Jefferson's times, we still see students of less privileged backgrounds than your own, or people who are just less lucky, being denied quality education at all levels. Voters turn down school financing referenda, legislatures oppose integration of school systems. There is appalling ignorance even among some of the supposedly well-educated youth of our country, and the extent of illiteracy remains staggering. Ecducation towards the goal of an informed citizenry requires all of the qualities that Jefferson embodied: committment to difficult projects, confidence in the soundness of one's own vision and perseverance in working through a problem.

As the areas of human knowledge have expanded, so have the aspirations of the American people. It is vitally important that the aspirations of our government keep pace with the knowledge and expectations of our people. With the explosion in human knowledge and expertise, it sometimes seems very difficult to understand what the Government is doing, to understand what our problems are, and to keep up. Yet the duty to keep up, to be informed, to be knowledgedable in some area of human endeavor, is an essential one, not only for the continued survival of our government but in the long run for our civilization. It is hard work being well-informed; but it is essential work for the citizens of a democracy.

It is a work, morover, for which people in your position have been specially prepared. The privilege of attending so fine a university as this one must bear with it an unceasing responsibility to use your knowledge and training for improving the lives of others. Whether you pursue this as a lawyer dedicated to the public interest; a doctor serving those in pain and sickness; a scholar adding to the store of human knowledge and sharing that knowledge with others; an engineer applying new technologies to serve human needs; an artist improving the quality of life by creative efforts; or just by seeking to be a good person who values helping others — matters not. What matters is to remember always the obligation you bear to the society that has placed you in a position where you could afford to spend four years of your lives — and for many of you, there have been and will be several more — in an institution of learning.

I said at the beginning of my talk that there were several reasons why I was truly honored to be here today. I have already mentioned the first — that this University represents something special in the American tradition. The second one is because you are young, you are a new generation just starting out. Those of us who are a bit older (like myself — and I said, just a bit), no matter how hard we may have worked to serve humanity — our time is coming to a close. I don't for a moment mean our *lives*, since I for one intend to keep on plugging at my present job for many years to come. But I recall to you now Thomas Jefferson's answer to the pleas of a friend in 1814. His friend begged Jefferson to take a stand then and there as a leader in the fight against slavery. Jefferson's answer, though hardly commendable, shows a human truth; he said, "No, I have outlived the generation with which mutual labors and perils begat mutual confidence and influence. This enterprise is for the young — for those who can follow it up, and bear it through to its consummation."

You people here today, about to use your degrees, it is for you now to undertake the projects of this age — in Jefferson's words, to follow them up and bear them through. It is not for me to tell you what these are — each generation must find its own calling. But you have the energies of youth — and while you have them, use them, that you may look back on your lives with as much of a sense of accomplishment as Jefferson no doubt did.

This is a great country, but fortunately for you it is not perfect. There is much to be done to bring about complete equality. Remove hunger. Bring reality closer to theory and democratic principles.

Each of you as an individual must pick your own goals. Listen to others but do not become a blind follower. Do not wait for others to move out — move out yourself — where you see wrong or inequality or injustice speak out, because this is your country. This is your democracy — make it — protect it — pass it on. You are ready. Go to it.

John McDermott

John McDermott

PREAMBLE

Mr. William McKenzie of the Board of Regents, Dr. Arthur Hansen, Chancellor of The Texas A&M University System, Dr. Frank Vandiver, President of Texas A&M University, Mr. Jack Fritts, President of the Association of Former Students, distinguished platform guests and my distinguished colleagues of the faculty here at Texas A&M University.

To the graduates, I offer my congratulations and commend to you wisdom from the American poet Emily Dickinson, who wrote "Sweet is the end of Grief." To the parents, relatives, friends and supporters of the graduates, I offer a special greeting of affection and admiration. As the parent of five children, four of them college graduates, two of them from Texas A&M University and a fifth child making her way through this university, I can attest to the financial, psychological and logistic forebearance and sacrifice necessary to arrive at this auspicious day. Sharing the sentiments of my wife Virginia, and, if I may be allowed a colloquialism on this August occasion, pun intended, I say to you, plaintively, "it ain't been easy."

I trust, dear graduates, that when the heady sense of self-achievement fades somewhat, that you will remember the largesse of your benefactors, far into the future, for they have done well by you.

Finally, on behalf of the faculty, I thank President Vandiver for giving me this rare opportunity to present a state of the university commencement address from the perspective of a member of the non-administrative faculty.

TEXT

The University: The Nectar is In the Journey

I take as my headnote, a passage from the Gospel of Mark, 8:36.

"For what shall it profit a man, if he shall gain the whole world, and lose his own soul."

I urge you to substitute the word university for man, and by analogy, you will have the intent of my address.

The growth of the American university system is not only one of the masterful achievements of American culture but ranks as a dazzling event in the history of world culture. It is almost 350 years since the founding of Harvard College in 1636. Since that time we have seen a proliferation of colleges, universities and schools representing every conceivable interest and need of the human quest. The building of the university is not a casual activity in America, for its health is essential to the salvation of this nation. As a people, we are religiously, ethically, politically, socially, linguistically and regionally diverse. To manage this extraordinary panopoly of styles and beliefs, we have woven into the very fabric of American life, the most important insight in the history of the Modern World, that of pluralism. Pluralism is not a fall from grace, awaiting some total agreement. I take as bald fact that diversity and disagreement are with us forever. The enemies of pluralism are intolerance, demands for exclusivity and moral self-righteousness. The defense of pluralism requires informed intelligence, a rich sense of the past, an experimental attitude to new ideas and new experiences, and, above all, a pervasive sense of tolerance for a range of beliefs and values. The sophistication of the defense of pluralism is a major task of the American university.

We are gathered here in one such university, Texas A&M. Its recent growth is startling. Its achievements and its mishaps are of national import. One question which confronts us is the future of this potentially great university, and by virtue of that future, whether we are to become a symbolic representation of the future of the American university as such. The use of universities as symbolizing shifts in the energy centers of American culture is not new. Early in the 18th century, in a prescient statement, the Irish philosopher George Berkeley predicted our scenario. In his work, "On the Prospect of Planting Arts and Learning in American," he wrote:

> Westward the course of empire takes its way;
> The first four acts already past,
> A fifth shall close the drama with the day;
> Time's noblest offspring is the last.

At the end of the 19th century, Harvard University and New England were still at the center of American intellectual life. In rapid succession, following shifts in population, resources and self-consciousness, the University of Chicago, Columbia University, Stanford and the University of California at Berkeley assumed the mantle as the center of the American intellectual vortex. The fifth phase is upon us as the nation looks to the Southwest to take its historical turn. Without any doubt, if the Southwest is to generate and preserve learning in the coming decades, the state of Texas must come to the fore.

Concomitantly, if Texas is to lead the way in science, art, letters and technology, one of its two flagship universities, Texas A&M, must explode with vision, imagination, courage, and especially maturity.

We have come a long way since 1876. The university historian, Dr. Henry Dethloff, tells us that "the location of the new college was in a rather unsettled and wild environment for the beginning of a great institution of higher learning. Horned toads, scorpions, rabbits and deer vied with wolves for life." I cannot vouch for the wolves, but a similarly isolated beginning occurred some 2400 years ago. After the death of Plato in 347 B.C.E., a struggle was waged to determine his successor as head of the Academy, until then, the most important institution of learning in the western world. As academic politics would have it, Plato's student, Aristotle, the greatest intellect in the history of the West was not chosen to succeed. After a hiatus of some 10 years, Aristotle returned to Athens to open a school, the Lyceum. Significantly, however, he did not locate the Lyceum in Athens, selecting rather a sparse and unsettled location north of the city, something like Brazos County. From those humble beginnings we find the Arabs and the Jews reading Aristotle in Damascus in the fifth century. With the spread of Islam, the thought of Aristotle and his students moved across northern Africa and into Spain. By the 13th century, Aristotle is the central figure in the intellectual life of Christendom. During the Renaissance, Aristotelian thought remains a worthy adversary in the speculative and empirical battles within biology, astronomy and physics. His scientific claims are not superseded until the invention of the telescope and microscope in the 16th century. To this day, Aristotle's logic, ethics and politics are a permanent deposit in our thought. Now that was a school. If we are to deserve the appellation "Great" before the name of Texas A&M University, we must achieve the influence and staying power of Aristotle's Lyceum as well as the Cambridge of Newton and the Padua of Galileo. It can be done. Brilliance of intellect, both speculative and empirical, transcends the environment, wending its way through the precincts of need and interest. Our bequest will be judged on its worth, not on its geographical origin.

Texas A&M University is no stranger to outreach. As a land-grant and sea-grant institution, the activities of extension and experiment are second nature to us. For countless Texans, it is assumed that Texas A&M University is the premier university in the state, for our extension and experiment stations have brought knowledge, solution and concern to virtually every county. In that way, we have overcome the provinciality and insularity which hazards many American universities. As a public university, we are supported by the citizens of the state.of Texas and through grants, by the citizens of this nation. Consequently, our mandate is clear. In response to these citizens and to the exquisite generosity of our former students, we are called upon to climb the highest mountain and probe the deepest sea. We are called upon to forge the rivers, purify the water and generate the crops; we are called upon to plan and to build. But not by bread alone do we live. We are also asked to soar, to prance, to sing, to pirouette and to write glowingly, fruitfully and prophetically. And it is not only the future to which we must attend, but the past as well. Listen to the poem of Emily Dickinson, "For a Library."

> A precious, mouldering pleasure 'tis
> To meet an antique book
> In just the dress his
> century wore.

The pilgrimage of Texas A&M University to possible greatness is not sheerly physical. It is more so a spiritual journey. Those who know best shall not revere our size, our money or our buildings, although each is an impressive ingredient in our growth. Rather, they shall evaluate the quality of our claims, our work, and above all, the personal quality of our students. How we carry on is as important as what we do. One version of greatness calls for us to become a national resource for the marriage of learning to a commitment to the needs of society. Another version of greatness calls upon us to merge the past, the present and our dreams for the future in all of our activities. In this vein, I would urge that every academic discipline teach its own history and celebrate the storied, courageous, frequently martyred lives of its progenitors. Told too, should be the false starts, broken promises and outright chicanery which actually mottles the historically innocent tapestry which is too often naively passed on to our students. In a word, we of the university should replicate our ancient forbearers, who were gatherers and hunters. We should scavenge and save both the fabled and the usable past. And we should hunt up the novel, the mysterious and press on to the frontiers, to the very edge of human endurance, human need, human hope and imagination.

While on this spiritual pilgrimage, the university faces serious dangers which lurk within and without. I would be derelict in my duty to this audience and to this university if I did not issue a warning as to their presence. A most serious affliction is institutional arrogance and the absence of intense, forthright, public self-criticism. Given the inordinate complexity of the modern world, no university is an island unto itself. We are members of a community of inquiry, sharing common goals, resources and methods. Self-preening braggadocio is vulgar and a denial of deep interdependence with scholarship, learning and research from every quarter. We cannot rank the quality of our spiritual life in a Southwest Conference format.

The reverse of the charge of arrogance is to succumb to the bleatings of self-appointed vigilante groups. We can have no truck with single-cause individuals, whether of the left or right, whether religious, economic or political in ideology, who attempt to tell us what to do. The direction of a university, for better or for worse, is the responsibility of its faculty, who in turn are entrusted to nurture its students and to progress in research. Without the faculty, the university is but a creaking skeleton, accompanied only by a Xerox machine, turning out purposeless memoranda. The faculty of a university is both the guardian and the explorer of the reflective life. In a democratic society, the community supports and sustains its public universities. But the marvelous paradox which protects the integrity of this relationship is that the university is expected to lead rather than follow the community. The university must be deeply sensitive to the needs of the community and yet, be equally resistant to any efforts from any quarter to dominate ideologically our mission and our trust.

Further warnings are in order. In America, of late, alas, two nefarious images of the university have emerged. The first is that the university is a business and consequently, must be permeated by that banal phrase, bottom-line accountability. The university, of necessity, does business. The university also teaches students how to conduct business, and both activities are absolutely essential to our survival and well-being. The university, itself, however, is not a business. If the teaching of Greek is more expensive than a more fashionable and career-oriented program, so be it. It is sheer folly and profoundly shortsighted to expect the humanities and the pure sciences to match the return on investment found in more allegedly practical university activities. On this very day, major universities throughout this country are being savaged by a narrow and economically parochial view of what constitutes the necessary requisites for the life of a civilization, let alone a culture. In the effort to placate the recent and frenetic move to university education as primarily a career opportunity, we run the risk of losing our soul. A career is but a strand in our lives. We shall be husbands, fathers, wives, mothers, lovers, and enemies. We shall vote and face sickness and death. We shall laugh and we shall cry. We shall succeed and we shall fail. We shall stay and travel and move. Who and what will teach us to drink deeply at that trough? The answer is obvious; the poets, the philosophers, the historians and the language and literature of world culture. They are the watchers over our soul. Without them we shall not survive as a people. Witness, for example, the contemporary emergence of a stunning cultural illiteracy in every nook and cranny of American society. Historically, this has foretold subsequent violence by an alienated and culturally deprived underclass.

A second baleful image of the university is briefly but more painfully reported. The university is not a farm team for the economic aggrandizement of professional sports. A season ticket holder in two major sports, no "twopercenter," I, for I thrill to our victories and lament our losses. Nonetheless, it is an embarrassment and an affront to our social and educational mission when negative and nationally publicized hoopla surrounds one of our more transient endeavors. I assure you, as the University of Chicago long ago taught us, and the University of San Francisco is now teaching us, there are far better and more worthy avenues to true distinction as a university. Perhaps in the future we can again do both, *mena sana, corpore sano,* that is athletics and intellect, for we are, above all, the inheritor of the noble tradition of the twelfth man, or should I say person, for in recent times the most notable athletic achievement of this university has been the national championship as garnered by the women's softball team. Comparatively unheralded, they represent university athletics at its very best.

One further caveat in our quest for excellence. The warning here is clear and politically explosive. As a public university, we have the moral obligation to mirror the ethnic and racial constituency of the state of Texas. Suffice it to say that until and unless we so do, our quest for distinction will be mired in self-deception. Under the prodding of former Chancellor Frank Hubert and the present leadership of President Vandiver, and with all deliberate speed, it is our intention to widen, dramatically, the ethnic and racial constituency of both our faculty and our student body. We cannot fail in this endeavor, for if we do, we shall either drop out of American university history, or worse, be lamentably remembered.

I now come to address the central figures of this occasion, the degree candidates from Texas A&M University on this fourteenth day of August, in the year 1982. If I may ask your indulgence, allow me to introduce myself. I am 50 years of age, the oldest of eight children in a lower middle class Irish Catholic family. We had no books. We did have a tradition of compassion and tolerance. Like the American Indians, we were taught to walk in the mocassins of another before we criticized anyone. In academic terms, I have a comparatively unsung pedigree. I did not go to Harvard or, for that matter, to Yale. Nonetheless, they do not exhaust the possibility of learning, as you well know, and so through the back door of a proletarian education, I became a teacher. During more than 30 years, I have taught more than 20,000 students. Most of this teaching has been in gigantic public universities, although I have taught also in small, fancy, private colleges. The bulk of my students have been regulars, ages 18 to 22. Still, along the way, I have taught preschool children, secondary school, middle aged adults and some others who were more than 80 years old. My clientele came from the ghetto and the farms, from the city and the suburbs. I have taught the blind, the deaf, the spastic and weird people of every cause and persuasion. I taught prisoners, parolees, mental patients and the bourgeoisie. Cutting through all these categories were Whites, Blacks,

Hispanics, Orientals and even the Irish. The upshot of all this experience is complex; some liked me, some disliked me; some remember me; some forgot me; sometimes it went well; sometimes it went badly; sometimes it was my doing or my fault; sometimes it was their doing or their fault. Unfortunately we do not have time for me to regale you with stories that illustrate the majesty and exhilaration of one of the most spiritual and rewarding professions, that of teaching. As for my students here at Texas A&M University — they are the most gentle, cooperative, and industrious of my experience. Of late, I have witnessed in them a remarkable increase in imagination and a bolder intellectual horizon. Putting all this together, if it is possible, will make our students premier in the nation. From all of my students, I can say that I have learned far more than I have taught.

To you, graduates, as Emerson said to Whitman, I greet you at the beginning of a great career. I do not mean a career in the narrow sense of a job or even a profession. No, I mean it in the sense of the Spanish philosopher Santayana, a moral career, that is, to build a life, a human community; nay, in our time, a global community. The key word is to build; to build a covenant in the bowels of time, although we have no guarantee of our future. Indeed to the contrary, for those of the last half of the 20th century, the future is precarious, as the last week has well reminded us in its annual memorial to the victims of Hiroshima and Nagasaki.

For those of you who are of the book, you no doubt read the warning of Deuteronomy 32:35, "Their foot shall slide in due time." Some others of us, however, remember also the text of Emerson:

> Why should not we also enjoy an original relation to the universe? Why should not we have a poetry and philosophy of insight and not of tradition, and a religion by revelation to us, and not the history of theirs?

Why not? Why cannot we build a genuine human community, focusing on the enemies of the Apocalypse rather than on each other as enemy? William James tells us that the world is malleable to our touch. And the American poet, Walt Whitman, reminds us that "the press of my foot to the earth springs a hundred affections." Yea, to build, to build a family, a community, a life, a career; always alert to the drama of experience, its surprises attendant on every turn of our body, our person. Again with William James, "life shall be built in doing and suffering and creating." In so building, we must pay close attention to the inevitable rotation of the sacred and the accursed, of the stable and the precarious. This alternating rhythm is the rhythm of our embodiment in nature, yielding both the penalties and possibilities of our being creatures in time.

Each of us has our own rhythms, our own needs. Our experiences move from the inchoate to the consummatory, a journey striated with blocked expectations, surprises, disasters, bypasses and periodic realizations. Our ultimate goal may be illusory, but the journey is clearly real. The nectar of human living is to be found in the journey, rarely in our accomplishments, for they seem always to be accompanied by still another goal. Much of the great literature of western civilization is journey literature: Homer's *Odyssey*, Virgil's *Aeneid*, Dante's *Divine Comedy*, Chaucer's *Canterbury Tales*, Goethe's *Faust* and the interior saga of that middle class American, Harry Angstrom, in the novels of John Updike. They teach us that if we are to have a genuine experience of the nectar of the journey, we must avoid second-handedness, by which we live out our lives at the bequest of our parents, siblings, relatives, teachers and other dispensers of already programmed possibilities. Despite its frequent majesty, and despite our critical need for an understanding and appreciation of the past, we should be wary of tradition, however noble in intention, for it is the quality of our own experience which is decisive. Failure and suffering, deeply undergone, often enriches, whereas success, achieved mechanically and by rote, through the path set out for others, more often blunts human sensibility. We are not tossed into the world as a thing among things. To the contrary, we are live creatures who eat experience. How, rather than what we experience, makes us who we are.

And now I come full circle. We are approaching the end of a century; more we have in our sight the end of a millenium. The journey is fraught with perils and rich with possibilities not yet in our present vision. In the deepest and most profound way, we are called to show up. In the works of Voltaire, we find a reference to a letter from Henry IV, the King of France, to an ill-knighted person by the name of Crillon, who, most unfortunately, arrived after a great battle had been fought. To the tardy Crillon, Henry IV wrote: "Hang yourself, brave Crillon! We fought at Arques, and you were not there."

The nature of the battle in our time is appallingly clear. The site of world hunger, mindless violence and the threat of nuclear obliteration. Unlike Crillon, I plan to be at that battle and I trust that you will do likewise, for to do less is to abandon all that is truly human. I tell that to our children and to my students. I ask them to pass this message to their children and to their students. We are the only generation in history who can create our own apocalypse. Likewise, we are the only generation who have the means to create a genuine, viable human world community. Which shall it be? I ask you. Graduates of Texas A&M Unlverslty, help us to build a new world. In so doing we shall be a truly great university, a great state, a great nation and we shall reach out with compassion and wisdom to all of our brothers and sisters on the planet earth.

Ave atque vale

Franklin D. Murphy

Franklin D. Murphy

COMMENCEMENT ADDRESS
UNIVERSITY OF HARTFORD
May 18, 1980

"PRIVATE HIGHER EDUCATION IN THE 1980s"

May I first take note of the reason for the ceremonies today and join with the audience in congratulating the members of this Class of 1980 on the occasion of their graduation from the University of Hartford. It is a time for self-satisfaction and appreciation to parents, friends and perhaps most of all to the University and its faculty. If the institution has done its job, you graduates should be well prepared for your participation in what is surely a complicated but nonetheless a challenging world.

On these occasions, it is customary to talk to the graduates about the future and their role in it. But I will not do so today. Because of the vast expansion of the electronic and print media, you are as aware as any of us, and much more aware than earlier generations of graduates, of the problems, complexities and opportunities in the society today. I could not usefully add to your perceptions by any comments I might make now.

Rather, I would like to remind you of an obligation that all of you have in common—namely, to see to it that the University of Hartford, which hopefully nourished your intellect and imagination and which has given you the tools to be competitive in the real world, will not only survive but grow even stronger and more productive. This institution will need the support of its alumni and friends as never before as higher education—and especially private higher education—moves into the complex and perilous decade of the 1980s.

Although there are a variety of issues that confront our universities, there are two which I would emphasize today.

The first is government regulation and intervention. From the beginning of the modern university, in the twelfth and thirteenth centuries, its most treasured possession was the right of selfgovernance and self-direction, albeit with a recognition of societal needs. Now there has developed a wholly unprecedented intrusion into the affairs of the academy which mainly began with the adoption of the so-called great society programs in the 1960s. In the abstract, the objectives of these programs seemed proper enough, especially as they were accompanied by a massive outpouring of dollars. The members of the academy applauded, helped fashion the programs and eagerly accepted the largess offered by their benevolent uncle in faroff Washington. Too late did they realize the fallacy of the "free lunch" or remember that the road to hell is often paved with good intentions. The natural history of government regulation in our political system is really very simple. A group or groups who have an idea whose time they honestly believe has come convince Congress or a president, or both, of the righteousness of their idea.

Legislation is approved creating a program described in the broadest and noblest of terms and an agency is formed to administer the program. First, however, the agency, consisting of anonymous and often inexperienced bureaucrats, must write the detailed regulations which govern the program. At this point, nobleness of purpose degenerates into pages of often unintelligible nit-picking, sometimes nonsense, but always intrusion into internal affairs. What is the recourse? If one is displeased wth a president, governor or legislator, he has recourse at the polls. But what with the anonymous bureaucrat well protected by civil service? You know the answer, at least to date—grin, or more likely, frown and bear it—the federal dollars are in the institutional budget to stay and the lesson that a federal regulation invariably follows a federal dollar was learned too late.

There once was a time when concern for over regulation came almost exclusively from the business community. Today, the anger, frustration and outrage of university presidents and faculties more than matches that of the corporate executive. Furthermore, the size of this particular cloud has grown enormously overnight with the totally unnecessary creation of a cabinet level department of education, not as the result of manifest need, but purely as payoff for a political promise—and this from a president who committed himself to reduce the size and cost of government. O tempora! O mores!

University administrators, faculties and alumni have no alternative other than to organize themselves to fight as hard against this government intrusion, blackmail and erosion of academic freedom as they have fought in the past for federal dollars. If they do not, our distinguished, mainly independent and innovative colleges and universities could well become merely pedestrian arms of an ever expanding, insensitive, nonaccountable bureaucracy. I should add that, in this fight, they will find strong and eager allies in business, small and large alike, and members of the learned professions.

The second major danger lies in the economic pressures on our institutions of higher learning and, under this rubric, I unhesitatingly put at the top the evil of inflation. It is not an oversimplification to date the onset of our current inflationary disease with the determination of an American president, one foot in the New Deal and one foot on the Texas frontier, to fight an expensive and unpopular war and at the same time build the great society, paying for all of this not out of current income but with I.O.U.'s. And, if this were not enough, oil-producing countries then discovered the real value of their unique natural resource, especially to a country become wasteful and profligate in its use of energy.

Inflation injures all people and all institutions—but often unequally. Institutions which are labor intensive tend to suffer more and no institution in our society is more labor intensive than the university. And no institution is less able to pass along its increased cost than the university. The financial squeeze in American higher education is severe and becoming more so.

The average citizen, buffeted by double-digit increased cost of living and ever higher unindexed taxes, is more and more reluctant to redress this institutional problem with higher taxation or increased private giving in the face of relatively less disposable income. Until the back of inflation is broken by a combination of political courage and citizen restraint, the financial plight of colleges and universities will remain severe.

Compounding the financial problem of education in general is the fact that its share of the available dollar is shrinking. In 1969 education took 7.5% of the gross national product. In 1979 the number was 7.2% and in 1989 this share will shrink to 6.1%, having lost ground to spending for health care, national defense and environmental issues.

Finally, an even more severe problem for private institutions especially is the effort to reduce or eliminate the incentives for private giving.

One of the fundamental hallmarks of American society is the principle of pluralism. From the very beginning of the United States, different groups of people with different objectives, different commitments and different points of view have gathered together to create their kind of institution, be it educational, religious or cultural.

Thus, over the years there has developed in this country, unlike most of the rest of the world, a rich mix of institutions—guaranteeing multiple choices for our citizenry. As a result, people worship in churches of their choice—we have no state religion. People attend concerts and museum exhibitions, and participate in activities running the full gamut of man's creative capacity, activities carried out without direct or indirect political control or censorship.

And finally, through a remarkable mix of private and public institutions at all educational levels, we have built in the United States the greatest and most innovative educational system in the world.

All of these institutions serve in different but important ways the full range of man's interest, ambitions, enlightenment and personal and social fulfillment.

In short, by committing ourselves to pluralism, we have guaranteed maximum freedom of responsible choice. It must be clearly understood, however, that pluralism is only an empty word wthout voluntarism and private philanthropy.

There is no other country in the world in which the principle of private giving for the support of all kinds of institutions is so deeply ingrained. This is, of course, the reason we have the freest, most open and pluralistic society in the world.

But now, financial and other problems in our institutional sector— including higher education— have tended to obscure a very serious threat, a subtle and growing attack on voluntary giving, without which pluralism withers and dies.

For fifty years the Congress of the United States has legislated to encourage private giving. The legislated tax devices designed to achieve this end have by and large succeeded. Of course, there have been some abuses and excesses, and in 1969 Congress passed a tax reform act which, among other things, dealt with private giving and—in my view—mainly in a constructive manner by eliminating actual or potential abuses.

During the hearings and congressional debates on these matters, however, it became clear that there was a segment of society and of the Congress that has serious reservations about private philanthropy, and I believe there is a growng attempt to restrict or cripple private giving.

There are several reasons given for these moves.

1. The revenue needs of government. We all know and are sadly aware of the mushrooming growth of the costs of government. Money, it is said, must be found to support this growth. An alternate—and to me more desirable solution—slowing the growth of government, seems to have had little political appeal in the recent past, although the plight of some of our major cities plus inflation has now given many people and politicians pause for thought.

2. There is a concern, in some measure a proper one, about "loopholes" and "fairness" in the tax laws. This concern is aided and abetted by some infrequent but often highly visible acts, such as tax deductions for gifts of overvalued so-called private papers, now impermissible, and people with six-and even seven-figure incomes paying little or no income tax—all indefensible.

3. Then, there are those who oppose private giving on straight ideological grounds. Their most persuasive and articulate spokesman is Professor Stanley Surrey of Harvard University, who refers to private giving with such cliches as "cost to government" or "government subsidy." He speaks for that group of people who have long believed privately—and increasingly state publicly—that government really can spend money more efficiently and more wisely than private agencies or individuals.

The attack on private giving takes many forms, mostly in the name of so-called "tax reform."

Many reasons, technical and other, are given in support of changes in the tax laws. The one heard most often is that the rich person gets a better tax break on gifts than does the average earner. What is forgotten are two points:

1. The individual—rich or otherwise—is in fact making a gift of something that either he or she or their heirs would otherwise possess.

2. From a strictly pragmatic point of view, a study in 1972 showed that 75% of the total amount of gifts to educational institutions came from 5% of the donors in gifts of $5,000 or more.

Stripped of all technical verbiage, this movement is basically an ideological attack on voluntarism, and therefore on pluralism. It is, in fact, a significant push toward statism.

Without voluntarism over the years and in the future, this nation would not have had and cannot retain its rich and exciting mix of private and public educational institutions. We would not have had our great cultural institutions such as museums and our distinguished organizations in the performing arts.

Without voluntarism we would not have had the great foundations which, in the fields of medicine, science and agriculture, have led the way in supporting activities that have benefited all of mankind.

Without voluntarism we would not have had in this country a high degree of free choice, and we would have had much less innovation and creativity.

Without voluntarism we would not have had any kind of balance to political and bureaucratic controls.

My message today is that all people who are involved in or who benefit from our great educational institutions must make a counterattack on the statists. We must make it clear that cultural and political freedom, in the last analysis, flows from pluralism.

The alternative is bureaucratic control and conformity. We must insist that a basic distinction be made between "loopholes" in our tax laws, many of which are indefensible, on the one hand, and philanthropy and voluntary giving to educational and charitable institutions on the other.

Congress must be prevailed upon not to reduce but, in fact, to increase the tax incentive for private giving.

Educational institutions must lobby and fight as hard for the foregoing as for tax support. If they do not, they, in the end, become mere arms of an everexpanding, anonymous, nonaccountable government bureaucracy.

When I entered higher educational administration right after the disruption of World War II, the issues were simple and clear. We were to return the academy to its time honored traditions of teaching, research and scholarly contemplation and disputation, activities which, when carried out wth integrity, have proven to be indispensable to the evolution of a free and decent society. At that time, the prospect was exciting, the implementation fulfilling and, in retrospect, compared to today, relatively simple.

In 1980, the stewardship of American higher education is fraught with much greater complexity. But I am sanguine that, once again, the academy will prove its permanence and resilience. It has survived wars, political intervention, economic dislocations and internal as well as external aggression, for the reason that after seven hundred years of experience, society has learned that the community of scholars is essential to man's continuing aspiration to move from barbarism and darkness to civilization and light.

As products of the University of Hartford and beneficiaries of the American commitment to higher education of the highest quality, you have a continuing obligation to see to it that this institution, and the tradition of which it is a part, remain healthy and vital. I trust that, when put to the test in the years ahead, your response will not be found wanting!

Laurence J. Peter

Laurence J. Peter

COMMENCEMENT ADDRESS
HEIDELBERG COLLEGE
May 16, 1982

"GOODBYE, AND REMEMBER WE LOVE YOU"

Today is called Commencement. You are partcipating in an academic ceremony that is hundreds of years old. It is an ending and a beginning. It is an opening of a door and the closing of a door. It is farewell and hello. It is one of those important times when, in parting, we feel that something relevant should be said. Parents say it all when they say, "Goodbye, and remember we love you." In Hamlet, Polonius gives his son Laertes some parting advice, ending with, "This above all: to thine own self be true, and it must follow, as the night the day, thou canst not then be false to any man." Although these special times may call for beautiful sentiments like these, not all parting shots are so idealistic. In the play, Poppy, W. C. Fields' departing words to his daughter were, "Let me give you a little fatherly advice. Never give a sucker an even break, and never smarten up a chump."

If I am to summarize my experiences into a few words that may have some meaning for your lives, I will first have to share some of these experiences with you. Early in my teaching career I became fascinated with why one teacher was more successful than another. This led to my lifework—research into what constitutes teacher competence. I was trying to answer a question, "What is it that teachers do that causes students to learn?"

During my observations of teachers in action I saw a lot of both competence and incompetence. Because my objective was to find competence, the incompetence I observed was a waste product. But I found a use for the examples of incompetence—they provided comic relief in my lectures and in my writing about the educational system.

I wrote about a competent student in teachers' college. She was almost perfect. She did exactly as expected of her. She was punctual, attentive, and turned in neat, precise assignments. She was a highly competent consumer of knowledge who had no difficulty in graduating. She got a job as a classroom teacher and reached her level of incompetence in her first job. She was a humorless bore who couldn't interest her students in anything. She was a competent consumer of knowledge, who had been promoted to become an incompetent dispenser of knowledge.

I went on to write about the competent classroom teacher who was promoted to principal of the school. He got on perfectly with children so was promoted to become a manager of adults. He was a competent teacher promoted to be an incompetent administrator.

I called this phenomenon The Peter Principle: In a hierarchy individuals tend to rise to their levels of incompetence. This bit of satire caught on and became internationally famous. While I was studying the education system I had discovered a universal principle. From this I learned two things. When you're looking for something you'll find something else, and you can reach more people with humor than you can with research.

The satire of the Peter Principle is in its making fun of the traditional ladder of success—the idea that up is better and more is better. It reminds me of Richard Armour's poem that says,

> Now that I'm almost up the ladder
> I should, no doubt, be gladder.
> It is quite fine, the view and such,
> If just it didn't shake so much.

Am I saying you shouldn't go out there and climb the ladder of success? Of course not. You are at Commencement because you've climbed the secondary school ladder, and you've survived the higher education hierarchy. We are all where we are because of climbing.

What I am suggesting is that success is not just climbing. It is not just escalation.It is not just accomplishment. Success is more, much more. It is fulfillment. It is self Actualization. It is satisfaction. It is not just the quantity-of your accomplishments—it is the quality of your own being and life.

We have seen that moving up has not always lead to success for individuals or for society. We know individuals who sacrificed their integrity in their lust for power or possessions. We know individuals who have ruined their emotional and physical health in the name of ambition. We know individuals who have destroyed their family life and harmed the people they care for in order to advance their careers. In spite of their accomplishments these individuals are failures.

As a society our accomplishments are phenomenal. We have produced food in abundance, created the electronic age, eliminated many infectious diseases and plagues, and travelled in space.

We have also polluted and destroyed much of our natural world and blighted the promise of this century. Conceivably we are all doomed. We have converted the miracles of science into a chamber of horrors as we feverishly go on inventing and building and planning and scheming and revising and escalating a supercolossal disaster. If we think seriously about our air and water pollution, destruction of resources, acid and yellow rain, industrial wastes turning our environment into a chemical minefield, and the possibility of a nuclear holocaust, can we really call our society a success?

Our accomplishments are impressive, but the meaning, the value, and the quality of what we do is questionable in terms of human survival. The answer seems obvious. If the world that will soon be in your hands is to survive as a beautiful, hospitable place, you must quit playing my generation's games. You must get off this treadmill to oblivion that we have created. This is the challenge before you. You will have to abandon the idea that more is better and up is better in favor of moving forward to solutions of the problems we have created. You will have to find ways to live in harmony with the natural world around you and with your fellow inhabitants of this planet. You will have to find a way to end escalation of the suicidal arms race that continues even when we can klll all the world's people many times over. You will have to stop being a throw-away society and find ways to recycle to conserve the earth's natural resources. You will have to be the adults when the leaders of the world behave like children and make demands of each other that are not negotiable. You must succeed in solving these problems because your survival depends on it.

There are no easy solutions to these problems but your college has done the most it can to help you—you've learned how to learn. If you keep on learning you will find solutions. Always remember that what you do makes a difference. If you continue in the ways of my generation you will escalate these problems. If you doubt yourself and leave these problems to others, you will become victims of wanton and corrupt leaders. If you accept the challenge of these problems and work on them, you will experience the joys of knowing that you do make a difference.

In these, my parting words, I wish to add one more challenge. Make your life a work of beauty. Be brave enough to live creatively. Soon you will be engaged in your profession. Learn to love your profession. If you put your heart into your work, you cannot fail. Try to be strong where strength is required and gentle where gentleness can help. Take your responsibilities seriously, but don't take yourself too seriously. Laugh at yourself. Laugh at adversity and help others laugh at their troubles. Love and laughter are truly the best medicines. May your lives be full of both.

John Powell, S.J.

John Powell, S.J.

COMMENCEMENT ADDRESS
JOHN CARROLL UNIVERSITY
May 23, 1982

First of all, let me say sincerely that I am very honored and very happy to be with you on this memorable day. However, I must quickly add that this is the first Commencement Address I have ever delivered. In effect, this means that "it may not fly, Wilbur." Please do not conclude that this is my first speech. In fact, I happen to have a lot of mileage on my mouth. It's just that occasions like this are usually very solemn and dignified, and I have real doubts about my own capacities for solemnity and dignity. My final disclaimer and confession is that I very proudly am . . . a Jesuit: and you know what that means—this could go either way.

A mystical friend of mine, who has direct connections with heaven, tells me that last Christmas the citizens of heaven were having a reenactment-celebration. The Baby Jesus lay peacefully in the crib. Mother Mary was kneeling at the side of the crib, and St. Joseph was standing off to the side with a group of shepherds. No one could find the original wise men, so the founders of religious orders were invited to bring up the gifts.

St. Benedict appeared first, carrying a solid gold missal, symbolic of the long and strong Benedictine liturgical tradition. The people in heaven reportedly ooohed and aaahed, whispering: "That missal is solid gold!" Next in line, St. Dominic appeared with a diamond-beaded rosary on a 24 karat gold chain. Again, there were audible ooohs and aaahs. Dominic was followed by St. Francis of Assisi, who brought in his gently cupped hands a small sculptured bird. The ooohs and aaahs of awe became a gentle murmur.: "Isn't that darling!"

The last of the gift-bearers was St. Ignatius of Loyola, the founder of the Jesuits. All the eyes of the heavenly court followed him as he limped toward the crib. You will remember that his knee had been shattered at the battle of Pamplona during his youth when he was more a soldier than a saint. In fact, this became the occasion of his conversion. He had to lie in traction for a year during which he read the lives of the saints. The question, "Are you pulling my leg?" is attributed to this period in the life of St. Ignatius. At any rate, Ignatius was, in the long Jesuit tradition, carrying no gift. This, of course, arched many heavenly eyebrows and drew some unpublishable comments. When St. Ignatius walked past the crib, the heavenly onlookers concluded that he was, in the long and strong Jesuit liturgical tradition, lost. Quietly Ignatius moved into a position next to St. Joseph. At this point the heavenly court was agreed that Ignatius had misunderstood his role, and possibly thought he was supposed to be a shepherd.

It was at this point that St. Ignatius put his arm around the shoulder of St. Joseph and is reported to have whispered into his ear: "Where are you going to send the boy to school?"

When thinking about what I really wanted to say to you, Class of 1982 on this occasion, I asked myself: What do I wish someone had said to me when I was your age?

Above all, I want to say *Bon Voyage!* A clergyperson friend of mine was recently visiting in the Bahamas. While there he saw a large crowd gathered at the end of a pier. There was considerable excitement among those gathered there. Fearing that there might have been a tragedy and thinking that he might be of help, my friend ran down the pier and "pardoned" his way through the crowd, only to discover that the attraction was a solitary man, in a homemade boat about to set sail on a voyage around the world. The uninvited comments of the crowd were all negative. "You'll never make it . . . You'll broil to death in the sun . . . You haven't got enough provisions . . . That little boat of yours will never make it through an ocean storm . . ."

My friend thought it very important that someone be saying something positive and encouraging. So he stood at the end of the pier, as the small craft drifted out on its daring course, waving his arms like semaphors and shouting: "*Bon Voyage,* Sailorman! You're gonna make it. Our love and prayers go with you. Have a great trip. We'll all be waiting to welcome you home."

This is your commencement: it is the beginning of a new chapter in your lives. You are beginning a voyage that has never been made before. I think it is this that I would most of all want to say to you today: "*Bon Voyage!* You are going to make it. Our love and our prayers go with you. Have a great trip. We'll all be seeing one another when we are finally reunited in the eternal home of our Father."

As you go forth to take your place in the world, I want to reassure you that our world really needs you, needs your goodness and giftedness. Someone has said that a secular humanist philosophy of life has entered our world, like a saboteur in a department store, and changed all the price tags. The values once held in high esteem by our Christian tradition have been deemed trivial and unimportant. Even the sacred value of every human life has itself been questioned and even denied. Other realities traditionally regarded as transient and unimportant by gospel standards have been dramatically overvalued in our contemporary society. The gospel imperative to love persons and use things has been inverted by many who are committed to loving things and using people to get those things. The words of Jesus are almost haunting: "Where your treasure is, there your heart will be."

These past four years in your lives have been years of risk and revision. You have tested your values and commitments. You have grown your own roots. You are no longer an echo or carbon copy of anyone else. The values you have determined to honor will be the chief authors of your personal lifescript. These values will be the source of your greatest contribution to the world which needs you. And please do not underestimate your capacity to leave this world better than you found it. One person who truly believes and who truly loves is a majority.

In many ways your education at this fine University has not prepared you for the future. There was no way it could have prepared you completely for life in a world that does not yet exist. The explosion of knowledge and skill that brings about "future shock" will profoundly change the face of the earth and the pace of human life by the time your children arrive at college. But your Christian values, nourished by your experience at John Carroll, will stand the test of time and the attrition of change. These gospel values are timeless and changeless.

One of the gospel values is, of course, the primacy of persons and interpersonal relationships. "Where your treasure is, there your heart will be." It is probably a truism that your individual lives will be as successful as your interpersonal relationships. Your mental and emotional health will be as sound as your relationships. The satisfaction and happiness of your life will be derived from and measured by your ability to know and to be known, to love and to be loved. And of all such relationships, the most vital and decisive are those with your parents, your families of origin and with the families which you will originate. No matter how many miles lie between you, and even after separation by death, your parents will always be a tremendous influence on you, just as you will always be a lasting and living force in their lives.

In Thornton Wilder's play, *Our Town,* the dead Emily is allowed to relive one day of her life. She chooses to relive her twelfth birthday. In the midst of the celebration she is saddened by a strange, interior sense of alienation, a painful distance from those she loves. At one point she takes her mother's hands into hers and pleads with her mother: "Mother, let's look at each other, I mean, *really* look at each other." I suppose that Emily's "really" looking at one another means much more than mere recognition of the presence of another. I suppose it means that you gather in the total reality of that other person—as far as that is possible—and all that person has been and is to you. It is to feel as deeply as possible the impact of that other person on your own life.

Dear Graduates and dear Parents, could I suggest that, in the rush and the crush of this exciting graduation day, you "really look at" each other?

As you really look at your parents, dear Graduates, try to imagine the much younger mother and father showing off their new baby, the flesh of their flesh, the bones of their bones . . . you. Try to remember the hands that held yours in the darkness, that chased away bad dreams and tied your shoes, the hands that stroked your feverish brow and, when necessary, spanked you. Try to get inside their proud feelings in all those glorious moments of your personal triumphs: when you won the spelling contest, got the braces off your teeth, when you made the all-star team or the pom pom squad. Maybe they didn't tell you in ways you could understand, but you played a very important role in their lives, and you occupied a great part of their hearts. An old Roman poet, Marcus Annaeus Lucanus, once observed that a pigmy on the shoulders of a giant can see more than the giant. It may well be that you are academically better educated than your parents, but look long and thoughtfully at your mother and father today and reflect on what giant figures of affirmation, affection and support they have been to you.

And, dear Parents, when you look at the little girl you carried who has become such a beauty and your little boy at play who has grown so tall: remember proudly all the life, the laughter and tears of the purest pride that child of yours has brought into your life. Remember her in her first party dress, remember him on the day of First Holy Communion. Remember the Valentine card brought home from school "for Mom and Daddy." Watch the parade proudly as your child marches from infancy into adulthood, always looking sideways to find your face in the crowd, always looking for your support, approval and recognition.

The Irish say that "the apple does not fall far from the tree." All of your own goodness and giftedness, all of your own efforts over the years, are blossoming today in that fine young man, in that beautiful young woman, who was once your baby, your child. Something of you will always live on in your child: a promise of your immortality.

And when you "really look at" each other later today, would you try to find the words that say something of what is really in your heart? Say it now before it is too late. We humans have developed an extensive vocabulary for hostility and suspicion. What we really need are new ways to say, "Thank you," and "I love you." We need a much bigger vocabulary of affection — and affirmation.

If we tell one another of gratitude and love, the words will surely become indelible memories. Today's experiences are tomorrow's memories. When we tell one another of gratitude and love, we will be creating messages that will play forever on the recorders of our minds and hearts. "It only takes a moment to be loved a whole life through."

Dear Graduates, dear Mothers and Fathers: I would like to suggest that, if you can find some time today to "really look at" each other, and if you can talk to one another of grateful love, it will be the most important thing you will do today, and perhaps the most important thing you will ever do.

The ancient Chinese philosopher, Confucius, once said that "When there is happiness in a family, there will be contentment in the community and prosperity in the nation. And when there is prosperity in the nation, there will be peace throughout the world."

If this be true, and I think it is, then when we "really look at" one another and contribute to a larger vocabulary of love and gratitude, a larger vocabulary of affirmation and affection, we will be dealing with the roots of many other problems. We will be dealing with the ultimate causes of crime delinquency and addiction, emotional and mental sickness; we will be dealing with the quiet desperation in which so many human beings spend their lives.

In closing, dear Graduates of 1982, I would like to remind you that we all share your happiness and that we are all proud of you. I myself teach in a Jesuit University, much like your own. I know the joy that a member of the faculty or staff feels in your achievement. I know the consoling and rewarding feelings that follow upon the thought that we were joined with you in your effort and can now rejoice with you in your success.

I would also like to remind you of an old Jewish-Christian tradition that God sends each person into this world with a special message to deliver, with a special song to sing for others, with a special act of love to bestow. No one else can speak your message, sing your song, or offer your act of love. These have been entrusted only to you.

According to this tradition, God may intend your personal message, song and act of love only for a few, or maybe for all the folk in a small town, or for all the people in a large city, or even for all the people in the whole world. It all depends on God's unique plan for each unique person.

With all the sincerity of which I am capable, I want to say this to you: Never lose faith in the fact that you have an important message to deliver, a beautiful song to sing, and a unique act of love with which to warm this world and brighten its darkness.

When the final history of this world is written, your message, your song, and your act of love will be recorded gratefully and forever.

May love be the rule of your life, and please remember me as loving you. Thank you and God bless you.

Ronald W. Reagan

Ronald W. Reagan

COMMENCEMENT ADDRESS
NOTRE DAME UNIVERSITY
May 17, 1981

Nancy and I are greatly honored to be here today sharing this day with you. Our pleasure is more than doubled because we also share this platform with a long-time good friend, Pat O'Brien.

I haven't had a chance to tell Pat that I've only recently learned of another something we hold in common. Until a few weeks ago. I've known very little about my ancestry on my father's side. He had been orphaned at age 6. Now I've learned my great-grandfather left the village of Ballyporeen in Ireland to come to America. Ballyporeen is also the ancestral home of Pat O'Brien.

If I don't watch myself.this could turn out to be less a commencement than a warm bath in nostalgic memories. During my growing-up years in nearby Illinois. I was greatly influenced by a sports legend so national in scope and so almost mystical, it is difficult to explain elements — a game, football: a university, Notre Dame: and a man, Knute Rockne: there has been nothing like it before or since.

My first time to ever see Notre Dame was to come here as a sports announcer only two years out of college to broadcast a football game. You won or I wouldn't have mentioned that.

A number of years later I returned in the company of Pat O'Brien and a galaxy of Hollywood stars for the world premiere of "Knute Rockne — All American" in which I was privileged to play George Gipp. There were probably others in the motion picture industry who could have played the part better. There were none who could have wanted to play it as much as I did. And I was given the part because the star of the picture, Pat O'Brien, kindly and generously held out a helping hand to a beginning young actor.

Having come to Hollywood from the world of sports, I had been trying to write a story treatment based on the life of Knute Rockne. And I must confess, my main purpose was because I had someone in mind to play the Gipper. On one of my sports broadcasts before going to Hollywood, I had told the story of his career and tragic death. I didn't have many words down on paper when I learned the studio where I was employed was already preparing to film that story.

And that brings me to the theme of my remarks. I am the fifth President to address a Notre Dame commencement. The temptation is great to use this forum for an address on some national or international issue having nothing to do with the occasion itself. Indeed this is somewhat traditional so I haven't been surprised to read in a number of reputable journals that I was going to deliver a major address on foreign policy. Others said it would be on the economy. It will be on neither.

By the same token I will not belabor you with some of the standard rhetoric beloved of graduation speakers over the years. I won't tell you that "You know more today than you have ever known or than you will ever know again," or that other standby — "When I was 14 I didn't think my father knew anything. By the time I was 21 I was amazed at how much the old gentleman had learned in 7 years."

You members of the graduating class of 1981 are what the behaviorists call "achievers." And while you will look back with warm pleasure on the years that led to this day, you are today also looking toward a future which for most of you seems uncertain but which I assure you offers great expectations.

Take pride in this day, thank your parents and those who over the last four years have been of help to you, and do a little celebrating. This is your day and whatever I say should take cognizance of that fact. This is a milestone in your life and a time of change.

Winston Churchill during the darkest period of the "Battle of Britain" in World War II said:

> "When great causes are on the move in the world...we learn we are spirits, not animals, and that something is going on in space and time, and beyond space and time, which, whether we like it or not, spells duty."

I'm going to mention again that movie Pat and I and Notre Dame were in for it says something about America. Knute Rockne as a boy came to this country with his parents from Norway. He became so American that here at Notre Dame he was an All American in a sport that is uniquely American.

As a coach he did more than teach young men how to play a game. He believed that the noblest work of man was molding the character of man. Maybe that's why he was a living legend. No man connected with football has ever achieved the stature or occupied the singular niche in our nation that he carved out for himself, not just in a sport, but in our entire social structure.

"Win one for the Gipper," has become a line usually spoken now in a humorous vein. I hear it from members of the Congress who are supportive of the economic program I've submitted. But let's look at the real significance of his story. Rockne could have used it any time just to win a game. But eight years would go by following the death of George Gipp before Rock ever revealed Gipp's deathbed wish.

Then he told the story at half time to one of the only teams he'd ever coached that was torn by dissension, jealousy and factionalism. The seniors on that team were about to close out their football careers without ever learning or experiencing some of the real values the game has to impart.

None of them had ever known George Gipp. They were children when he played for Notre Dame. Yet it was to this team that Rockne told the story and so inspired them that they rose above their personal animosities. They joined together in a common cause and attained the unattainable.

We were told of one line spoken by a player during that game that we were afraid to put in the picture. The man who carried the ball over for the winning touchdown was injured on the play. We were told that as he was lifted on the stretcher and taken off the field he was heard to say, "That's the last one I can get for you, Gipper."

Yes, it was only a game and it might seem somewhat maudlin, but is there anything wrong with young men having the experience of feeling something so deeply that they can give so completely of themselves? There will come times in the lives of all of us when we'll be faced with causes bigger than ourselves and they won't be on a playing field.

This nation was born when a little band of men we call the founding fathers, a group so unique we've never seen their like since, rose to such selfless heights.

Lawyers, tradesmen, merchants, farmers — 56 men in all — who had achieved security and some standing in life, but who valued freedom more. They pledged their lives, their fortunes and their sacred honor. Some gave their lives, most gave their fortunes, all preserved their sacred honor.

They gave us more than a nation. They brought to all mankind for the first time the concept that man was born free; that each of us has inalienable rights, ours by the grace of God, and that government is created by us for our convenience having only those powers which we choose to give it.

This is the heritage you are about to claim as you come out to join a society made up of those who have preceded you by a few years and some of us by many.

This experiment in man's relation to man is a few years into its third century. Saying it that way could make it sound quite old. But look at it from another perspective. A few years ago someone figured out that if we could condense the history of life on earth down to a film that would run 24 hours a day for one year, 365 days (on leap year we could have an intermission), this idea we call the United States would not appear on the screen until 3½ seconds before midnight on December 31.

As you join us out there beyond the campus, you already know there are great unsolved problems. The careful structure of federalism with built-in checks and balances has become distorted. The Central Government has unsurped powers that properly belong to state and local government; and in so doing has in many ways failed to do those things which are the responsibility of the Central Government.

All of this has led to a misuse of power and a preemption of the prerogatives of the people and their social institutions. You are graduating from one of our great private, or if you will, independent universities. Not many years ago such schools were relatively free of government interference. But in recent years as government spawned regulations covering virtually every facet of our lives, our independent and church-supported colleges and universities found themselves included in the network of regulations, and the costly blizzard of administrative paperwork government demanded. Today 34 congressional committees and almost 80 subcommittees have jurisdiction over 439 separate laws affecting education at the college level. Virtually every aspect of campus life is now regulated — hiring, firing, promotions, physical plant, construction, record keeping, fundraising and to some extent curriculum and educational programs.

I hope when you leave this campus you will do so with a feeling of obligation to this, your alma mater. She will need your help and support in the years to come. If ever the great independent colleges and universities like Notre Dame give way to and are replaced by tax-supported institutions, the struggle to preserve academic freedom will have been lost.

Yes, we are troubled today by economic stagnation, brought on by inflated currency, prohibitive taxes, and those burdensome regulations. The cost of that stagnation in human terms mostly among those who are least equipped to survive it, is cruel and inhuman.

Now don't decide to turn in your diplomas and spend another year on campus. I've just given you the bad news. The good news is that something is being done about all this — being done because the people of America have said 'enough already.' We just had gotten so busy, that for awhile we let things get out of hand, forgot we were the keeper of the power. We forgot to challenge the notion that the state is the principal vehicle of change; forgot that millions of social interactions among free individuals and institutions can do more to foster economic and social progress than all the careful schemes of government planners.

Well, at last we are remembering: remembering that government has certain legitimate functions which it can perform very well; that it can be responsive to the people; that it can be humane and compassionate; but that when it undertakes tasks that are not its proper province, it can do none of them as well or as economically as the private sector.

For too long government has been fixing things that aren't broken and inventing miracle cures for which there are no known diseases.

We need you, we need your youth, your strength and your idealism to help us make right that which is wrong. I know you have been critically looking at the mores and customs of the past and questioning their value. Every generation does that. But don't discard the timetested values upon which civilization is built just because they are old.

More important don't let the doom criers and the cynics persuade you that the best is past — that from here it's all downhill. Each generation sees farther than the generation preceding it because it stands on the shoulders of that generation. You will have opportunities beyond anything we've ever known.

The people have made it plain they want an end to excessive government intervention in their lives and in the economy. They want an end to burdensome and unnecessary regulations and to a punitive tax policy that takes "from the mouth of labor the bread it has earned."

They also want a government that not only can continue to send men through the far reaches of space but can guarantee the citizens they can walk through a park or in their neighborhoods after dark without fear of violence. And finally they want to know that this nation has the ability to defend itself against those who would try to pull it down.

All of these things we can do. Indeed a start has already been made. A task force under the leadership of Vice President George Bush has identified hundreds of regulations which can be wiped out with no harm whatsoever to the quality of life. Their cancellation will leave billions of dollars for productive enterprise and research and development.

The years ahead will be great ones for our country, for the cause of freedom and for the spread of civilization. The West will not contain communism: it will transcend communism. We will not bother to denounce it; we'll dismiss it as a sad, bizarre chapter in human history whose last pages are even now being written.

William Faulkner at a Nobel Prize ceremony some time back said man "would not merely endure: he will prevail" against the modern world because he will return to "the old verities a truths of the heart."

"He is immortal," Faulkner said of man, "because he alone among creatures . . . has a soul, a spirit capable of compassion and sacrifice and endurance."

One cannot say those words without thinking of the irony that one who so exemplifies them — Pope John Paul II, a man of peace and goodness, an inspiration to the world — would be struck by a bullet from a man towards whom he could only feel compassion and love.

It was Pope John Paul II who warned last year in his encyclical on mercy and justice, against certain economic theories that use the rhetoric of class struggle to justify injustice; that "in the name of an alleged justice the neighbor is sometimes destroyed, killed, deprived of liberty or stripped of fundamental human rights."

For the West, for America, the time has come to dare to show the world that our civilized ideas, our traditions, our values are not — like the ideology and war machine of totalitarian societies — a facade of strength. It is time the world know that our intellectual and spiritual values are rooted in the source of all real strength — a belief in a Supreme Being, a law higher than our own.

When it is written, the history of our time will not dwell long on the hardships of our recent past. But history will ask — and our answer determine the fate of freedom for a thousand years — did a nation born of hope lose hope? Did a people forged by courage find courage wanting? Did a generation steeled by a hard war and a harsh peace foresake honor at the moment of a great climactic struggle for the human spirit?

If history asks such questions, history also answers them. These answers are found in the heritage left by generations of Americans before us. They stand in silent witness to what the world will soon know and history someday record: that in its third century the American nation came of age — affirming its leadership of free men and women — serving selflessly a vision of man with God, government for people and humanity at peace.

This is a noble, rich heritage rooted in the great civilized ideas of the West — and it is yours.

My hope today is that when your time comes — and come it shall — to explain to another generation the meaning of the past and thereby hold out to them the promise of the future, you will recall some of the truths and traditions of which we have spoken. For it is these truths and traditions that define our civilization and make up our national heritage. Now they are yours to protect and pass on.

I have one more hope for you: that when you do speak to the next generation about these things, you will always be able to speak of an America that is strong and free, that you will always find in your hearts an unbounded pride in this much-loved country, this once and future land, this bright and hopeful nation whose generous spirit and great ideals the world still honors.

Congratulations and God bless you.

Frank H. T. Rhodes

Frank H. T. Rhodes

COMMENCEMENT ADDRESS
CORNELL UNIVERSITY
May 31, 1981

The chief function of the Commencement speaker is to be brief. Lord Canning was once asked by a preacher how he enjoyed his sermon. Canning replied, "You were brief." "ah," said the preacher, "I always like to avoid being tedious." Canning thought for a moment and then replied, "You were also tedious." So there is no absolute guarantee of success.

Specifically I want to remind you of a gift from these four years that you will take with you when you leave Cornell. This will not appear on your transcripts. It is not inscribed on your diplomas. But it should be noted, for it will serve you well.

This is a sense of the priority of the present, for the present is literally all that there is. Those of you who studied history or literature during your Cornell years may be tempted to revel in the glories of the past — the great loves, the great wars, the Age of Chivalry, the Age of Reason. But if great deeds and great heroes of the past provide only an escape from the present, they become hollow facts, devoid of context. It is only when the past is prologue, when it provides the perspective that equips us for the "insistent present," that its value is realized.

But today, you reply, is focused, not on the past, but the future. But we should not be dazzled by all the tomorrows, with their vague promises, stretching to a seemingly endless horizon. So often, living for tomorrow becomes an excuse for not living fully today, an excuse for not extending ourselves to others as loving, caring, listening, giving human beings. It becomes an excuse for seeking the safe and sure today — to meet better the risks of tomorrow. In pursuit of a distant rainbow, we heap the gifts of each new day on the "altar of the future", never fully happy in the present and never pausing to savor its joys, never stopping to smell the roses. "You cannot smell the flowers from a galloping horse," an ancient Chinese proverb reminds us. If we live for the future, life, real life, will always be one step removed, joy, real joy, will always be deferred.

"Never, . . . commit your virtue or your happiness to the future," C. S. Lewis has written. "Happy work is best done by the man who takes his long-term plans somewhat lightly and works from moment to moment. . . . It is only our *daily* bread that we are encouraged to ask for. The present is the only time in which any duty can be done or any grace received."

Of course that does not mean that we should reject the past or that we must renounce the future. It requires discernment to see the present in the past. It requires not only discernment but courage to see the future — with all its potential — in the present. Nor does a commitment to the present mean blind hedonism. We are not required to live *for* the moment, but *in* the moment, embracing the joy of relationships and the splendor of the earth, thanking that parent or encouraging that friend today — for there may be no tomorrow. For it is the faithful and cheerful devotion to the common tasks of each new day, rather than commitment to brave but vague new worlds, that carries society forward. Sir William Osler, the renowned physician, once said, "Nothing will sustain you more potently than the power to recognize in your humdrum routine the true poetry of life - the poetry of the commonplace, . . ."

Nor does this mean that we should reject the familiar contemporary exhortation to establish goals for ourselves. But it does mean that we should not be consumed by them. Goals are admirable purposes to develop, commendable objectives for which to strive. But they are hollow if the true end of life becomes the act of achievement of the goal, rather than the enrichment that comes from fulfilling the part demanded by the goal. We speak with contempt and even pity of politicians who are always running for re-election, even from the moment they assume the office they seek, but in some ways they reflect our own condition. We, too, are always running for re-election, constant candidates for the ceaseless future, discarding the richness of the present for the abstraction of a future achievement. But the achievement becomes hollow even at the moment we attain it; it crumbles, trampled beneath our feet as we press on to the next goal. The future, for all its shimmering light, is a mirage to those who sacrifice the present.

Life brings no less frustration to those who sacrifice the immanent for the transcendant. To cherish the present is not to reject the transcendant, for it is through the immanent that the transcendant is disclosed; it is through the perishable that the imperishable may be glimpsed.

That, surely, is the crucial thing that all art and all literature teach us: that no moment, no scene, no situation, no person is to be neglected or despised as merely familiar, as just ordinary, as nothing but another example of a general category, long known to us. We can insist, if we will, that the world conform to our categories — that each experience, each encounter is nothing but another instance of something we have already met — but we shall pay a terrible price. For that will remove all possibility of the new, the unexpected, the unique; it will destroy the very possibility of joy. In preserving our personal categories, in establishing the world in our own image, we shall have lost our souls.

To cherish the many sidedness of the present does not require the rejection of the rigor or the beauty of science: they are amongst the glories of our age. But it does require an acceptance of the need for complementary modes of thought. We should be very parsimonious in our use of the word "merely" or "nothing but." The person who claims that light is *"nothing but"* an electromagnetic radiation has either overlooked or undervalued the splendor of sunrise across misty fields on a summer morning. Elizabeth Barrett Browning expressed it well when she wrote:

Earth's crammed with heaven
And every common bush afire with God;
But only he who sees, takes off his shoes,
The rest sit round it and pluck blackberries . . .

One need not necessarily accept her theology to accept her conclusion; each moment, each object is sacred. Each is — in Dr. Wexler's phrase — a means of grace.

So we savor this special moment of the present, this turning point of graduation, posed between the half-forgotten recollection of the past and the half-formed hopes of the future. Savor it well, for if we truly live in the present, we shall see the immense significance of this moment, and the reason that all of us celebrate your achievement.

Tomorrow, when Schoellkopf is empty, the parties are over and friends and family have scattered to the corners of the nation and beyond, today will be but a memory. And tomorrow's tomorrow will be but a possibility.

But today there is opportunity. Only the present is real. Marshall Lyautey, the great French soldier, once irritated his gardener by insisting that he plant a certain tree and do it before lunch. "But Marshall," the gardener complained, "What's the hurry? That tree is so slow growing that it will take a hundred years to reach maturity." "In that case," replied Lyautey, "there is not a moment to lose. Plant it at once."

And so, Class of 81, here's to you and here's to the past four years, and all they've meant; here's to the future and all it may be; but also — and especially — here's to the present, and all it now is.

There is an old Gaelic blessing that may serve to bid you well on the long journey you now begin:.

"May the sun shine gently on your face,
May the wind be at your back,
May the road rise to meet you,
May God hold you in the hollow of His hand,
Until we meet again."

Adrienne Rich

Adrienne Rich

COMMENCEMENT ADDRESS
SMITH COLLEGE
1979

I have been very much moved that you, the Class of 1979, chose me for your commencement speaker. It is important to me to be here, in part because Smith is one of the original colleges for women, but also because she has chosen to continue identifying herself as a women's college. We are at a point in history where this fact has enormous potential, even if that potential is as yet unrealized. The possibilities for the future education of women that haunt these buildings and grounds are enormous, when we think of what an independent women's college might be: a college dedicated both to teaching women what women need to know, and, by the same token, to changing the landscape of knowledge itself. The germ of those possibilities lies symbolically in The Sophia Smith Collection, an archive much in need of expansion and increase, but which by its very existence makes the statement that women's lives and work are valued here, and that our foresisters, buried and diminished in male-centered scholarship, are a living presence, necessary and precious to us.

Suppose we were to ask ourselves, simply: What does a woman need to know, to become a self-conscious, self-defining human being? Doesn't she need a knowledge of her own history; of her much-politicized female body; of the creative genius of women of the past — the skills and crafts and techniques and visions possessed by women in other times and cultures, and how they have been rendered anonymous, censored, interrupted, devalued? Doesn't she, as one of that majority who are still denied equal rights as citizens, enslaved as sexual prey, unpaid or underpaid as workers, withheld from her own power — doesn't she need an analysis of her condition, a knowledge of the women thinkers of the past who have reflected on it, a knowledge too of women's world-wide individual rebellions and organized movements against economic and social injustice, and how these have been fragmented and silenced? Doesn't she need to know how seemingly natural states of being, like heterosexuality, like motherhood, have been enforced and institutionalized to deprive her of power? Without such education, women have lived and continued to live in ignorance of our collective context, vulnerable to the projections of men's fantasies about us as they appear in art, in literature, in the sciences, in the media, in the so-called humanistic studies. I suggest that not anatomy, but enforced ignorance, has been a crucial key to our powerlessness.

There is — and I say this with sorrow — there is no women's college today which is providing young women with the education they need for survival as whole persons in a world which denies women wholeness — that knowledge which, in the words of Coleridge, "returns again as power." The existence of Women's Studies courses offers at least some kind of lifeline: but even Women's Studies can amount simply to compensatory history; too often they fail to challenge the intellectual and political structures that must be challenged if women as a group are ever to come into collective, non-exclusionary freedom. The belief that established science and scholarship — which have so relentlessly excluded women from their making — are "objective" and "value free" and that feminist studies are "unscholarly," "biased," and "ideological" dies hard. Yet the fact is that all science, and all scholarship, and all art, are ideological; there is no neutrality in culture. And the ideology of the education you have just spent four years acquiring in a women's college, has been largely, if not entirely, the ideology of white male supremacy, a construct of male subjectivity. The silences, the empty spaces, the language itself, with its excision of the female, the methods of discourse, tell us as much as the content, once we learn to watch for what is left out, to listen for the unspoken, to study the patterns of established science and scholarship with an outsider's eye. One of the dangers of a privileged education for women is that we may lose the eye of the outsider, and come to believe that those patterns hold for humanity, for the universal, and that they include us.

And so I want to talk today about privilege, and about tokenism, and about power. Everything I can say to you on this subject comes hard-won, from the lips of a woman privileged by class and skin-color, a father's favorite daughter, educated at Radcliffe, then casually referred to as the Harvard "Annex." Much of the first four decades of my life was spent in a continuous tension between the world the Fathers taught me to see, and had rewarded me for seeing, and the flashes of insight that came through the eye of the outsider. Gradually those flashes of insight, which at times could seem like brushes with madness, began to demand that I struggle to connect them with each other, to insist that I take them seriously. It was only when I could finally affirm the outsider's eye as the source of a legitimate and coherent vision, that I began to be able to do the work I truly wanted to do, live the kind of life I truly wanted to live, instead of carrying out the assignments I had been given as a privileged woman and a token.

For women, all privilege is relative. Some of you were not born with class or skin-color privilege; but you all have the privilege of education, even if it is an education which has largely denied you knowledge of yourselves as women. You have, to begin with, the privilege of literacy; and it is well for us to remember that, in an age of increasing illiteracy, sixty per cent of the world's illiterates are women. Between 1960 and 1970, according to a UNESCO report, the number of illiterate men in the world rose by 8 million; while the number of illiterate women rose by 40 million. And the number of illiterate women is increasing. Beyond literacy, you have the privilege of training and tools which can allow you to go beyond the content of your education and re-educate yourselves — to debrief yourselves, we might call it, of the false messages of your education in this culture, the messages telling you that women have not really cared about power or learning or creative opportunities, because of a psychobiological need to serve men and produce children; that only a few atypical women have been exceptions to this rule; the messages telling you that woman's experience is neither normative, nor central, to human experience. You have the training and the tools to do independent research, to evaluate data, to criticize, and to express in language and visual forms what you discover. This is a privilege, yes; but only if you do not give up in exchange for it the deep knowledge of the unprivileged, the knowledge that, as a woman, you have historically been viewed and still are viewed as existing, not in your own right, but in the service of men. And only if you refuse to give up your capacity to think like a woman; even though in the graduate schools and professions to which many of you will be going, you will be praised and rewarded for "thinking like a man."

The word "power" is highly charged for women. It has been so long associated, for us, with the use of force, with rape, with the stockpiling of weapons, with the ruthless accrual of wealth and the hoarding of resources, with the power that acts only in its own interest, despising and exploiting the powerless — including women and children. The effects of this kind of power are all around us; even literally in the water we drink and the air we breathe, in the form of carcinogens and radioactive wastes. But for a long time now, feminists have been talking about redefining power; about that meaning of power which returns to the root: *posse, potere, pouvoir* — to be able, to have the potential, to possess and use one's energy of creation: *transforming power.* An early objection to feminism — in both the 19th and 20th centuries — was that it would make women behave like men — ruthlessly, exploitatively, oppressively. In fact, radical feminism looks to a transformation of human relationships and structures in which power, instead of a thing to be hoarded by a few, would be released to and from within the many, shared in the form of knowledge, expertise, decision-making, access to tools, as well as in the basic forms of food and shelter and health care and literacy. Feminists — and many non-feminists — are, and rightly so, still concerned with what power would mean in such a society, and with the relative differences in power among women as a group here and now. Which brings me to a third meaning of power where women are concerned: the false power which masculine society offers to a few women, on condition that they use it to maintain things as they are, and that they essentially "think like men." This is the meaning of female tokenism: that power withheld from the vast majority of women is offered to a few, so that it may appear that any truly qualified woman can gain access to leadership, recognition and reward; hence, that justice based on merit actually prevails. The token woman is encouraged to see herself as different from most other women; as exceptionally talented and deserving; and to separate herself from the wider female condition; and she is perceived by "ordinary" women as separate also: perhaps even as stronger than themselves.

Because you are, within the limits of all women's ultimate outsiderhood, a privileged group of women, it is extremely important for your future sanity that you understand the way tokenism functions. Its most immediate contradiction is that, while it seems to offer the individual token woman a means to realize her creativity, to influence the course of events, it also, by exacting of her certain kinds of behavior and style, acts to blur her outsider's eye, which could be her real source of power and vision. Losing her outsider's vision, she loses the insight which both binds her to other women and affirms her in herself. Tokenism essentially demands that the token deny her identification with women as a group, especially with women less privileged than she: if she is a lesbian, that she deny her relationships with individual women; that she perpetuate rules and structures and criteria and method-ologies which have functioned to exclude women, that she renounce or leave undeveloped the critical perspective of her female consciousness. Women unlike herself — poor women, women of color, waitresses, secretaries, housewives in the supermarket, prostitutes, old women — become invisible to her; they may represent too acutely what she has escaped or wished to flee.

Jill Conway tells me that ever-increasing numbers of you are going on from Smith to medical and law schools. The news, on the face of it, is good: that, thanks to the feminist struggle of the past decade, more doors into these two powerful professions are open to women. I would like to believe that any profession would be better for having more women practicing it, and that any woman practicing law or medicine would use her knowledge and skill to work to transform the realm of health care and the interpretations of the law, to make them responsive to the needs of all those — women, people of color, children, the aged, the dispossessed — for whom they function today as repressive controls. I would like to believe this, but it will not happen *even* if fifty per cent of the members of these professions are women, unless those women refuse to be made into token insiders, unless they zealously preserve the outsider's view and the outsider's consciousness.

For no woman is really an insider in the institutions fathered by masculine consciousness. When we allow ourselves to believe we are, we lose touch with parts of ourselves defined as unacceptable by that consciousness; with the vital toughness and visionary strength of the angry grandmothers, the shamanesses, the fierce market-women of the Ibo, the marriage-resisting women silk-workers of pre-revolutionary China, the millions of widows, midwives and women healers tortured and burned as witches for three centuries in Europe, the Beguines of the 12th century, who formed independent women's orders outside the domination of the Church, the women of the Paris Commune who marched on Versailles, the uneducated housewives of the Women's Cooperative Guild in England who memorized poetry over the washtub and organized against their oppression as mothers, the women thinkers discredited as "strident," "shrill," "crazy," or "deviant," whose courage to be heretical, to speak their truths, we so badly need to draw upon in our own lives. I believe that every woman's soul is haunted by the spirits of earlier women who fought for their unmet needs and those of their children and their tribes and their peoples, who refused to accept the prescriptions of a male church and state, who took risks and resisted as women today — like Inez Garcia, Yvonne Wanrow, Joan Little, Cassandra Peten — are fighting their rapists and batterers. Those spirits dwell in us, trying to speak to us; but we can choose to be deaf; and tokenism, the myth of the "special" woman, the unmothered Athena sprung from her father's brow, can deafen us to their voices.

In this decade now ending, as more women are entering the professions (though still suffering sexual harassment in the workplace, though still, if they have children, carrying two full-time jobs, though still vastly outnumbered by men in upper-level and decision-making jobs), we need most profoundly to remember that early insight of the feminist movement as it evolved in the late sixties: *that no woman is liberated until we all are liberated.* The media flood us with messages to the contrary: telling us that we live in an era when "alternate life-styles" are freely accepted, when "marriage contracts" and "the new intimacy" are revolutionizing heterosexual relationships: that shared parenting and the "new fatherhood" will change the world. And we live in a society leeched upon by the "personal growth" and "human potential" industry, by the delusion that individual self-fulfillment can be found in thirteen weeks or a weekend, that the alienation and injustice experienced by women, by Black and Third World people, by the poor, in a world ruled by white males, in a society which fails to meet the most basic needs, and which is slowly poisoning itself, can be mitigated or solved by Transcendental Meditation. Perhaps the most succinct expression of this message I have seen is the appearance of a magazine for women called "SELF." The insistence of the feminist movement, that each woman's selfhood is precious, that the feminine ethic of self-denial and self-sacrifice must give way to a true woman-identification, which would affirm our connectedness with all women, is perverted into a commercially profitable and politically debilitating narcissism. It is important for each of you, toward whom many of these. messages are especially directed, that you discriminate clearly between "liberated life-style" and feminist struggle, and that you make a conscious choice.

It's a cliche of Commencement speeches that the speaker ends with a peroration telling the new graduates that however badly past generations have behaved, their generation must save the world. I would rather say to you, women of the Class of 1979: try to be worthy of your foresisters, learn from your history, look for inspiration to your ancestresses. If this history has been poorly taught to you, if you do not know it, then use your educational privilege to learn it. Learn how some women of privilege have compromised the greater liberation of women, how others have risked their privileges to further it; learn how brilliant and successful women have failed to create a more just and caring society, precisely because they have tried to do so on terms that the powerful men around them would accept and tolerate. Learn to be worthy of the women of every class, culture, and historical age who did otherwise, who spoke boldly when women were jeered and physically harassed for speaking in public: who — like Anne Hutchinson, Mary Wollstonecraft, the Grimke sisters, Abby Kelley, Ida B. Wells Barnett, Susan B. Anthony, Lillian Smith, Fannie Lou Hamer — broke taboos: who resisted slavery — their own and other people's. To become a token woman — whether you win the Nobel Prize or merely get tenure at the cost of denying your sisters — is to become something less than a man indeed, since men are loyal at least to their own world-view, their laws of brotherhood and male self-interest. I am not suggesting that you imitate male loyalties; with the philosopher Mary Daly, I believe that the bonding of women must be utterly different, and for an utterly different end: not the misering of resources and power, but the release, in each other, of the yet unexplored resources and transformative power of women, so long despised, confined, and wasted. Get all the knowledge and skill you can, in whatever professions you enter; but remember that most of your education must be self-education, in learning the things women need to know, and in calling up the voices we need to hear within ourselves. I am going to end by reading a short poem of mine; it is called "Power":

POWER

Living in the earth-deposits of our history

Today a backhoe divulged out of a crumbling flank of earth
one bottle amber perfect a hundred-year-old
cure for fever or melancholy a tonic
for living on this earth in the winters of this climate

Today I was reading about Marie Curie:
she must have known she suffered from radiation sickness
her body bombarded for years by the element
she had purified
It seems she denied to the end
the source of the cataracts on her eyes
the cracked and suppurating skin of her finger-ends
till she could no longer hold a test-tube or a pencil

She died a famous woman denying
her wounds
denying
her wounds came from the same source as her power

Adrienne Rich

From *The Dream of a Common Language,* copyright 1978 by W. W. Norton Company
© Copyright 1979 by Adrienne Rich. Reprinted by permission of the author.

Felix G. Rohatyn

Felix G. Rohatyn

COMMENCEMENT ADDRESS
MIDDLEBURY COLLEGE
May 23, 1982

"THE FRAGILE SYSTEM"

It has been more than thirty years since I graduated, without the slightest distinction, from a small, idyllic, some might say Ivory Tower, college in Vermont called Middlebury. I had come to the United States in 1942, a refugee from Nazi occupied France. America meant freedom and opportunity for me; Franklin Roosevelt was America, Middlebury was part of a heady post-war period, of belonging somewhere, of becoming a U.S. citizen, of having a future. A small, bouncy, bald professor named Benjamin Wissler taught me the difference between a fact and an assumption, between reasoning and guessing. Even though, soon after graduation, I was drafted for the Korean War and graduated from that experience as a Sergeant of Infantry, also without distinction, nothing during that period dimmed my conviction that in the U.S. tomorrow would be better than today, as would every tomorrow thereafter. Insofar as I am concerned, America has far exceeded my personal expectations. No European country would have given a Jewish refugee, of Polish extraction, the opportunities in business and in public affairs that this country has given me.

And yet it would be disingenuous and unrealistic not to recognize that the world as a whole and the U.S. in particular, are profoundly changed from my graduating year of 1949.

A friend of mine, one of the more civilized corporate chairmen, said to me recently: "I no longer give commencement addresses; the graduates are entitled to an upbeat speech and I am no longer capable of delivering it." It gave me pause because I certainly do not have an upbeat speech; however, a realistic assessment of where we are cannot be equated with hopelessness. We saved New York City from bankruptcy against much greater odds than those facing this country today. But we did it by being ruthlessly realistic about the mess we were dealing with and by assuming, quite correctly, that when things look very bad, they usually turn out to be worse than they look.

Today, the United States and the world as a whole are messy, but they are better than they were. They have always been messy for that is the nature of

217

most societies, but things are clearly no worse today that they were in the 1930s, with a depression in America and Europe facing Hitler and Stalin. We are facing very complicated, some possibly intractable problems on a very large scale all over the world. We have at our disposal exploding levels of technology as well as instantaneous and almost infinite access to information. As a result, the United States today faces an uncertain, but certainly not hopeless future. Unfortunately, it faces this future with an ideology and a philosophy more suitable to the past than to the present.

After our most recent Presidential election, the nation was mesmerized, first by the theory, and then by the implementation, of supply-side economics. This turns out to be John Maynard Keynes in disguise. After all, running large deficits as a result of tax cuts and defense spending is little different from running large deficits as a result of social programs and public works. The country eventually goes bankrupt either way. However, while all the attention was focused on the economic program, the nation paid little attention to the true radicalism of the Administration's program, namely the deliberate use of huge deficits to bludgeon the Congress to reduce dramatically the role, and the responsibility, of government.

The American Revolution of 1981 was, therefore, as profound in its reach as it was little noticed in its underlying philosophy. The last fifty years have witnessed a basic continuity on the part of one Administration after another on two counts: First, that Government had a responsibility to improve the lot of those unable to help themselves. Secondly, from 1932 to 1980, one government after another, albeit with different levels of conviction, accepted the basic thesis that the American free enterprise system could not rely solely on the free market to provide opportunity for all our people. Even President Nixon, when forced by events, imposed wage and price controls and enacted sweeping environmental legislation in support of this philosophy. The Revolution of 1981 is changing all that.

The United States is more than a nation, it is a continent. Within this continent lie our greatest challenges and the most serious threat to our democratic form of government: Income and class disparities on the one hand, regional disparities on the other. The Reagan Administration's approach to these issues was to state that tax policy should not be used to effect social change and that citizens should vote with their feet. As a result, a completely laudable attempt to improve American productivity by stimulating investment has resulted in an economic program incoherent in its application.

Budget cuts have been largely concentrated on lower-income programs such as food stamps and welfare and have not, so far, touched the large, middle income support programs, indexed to the cost-of-living, such as Social Security and pensions. Massive tax cuts, coupled with enormous and apparently indiscriminate increases in military spending, have created the perspective of enormous federal deficits for years to come. The growth in the economy which was expected to pay for these programs is, time and again, choked off by high interest rates.

At the same time, a strong regional tide is running away from this part of the country. Unless vigorous actions are taken soon, Older America, the Northeast and Midwest — tied to traditional industries like autos, steel, glass and rubber, seriously wounded by Japanese competition — will not provide the jobs, the schools, the taxbase to maintain the physical plant of its cities, and the minimum requirements of its citizens. Half this country will be basking in the sun, swimming in oil and defense contracts while the other half will sink further and further into physical decay, social stress and despair.

The basic test of a functioning democracy is its ability to create new wealth and see to its fair distribution. When a democratic society does not meet the test of fairness, when, as in the present state, no attempt seems to be made at fairness, freedom is in jeopardy. Whether the attack comes from the left or from the right is irrelevant; both extremes are equally lethal.

We have seen, in 1981, that legislating sacrifice puts the burden on those least able to afford it and that moderating inflation can only come through the bitter medicine of steep recession. Those solutions are neither fair nor are they likely, ultimately, to be effective. At a time of stress, sacrifice has to be negotiated and not legislated.

Austerity and democracy do not walk hand-in-hand in the United States except in wartime. The near bankruptcy of New York City in 1975 created something like the "moral equivalent of war" for city and state politicians, as well as for business and labor leaders. Before then, the City had, for years, plunged ahead toward disaster.

It was only when this became apparent that Governor Carey called on business and labor to join forces with government in order to devise a program that would head off the crisis and bring the City back to life.

What ultimately saved New York City was a limited period of austerity, imposed under the direst of threats, followed by gradual relaxations while a prosperous city economy, together with inflation, generated the growth in revenues to bring about a balanced budget. Our imposition of extreme austerity was temporary and it required courageous political leadership as well as a true social contract with business and labor. We created structures, such as the Municipal Assistance Corporation, which are clearly intrusions into the *political* process; they have not, in any way, hurt the *democratic* process. And the people of the City were willing to make real sacrifices as long as they believed those sacrifices were fairly distributed, that there was an end in sight and that the result would be a better city, a better environment and a better life.

It is worth analyzing what we were able to do in New York as well as the limits beyond which we were not able to go, since New York is, in certain respects, a mirror of the United States.

Maybe for the first time in its history, the United States is faced with doubts about its destiny. In less than twenty-five years we have gone from the American century to the American crisis.

The United States today is a country in transition. It is in transition from being the world's dominant military power to sharing that role with the Soviet Union; it is in transition from an industrial to a service society; from being a predominantly white, northern European society based in the Northeast and Midwest to being a multi-racial society with its center of gravity in the Sunbelt. A society in transition cannot be governed by rigid dogma; on the contrary, it requires a government which is flexible, pragmatic, even sometimes deliberately ambiguous. Shared values must be clear, but the means to the end cannot be rigid. From Fascism to Communism, from monarchy to anarchy, the ends of government are purportedly the same. Justice with opportunity, higher standards of living, peace in our time. The means to the end are very different, however, and the means are what determine whether we live in a free society.

The critical issues we face today are not the levels of interest rates or what kind of package finally comes out of budget negotiations. These things are important, but our fascination with numbers must not obscure the real issues. These are, in no particular order:

The rapid growth of a permanent underclass in America. The residents of inner-city ghettos, black and Hispanic, undereducated, underskilled, without real hope of participating in the future of the country;

The regional split between Sunbelt and Frostbelt, which is accelerating and which will leave the northern half of the United States in serious difficulty;

The decline of our traditional manufacturing sectors, the decay of our older cities and the decline in the quality of urban life;

Illegal immigration in great numbers, especially from Mexico, which will create additional social tensions unless we produce enough jobs to absorb our own unemployed along with new arrivals;

Nuclear proliferation and the need to control and reduce the level of nuclear weapons while being realistic about Soviet power.

To be fair and even-handed, I should probably attempt to sketch the many reasons today to be optimistic about the future. The new technologies and inventions, the exploration of space and the oceans, communications and education, advances in medicine and knowledge of the human body, plus the myriad new developments we cannot even conceive of today. We must also be realistic in recognizing that we are today the strongest economic power in the world and that we are facing a Soviet system which is spiritually and financially bankrupt.

If I seem to dwell on the problems it is probably for two reasons. First, because I have been trained, professionally, to look after the bad news first and let the good news take care of itself. Second, because I believe that in our problems lie the most serious challenges to our system and in their resolution lie some of the greatest opportunities for tomorrow.

And yet the list of problems that I reviewed is by no means a complete list and their diversity and complexity indicate the futility of trying to deal with them by across-the-board economic theories and "hands-off" government. The role of government, in the last decades of this century, will be *the* paramount question to be decided.

Today, we are witnessing a paradox: A government which abdicates to a theoretical marketplace most of its responsibilities for the welfare of the people, while wishing to intrude on people's most private decisions. How does one equate the conservative passion to intrude on such issues as abortion, school prayer and the death penalty with its equally fervent passion for the free market as the fount of all benefits? Today's conservative experiment will fail because it has no relevance to the world we live in, just as yesterday's liberalism failed for exactly the same reason. We are soon, however, going to run out of time for experiments.

Benny Wissler once snappily explained to me that there was no such thing as *the wrong answer;* there was only a *wrong answer.* It was only recently however that I concluded that, especially in government and public life, there may not be any such thing as *the right answer.* There may, at best, exist a process whereby trends can be affected and the direction of social and economic behavior temporarily influenced. This is the antithesis of the planned, central domination of government, but it means government committed to oppose destabilizing trends before they become floodtides. It is a permanent but ever changing process.

A Rabelaisian friend of mine once compared saving New York City to making love to a gorilla. "You don't stop when you're tired," he said to me, "you stop when he's tired." The gorilla never tires and government can never abdicate its responsibilities.

At the same time, we must recognize that it was the unrealistic liberalism of the Great Society and the perceived wishy-washiness of the Carter Administration that brought us the 1981 Revolution. We may be heading for an economic and social catastrophe with supply-side economics and the Laffer curve; we were surely headed for one with runaway spending, runaway inflation, and the appearance of weakness symbolized by the Iranian hostage crisis.

What alternatives are we facing if the current social and economic experiment fails?

One scenario is rather frightening. Described by Kevin Phillips recently in an article entitled "Post-Reagan America," it involves far greater government control over the economy as well as authoritarian right-wing populism. Limiting political and social dissent in the name of law and order, corporate statism can lead to something far worse. To those who say it cannot happen here, I would simply say that democracy is a fragile system and that we are stretching it to the breaking point. The essential questions of fairness and opportunity cannot be answered in the affirmative today by an economic policy which seems to favor the wealthy and a government which invests mostly in the military.

Another scenario is scarcely more inspiring. The attacks on many of our institutions by liberals of the late 1960s and early 1970s reached a level of shrillness and violence which created the impression, among millions of Americans, that liberalism was the antithesis of some of our most basic values: love of country, love of family, the work ethic. While this was happening, many of the Great Society social programs, enacted in the 1960s for totally valid reasons, turned out to be uncontrollable spending machines, which threatened to bankrupt our economy. The Achilles heel of liberalism, in a world of limited resources, is its apparent unlimited capacity to cave in to pressures for runaway spending. A bankrupt country is also incapable of maintaining the freedom of its people.

Where can we go, then, if neither conservatism nor liberalism has the answers and if a failed attempt at a middle-ground, the quintessence of Jimmy Carter, winds up in shambles. Recently, the Head of the French Socialist Party compared the political center to the Bermuda Triangle. "Everyone who goes there, disappears forever," he said. And yet, the answers, if there are any, must come from a rational middle ground; however, it need not be wishy-washy.

There is no reason why a hard-headed liberalism cannot live with the reality that we cannot spend ourselves into bankruptcy.

There is no reason why social programs, impeccable in their objectives, have to be grossly abused, or expanded to include those who really don't need them.

There is no reason why an economy, geared mostly to private sector growth, cannot at the same time, permit limited government intervention where needed. A modern version of the Reconstruction Finance Corporation of the 1930s could help rebuild our cities and restructure our basic industries without threatening our basic free enterprise system.

There is no reason why limited and temporary protection for our hard hit industries cannot be conditioned on restrained wage and price behavior by labor and management; this might become the model for an incomes policy where wage and price behavior could be linked to productivity.

There is no reason why large savings cannot be effected in defense, and particularly in reducing nuclear delivery systems, if we are willing to pay the price of larger standing conventional forces.

There is no reason to abandon human rights abroad and deal with murderers from the right because they happen to be anticommunist. Nor is there reason to tolerate murderers from the left on the romantic notion that they are agrarian reformers.

However, although there is no reason why these results cannot be achieved, we must be realistic about the political difficulty of bringing this about. Without the active support of the American people and the active cooperation of business/labor/and government, it cannot happen.

In times of upheaval, the passions must be for moderation and not for extremes. As Anwar Sadat well knew, the passion for moderation may be one of the most dangerous passions today, and yet it is especially vital to our future. Sadat took the risks, and paid the price. Even though today's technology provides us with mountains of instant data, it is useless without judgment. And if judgments are to have value, policy decisions have to be made early. When the crisis is clear it is often too late to act. That is the dilemma of statesmanship and the possibly fatal flaw in a political system which only seems to act when it is too late.

France has given the world a lot; not least is the skepticism of Montaigne and of Voltaire. Skepticism is what is needed today, skepticism of easy solutions, of cant, of ideology of the left or right. Skepticism does not equate with cynicism; it is not inconsistent with the fiercest patriotism or the firmest belief in basic values. But it can be the anchor to windward when our basic institutions seem to be adrift with the tides.

Yesterday, your President spoke to you of the American dream; today, I speak to you of the American reality. They are not inconsistent with each other but unless you face the latter, you will never achieve the former. Ladies and Gentlemen of the Class of 1982, I do not envy you but I do not feel sorry for you. You will have an exciting time and it is likely to be hard going. The United States is in need of change and your challenge will be to provide it as well as to adjust to it. As the rate of change accelerates, as the problems become greater and the solutions more elusive, get involved in public affairs. It is a great adventure.

Politics is not the only way to become involved in public life. There will be many structures such as Municipal Assistance Corporation, where private citizens can play important roles. I had the privilege of participating in a great adventure, the rescue of New York City. It was an experience both terrifying and exhilirating which I would not have missed for anything. It taught me what you will find out. To be skeptical and always look over your shoulder, but to get involved deeply and to shoot for the moon. To beware of lawyers and consultants and people who do not take risks and who do not get their hands dirty. There are even more experts today than there are problems, but there is no greater strength than an open mind combined with a willingness to take risks. Middlebury opened my mind as I am sure it did yours. In order to take risks, however, you have to go in harm's way. What happens then and how you perform, will depend on the fates as well as on your character.

Terry Sanford

Terry Sanford

COMMENCEMENT ADDRESS
DUKE UNIVERSITY
May 6, 1979

"THE USES OF A LIBERAL EDUCATION"

In a day when many doubt the value of a liberal education, often measuring it as they measure too many elements of our society, chiefly in economic terms, it will not suffice for a university to take smug refuge in Plato's answer to the inquiry, "What is the good of education in general?," because there are legitimate doubts beyond the question of economic returns. How do we indeed know, as Plato had the Athenian reply, that "education makes good men, and that good men act nobly." While I claim for Plato that he surely would have said "men and women" had he understood the implications of Title IX, I am still not completely reassured. Who, today, acts nobly? Can we claim this result for liberal education as now provided in the colleges and universities?

Duke is dedicated to the concepts of a liberal education, but I have worried for the past ten years about how good we are, how we fulfill our mission, whether we enrich the lives of those who come to Duke as students, whether a liberal education makes any difference. Sometimes I despair, doubting that we spend productively the resources gathered over the years from founders and benefactors, and wondering if change produced in the lives of students justifies the sacrifice of student time and family money. Sometimes I think that it may all be frivolous, as suggested by the rathskeller philosopher that a college education is one of the few things a person is willing to pay for and not get. Mostly I am hopeful, for I suppose that there is no better way known than to bet on education of young people, and that there is no better definition of the educated person than the embodiment of liberal education. But an assumption is not enough.

Can a university demonstrate that the life of a graduate with a liberal education is any better than the life of a graduate with some other kind of education, or of a person who is no graduate at all? The frightening realization is that they might not be very different. Universities are constantly reassured by thousands who have defined and refined the meaning and purpose of liberal education. Liberal education, it is said, promotes, educates, and develops the ability to value, reason, solve problems, think critically, act creatively, make decisions, grasp ideas, communicate—even with the written word, and offer leadership to our society.

From the grand claims to the actuality is another matter. We can define liberal education, but can we provide it? Are we and most other liberal education institutions merely fooling ourselves and missing the mark? There is no final SAT scoring for liberal education, no mathematical way to measure the achievement of our purposes.

Our proof of performance in the short run is no proof at all, but merely an indication that students are happy enough with the experience to keep on recommending Duke to their friends in high school. I like that, but it is not proof. The proof lies in the lives of students decades beyond graduation day, and we have never had a thorough accounting from that far out.

For Duke, we must, with every entering class, reaffirm our philosophy and reexamine our purposes. For faculty members, officers, and trustees, that is a responsibility filled with dread and wonder, inspired by the majesty and promise of young lives, and driven by duty that we neither betray nor neglect tradition and hope.

My concern for your acquisition of knowledge is not as great as my concern for your education. We can measure what knowledge you have acquired, and predict your ability to acquire more knowledge. We cannot know whether you have been educated until we observe your lives, something we are not positioned to do. My uneasy feeling comes from this realization. We have tried so hard and spent so much, and we may have failed you. We have little way of knowing right now. Life is difficult, and a successful life is even more difficult, and I am not certain that we have even helped you define success.

In our preoccupation with the budgets, and housing, and curricula, and parking, and eight o' clock classes, and drop-add, and board plans, we may have neglected the fundamental. Last fall I called on the entering class to re-establish an honor code for Duke. They are working on it. Within the month the Carnegie Council on Policy Studies in Higher Education has reported an "ethical crisis" in higher education. Cheating, disdain of honorable conduct, success — superficial success — at any price, are noticeable traits among college students, so say the report. Could this apply at Duke? If we are not working and studying in a climate braced by ethical and honorable behavior, college can be a detrimental force, or an evil. If there is not honor, all the purposes of a liberal education are denied and abandoned.

I do not believe that Duke is yet guilty of forsaking honor, and it is my prayer on each graduation day that we have given the graduates of this University the capacity and the desire to measure their own lives by a humanistic standard. I resort to prayer because it is too late for any other action. If we have made a mistake, and your sense of right and honor is flawed, we cannot recall you, as a motor company regularly recalls defective automobiles.

I want Duke to be an increasingly outstanding place of learning, but of learning to be honorable men and women while acquiring knowledge and sharpening intellectual capacity. It may be that there is not much demand for this kind of learning, that the abounding illustrations teach students that power, position, and wealth come from being dishonest enough to get the job done, and crafty enough to stay out of jail, and further teach that the public demands scant integrity and honor if offset by what we call success. I do not intend to tolerate a Duke University that approaches the pattern of Carnegie's baleful portrait of higher education today.

True, the Carnegie Report observes in college students the deficiencies and shortcomings of society generally, but that is no vindication. Universities are influenced by society, but it is the responsibility of universities to elevate society more than to be degraded by the failings of society, and it is the responsibility of Duke to elevate your influence on society through liberal education.

How do we tell whether our students live different and more valuable lives because of their experience at Duke? How do we examine the product? I have reflected often on how we might measure the results of Duke's liberal education in the performance of our graduates, examined every day, not alone in items of newsworthy acclaim in the "Alumni Register," but in the daily lives which determine whether Duke made a difference, with the important question being, "What kind of difference?" What survey techniques might we apply? How can we prove beyond a reasonable doubt that liberal education does what the definitions claim? How can we examine the tens of thousands who have been exposed to liberal education in order to say whether liberal education is worth the candle? We are forced to conclude that we cannot devise a method. The proof of the value of a liberal education, the justification for the continuation of Duke University, the evidence we find impossible to assemble, is in your lives. We shall never know fully how effectively Duke has served you, for it is not within our capacity to monitor your lives. We can observe and greet our alumni, with love and understanding and pride, but you are the final witness five years hence, or fifteen, thirty or fifty years from now. We cannot measure the results; only you can, each for yourself.

You can observe yourself, and also others with whom you will associate and work, graduates of Duke and of other schools, and those whose schooling was less formal.

You can note your own ambitions. We will certainly note your achievement, but achievement can often be distorted, and only you can answer, "Achievement for what?" You can note creativity. Are the changes that are brought about by your creative touch useful, and do they uplift humankind? And you can measure your own sense of decency, of concern, of love, of compassion, of caring about the world, about others. There are many people of great achievement, even creative people, who haven't got a decent streak about them. Honor must be a part of education, for honor is the path to truth.

It is not enough to treasure good books, and to savor great music, and to cherish fine objects of art, although a graduate with a liberal education probably does those things, but that's not the purpose of a liberal education. The purpose is truth. Truth is the fixed star. How many highly educated people, educated in the sphere of the liberal education, jump to conclusions and swing into action on skimpy evidence? You can see them on our campus, meticulous in laboratory and dissertation, but careless and impetuous in accepting rumors and press accusations. You can see them in the community, the nation, and all around the world. In a day of rapid communication, getting more rapid all the time, who stops to question the truth of assertions flashed around the world? How can we expect to maintain a civilized society without an insistence on truth? The searching questions of what is correct, what is right, what is the fact, what is decent, what is compassionate, what uplifts humankind, what is useful for society—all of these bear on truth, all relate to truth. But how many seekers of truth do we graduate, and how many seekers of truth do we graduate who soon lose faith because it's easier to do things the other way?

The seeker of truth, the insister on truth, may be the ultimate mark of the person with a liberal education. All people are different, and all are going to have different levels of ambition, experience different levels of achievement, be creative or less creative, be decent or more decent, be committed more or less, with concern and love and compassion depending on a lot of things other than education, but the heart of the liberal education is the search for truth, and the insistence that truth be established.

It is enticingly easy to overlook the truth, because truth appears to get in the way of ambition and achievement. Yet it is more important to be right — noble — than powerful. It might not seem that way, but it is, for truth and right endure, and triumph; and power somehow passes and comes to naught, if not marked by truth.

Having observed a generation of politics, I can tell you that the spectacular life of the demagogue, rising to what seems to be power, is not as significant as the unheralded life of a person who has stood for the right.

I observed at first hand most of the political demagogues of the fifties, sixties, and seventies exploiting the racial difference for their own political popularity, degrading fellow human beings, playing upon and inflaming the ignorance and prejudices of others, and never hindered by truth and true values. In contrast, I can recall a small restaurant owner, whose name is not remembered by many, who understood the need for human dignity, and the truth of human values, who voluntarily integrated his restaurant, before the law required it, as an example for his community, and ultimately lost his business in bankruptcy, because people stirred by the demagogues and captured by their own demagogic spirits, quit coming. The man who made that harsh choice is living today in harmony and inner peace and no person who knows him doubts his civilized spirit or his civilizing influence on those around him. The demagogue is busy asserting that his purpose really was not racist, that he simply was a populist, whatever that is, but his denials pathetically demonstrate that he knows very well that he denied truth, that his life has been wasted, and that his part in history, attended daily by the press and cheered by frenzied crowds, was nevertheless insignificant and contributed nothing to the advance of civilization. I have observed too many similar contrasts, in large matters and in small matters, in business, government, education, and every human endeavor. Truth versus power.

You are our proof, our only verification, and yet I appear naive, even simplistic, in asserting that honor and truth are the basic goals. My deepest feelings come out as only words. It is a fearful duty that the University holds because we proclaim that we develop those who will seek the truth with all its facets. Every teacher, every course, every classroom, every activity, every decision becomes crucial because everything is at stake as we bet, somewhat blindly, on your future. Whether we win or not will be measured by your lives well into the next century; and you, looking back, can ask the question, "Do I fit the definition of a person of liberal education, or am I something else?" If something else, it will then be too late.

Whatever it was that inspired you to the accomplishments leading to this significant occasion, it got you involved with truth. It is our simple hope that because of your years at Duke you will prove that liberal education is all that we proclaim it to be.

Go, with our faith and fears, and may the spirit of humanity go with you.

John R. Silber

John R. Silber

COMMENCEMENT ADDRESS
BOSTON UNIVERSITY
May 17, 1981

"THE GODS OF THE COPYBOOK HEADINGS"

On March 4, 1825, only fourteen years before the founding of Boston University, John Quincy Adams came to the presidency of the United States. In his inaugural address he said:

> Since the adoption of (our) social compact, (a generation) has passed away. It is the work of our forefathers. We now receive it as a precious inheritance from those to whom we are indebted for its establishment, doubly bound by examples they have left us and by the blessings which we have enjoyed as the fruits of their labor to transmit the same, unimpaired, to the succeeding generation.

John Quincy Adams was the first President of the United States to speak of the Revolutionaries as belonging to a previous generation. Before him, each President had himself been one of the founders of the nation.

His position had a peculiar poignancy, but it is one in which all responsible individuals find themselves in every generation, and which affects most deeply young people like yourselves who are completing their education. You look in two directions, behind and ahead.

You look behind to your parents and mentors, to those who have been your teachers and who have passed on to you through many generations the legacy which 200 years ago was passed from John and Abigail Adams to John Quincy Adams and by him to his successors and eventually to us. Those of you who stand in this graduating class look backward, not only to the education you have received at Boston University, but to your great inheritance as Americans.

But you also look forward. You stand between the generation that is moving from the scene and the generation that is yet unborn. You, in your turn, now have the responsibility to create a generation and to pass on to it the tradition that has been given to you. It will be your responsibility to be the parents—both physically and spiritually—of the next generation, to pass on to the next generation an inheritance as good, if possible, as the one you have received, just as it has been our responsibility to pass that precious inheritance on to you.

As you commence your adult lives with these responsibilities, I suggest that you seek guidance from the education that earlier parents provided their children. In the provision of elementary and secondary education I am not sure that my generation has done as well as the generation that preceded it. I received a far better education in the public schools of San Antonio, Texas, than those schools provide their students today. I am convinced that the schools in Boston at this time are not equal to the schools in Boston fifty years ago, certainly not equal to those 100 years ago.

We should acquaint ourselves with earlier educational standards and expectations, so that we do not diminish the richness of our inheritance, but pass that treasure on to the next generation faithfully and undiminished.

The first objective of early education should be training in the reality principle. It has been argued that the child who grows up with television, finding that he can alter the reality of the screen by changing channels, believes that he can as easily alter the world itself, a point made brilliantly by Peter Sellers in the film *Being There*. In a world in which the very young are given such misleading intimations of omnipotence, concern for reality is more important than ever.

The child's confrontation with reality, a hundred years ago, began with the realization of death, which might come through the death of a sibling, a friend, or a parent, aunt, uncle or grandparent, any of which was far more likely to be experienced by the young. Today, in contrast, the death of a child is so rare a misfortune as to be thought nearly unbearable, and increases in the lifespan have significantly postponed the time at which most children experience the death of an elder.

Learning about the fact of death is a most shocking contact with reality. Sound education absolutely depends on it, because it is the condition on which our full humanity depends. Education should expose us to what is true, to a confrontation with what is real. A true education, therefore, must provide an acquaintance with death and with the conditions by which people can achieve happiness in the awareness of death. It must explain, for example, the essential role of virtue in the attainment of happiness: it must explain that virtue establishes one's worthiness to be happy. These are aspects of reality that must be introduced into the education of a child, if the child is to develop fully.

Long before a child went to school in nineteenth-century America, or even early twentieth-century America, he learned these things. This confrontation with reality has been provided for several hundred years through *Mother Goose* rhymes. In *Mother Goose,* we find important moral lessons that were thought to be far too important to be kept from the child until he entered school at age six. The child of three or four learned to repeat:"If wishes were horses, beggars would ride." The child was warned to remember the reality principle, and not to be misled by the attractions of wishful thinking.

Recently I reviewed some early books used to teach reading and writing—preprimers and primers used in the first grade and even earlier by parents who taught their own children at home. These books had a rhyme for every letter in the alphabet, for their authors capitalized on the delight that children take in verse. Let me read a few of them from the *New England Primer,* widely used in our local schools.

A. Adam and Eve their God did grieve.

B. Life to mend this book attend.

(This was accompanied by a picture of the Bible.)

C. The cat doth play and later slay.

(Cats, you see, were not just pets. They tormented, killed, and ate mice, and children were not protected from that grisly fact.)

D. A dog will bite a thief at night.

(This was an admonition to dogs and thieves alike.)

F. The idle fool is whipped at school.

(A self-explanatory point.)

H. Wrought by hand great works do stand.

J. Job felt the rod yet blessed his God.

Q. Queens and Kings must lie in the dust.

(A child who has not yet gone to school is thus reminded that Queens and Kings are mortal.)

T. Time cuts down the great and small.

(In case the child missed the point earlier or thought it was restricted to kings and queens, the point is generalized: all people must die.)

X. Xerxes the Great shared the common fate.

(Now the child, who has not yet learned to read and write, has been told this fact three times.)

This is the way Americans of earlier generations taught the alphabet. This book addresses the child at a far more dignified level than such contemporary efforts as, "Spot and Jane run and play. Run, Spot, run. Catch, Jane, catch. Dick and Jane are friends." This book was written in a period before condescension toward children had been developed into a dogma.

Reality provides the conditions on which pleasure can or cannot be achieved, and provides the moral conditions on which pleasure should or should not be achieved. This value-freighted reality reveals the conditions that must be met or avoided if there is to be any gratification at any time. The child learned that wishes were not horses because before he learned to read he was taught through these verses that if they were horses beggars would be riding, and every child knew that beggars went on foot. Thus *Mother Goose* taught the child that there's no such thing as a free lunch. Unfortunately, many politicians in Massachusetts and in Washington have never read *Mother Goose.*

This was the normal education of the young child before he went to school. It taught him the alphabet and prepared him to read. It also prepared him for something much more important than reading. It prepared him for life.

Consider, moreover, how children learned to write. (A skill on the endangered species list in contemporary America.) They did it through the use of copybooks, manuals with beautifully handwritten sentences—copybook headings—printed at the top of each page. The child was expected to imitate the excellent writing of the headings by copying them many times on the lined spaces below, until he had learned the headings by heart.

Now, what did these copybook headings say? I quote from *The Art of Penmanship,* one of the most widely used copybooks of the period: "Religion conduces to our present as well as our future happiness." This sentence was in the copybook of a child so young that he was just beginning to learn to write. And another, "Persevere in accomplishing a complete education." "Persevere in accomplishing a complete education." "Persevere in accomplishing a complete education." And on and on until the word "persevere" was learned by heart, and the meaning of perseverance learned by persevering long enough to write it twenty times.

The educators who prepared that copybook knew that children are naturally fascinated and excited by grown-up words. The educators of that period understood the attraction and the power of language. In these copybooks words appear as treasures, language as a treasure-house, and education as the key. Let me read a few more of those copybook headings.

Quarrelsome persons are always dangerous companions.
Employment prevents vice.
Great men were good boys.

(This thought somehow managed to survive the copybooks—at least in one corner of America. When I was growing up, the wall of the San Antonio YMCA boasted a large sign which said: "Don't wait to be a man to be great! Be a great boy.")

Praise follows exertion.
Trifles alienate friends.
X begins no English word.

(Presumably this was before xylophones.)

Build your hopes of fame on virtue.
Death to the good brings joy instead of terror.
Zinc is a white semi-metal useful in galvanism.

(If not edifying, this heading was at least semi-informative.)

One may perhaps understand better why the abolitionist movement began in Boston when one reads the copybook headings that shaped the minds of Boston children. "Justice is a common right." "Magnanimity ennobles." "Overcome all prejudice." "Justice will pursue the vicious." "Zeal for justice is worthy of praise." If there is to be an effective moral education, the education must begin in early childhood. The child's education started when he began learning the language. These copybook headings were the efforts of an earlier generation to pass on their moral heritage to their children, to acquaint their children with nature—not merely physical but moral and spiritual. By introducing moral and spiritual reality into the education of the child they expressed their concern to educate the child in all dimensions of reality, to prepare children, in short, for a true and complete human existence.

It was not enough to teach penmanship merely as beautiful writing. It was important to have something to write *about,* to have content in all the curriculum, a content that was the distillation of a high culture. It presented as aphorisms the things that thoughtful, understanding people would be expected to know about the nature of the world, about the nature of society, about the nature of the universe, and about themselves. The full meaning and justification of these aphorisms was provided in later stages in the curriculum in the works of Plato, Aristotle, Aquinas, Spinoza, Kant, and many others.

But it never crossed the mind of an eighteenth-century or a nineteenth-century parent or teacher that his principal responsibility was to be a pal to his children, or to try to make life easy, comfortable, convenient, or maximally pleasurable. Rather it was his duty to prepare the child, through exposure to reality, for the uncertainty of human life and the ever-present possibility of death. The child was led to the realization that virtue and achievement count, and that, since death cannot be avoided, he prepares for death by living well. It was fine to welcome pleasure when it came, but the child had to recognize the folly of basing his life on mere pleasure-seeking.

If we are to recapture this wisdom, we must go back to the copybooks and primers of the eighteenth and nineteenth centuries. I do not mean that we should literally reintroduce them into the curriculum. But we must reintroduce their subject matter, we must return to reality. And that requires us to look to the past because the past necessarily shapes the future. If our future is to be as strong, as good, as fine, and as just as our past has been, we must reassert what was best in a more distant past out of which that more recent past came to be.

A prophetic poem on this subject was written by Rudyard Kipling over sixty years ago: "The Gods of the Copybook Headings." Let me read it to you: the poet speaks as the voice of mankind.

> As I pass through my incarnations in every age and race,
> I make my proper prostrations to the Gods of the Market-place.
> Peering through reverent fingers I watch them flourish and fall,
> And the Gods of the Copybook Headings, I notice, outlast them all.
>
> We were living in trees when they met us. They showed us each in turn
> That Water would certainly wet us, as Fire would certainly burn:
> But we found them lacking in Uplift, Vision, and Breadth of Mind,
> So we left them to teach the Gorillas while we followed the March of
>   Mankind.
>
> We moved as the Spirit listed. *They* never altered their pace,
> Being neither cloud nor wind-borne like the Gods of the Market-place;
> But they always caught up with our progress, and presently word would
>   come
> That a tribe had been wiped off its icefield, or the lights had gone out in
>   Rome.
>
> With the Hopes that our World is built on they were utterly out of touch,
> They denied that the Moon was Stilton; they denied she was even Dutch.
> They denied that Wishes were Horses; they denied that a pig had Wings.
> So we worshipped the Gods of the Market Who promised these beautiful
>   things.

When the Cambrian measures were forming, they promised perpetual peace.
They swore, if we gave them our weapons, that the wars of the tribes would cease.

But when we disarmed they sold us and delivered us bound to our foe,
And the Gods of the Copybook Headings said: *"Stick to the Devil you know."*

On the first Feminian Sandstones we were promised the fuller Life
(Which started by loving our neighbour and ended by loving his wife)
Till our women had no more children and the men lost reason and faith,
And the Gods of the Copybook Headings said: *"The Wages of Sin is Death."*

In the Carboniferous Epoch we were promised abundance for all,
By robbing selected Peter to pay for collective Paul;
But, though we had plenty of money, there was nothing our money could buy,
And the Gods of the Copybook Headings said: *"If you don't work you die."*

Then the Gods of the Market tumbled, and their smooth-tongued wizards withdrew,
And the hearts of the meanest were humbled and began to believe it was true
That All is not Gold that Glitters, and Two and Two make Four—
And the Gods of the Copybook Headings limped up to explain it once more.

As it will be in the future, it was at the birth of Man—
There are only four things certain since Social progress began—
That the Dog returns to his Vomit and the Sow returns to her Mire,
And the burnt Fool's bandaged finger goes wabbling back to the Fire;

And that after this is accomplished, and the brave new world begins
When all men are paid for existing and no man must pay for his sins,
As surely as Water will wet us, as surely as Fire will burn,
The Gods of the Copybook Headings with terror and slaughter return.

If we have the courage to face reality, we will know and we will proclaim these harrowing truths. That the degenerate society consumed in pleasure-seeking will not suvive. "The wages of sin is death." That the society that will not defend its freedom will lose it. "Stick to the Devil you know." That a society that consumes more than it produces will go bankrupt. "If you don't work, you die." We, members of the graduating class, faculty, parents—all of us—we will ill serve ourselves and our children by preparing ourselves and them for a life of freedom and easy pleasure that may never come and most certainly will never last. We had better prepare ourselves and them for reality: a reality that is infused with moral laws as surely as it is infused with physical laws; a reality in which there is no consumption without production, no freedom without defense, no self-fulfillment and no self-government without self-disciplined persons who govern themselves, persons who are capable of subordinating their desires long enough to achieve the conditions on which freedom and surivival, and even pleasure, depend.

It is often said, and said mistakenly, that students at graduation go out into the real world. That is an expression of escapism. It suggests that we were avoiding the real world all the time we were in school and in college. No world is more real than the world of ideas in which students are, or should be, immersed from kindergarten through college. And we had better take hold of our educational program and see to it that reality is packed into the curriculum so that our graduates will confront reality with the ideas of the copybook headings in mind. They will then find themselves in the same world that they learned about in school and in college, and will be guided by ideas and principles that can anchor their lives, and can give meaning, direction, and support. That should be our legacy to them.

These ideas must prepare them for the disappointment which is an essential part of the joy of living. All of us must live with disappointment, accept limitations and imperfections. We live in a world of becoming and change. Inevitably you will sometimes be disappointed with friends. You will sometimes be disappointed in marriage, disappointed in institutions, and sometimes disappointed in yourselves. Thus if you are to retain your joy in life you must find much of that joy in spite of disappointment, for the joy of life consists largely in the joy of savoring the struggle, whether it ends in success or in failure. Your ability to go through life successfully will depend largely upon your traveling with courage and a good sense of humor, for both are conditions of survival. It is for this reason that I stress the importance of living with reality and therefore with disappointment.

The difficulties of life did not destroy John Adams' parents, or John Quincy Adams' parents. They did not destroy your teachers' parents or your parents. They need not destroy you. Hence there is room for hope. There is hope for fulfillment in your own lives and in the lives of your posterity.

When I look to the future of our country over the next twenty-five years, I find it very difficult to be hopeful in the conventional understanding of that word. But it is easy to be hopeful at a more profound level. The difficult years that lie before us may turn out to be far happier than the twenty-five years through which we have come. For the ancients knew that happiness is more often achieved in adversity than in luxury and affluence. Juvenal rightly said, "Luxury is more ruthless than war."

We now face the disappointments that follow affluence. And as affluence begins to wind down and the struggle for survival increases, and as we discover our ability to cope with disappointments, with limitations, with greater privations than most of us have ever known, we shall find at the same time increasing opportunities for personal achievement, fulfillment, and happiness.

We must quickly come to terms with our unavoidable imperfections and with the unavoidable imperfections of others and of our institutions. We must find it possible to live happily in an imperfect world with self-confidence and joy, for there is a stern reality to be faced and much hard work to be done. We must join with one another to build a more basic foundation than pleasure, a foundation of enduring happiness that comes through triumph over one's self in a world not of our making by achieving a disciplined and moral relation to reality. We must find courage, personal renewal, and, ultimately, happiness by regaining a sense of ourselves as a free people in a common cause on behalf of our free nation, prepared to do, and prepared to do without, whatever is necessary in order to preserve what is best in the American way of life. (The phrase may be shopworn but the reality behind the phrase is still our last, best hope.)

Rebuild our defenses, balance our budget, achieve energy independence, rid our cities of crime? Of course! Educate a new generation for reality, for responsible productivity rather than irresponsible consumption? Of course! Regain our sense of direction as a nation, a sense of direction as individuals who seek not pleasure but happiness? Yes, that too! All this or nothing. For we will either learn the lessons of the Copybook Headings and respond creatively and responsibly to those lessons or we will succumb to the consequences of ignoring them.

I am convinced that the graduating class of Boston University and other graduating classes all over the United States, this spring of 1981, are a worthy generation of young Americans, who are prepared for a return to reality and for a courageous moral existence. I am confident that you will savor and treasure your inheritance, that you will contribute substantially to it, and that you will transmit that inheritance unimpaired and perhaps enhanced to succeeding generations.

As John Quincy Adams said, "Think of your forefathers; think of your posterity." That is to say: think of yourselves.

Aleksandr I. Solzhenitsyn

Aleksandr I. Solzhenitsyn

COMMENCEMENT ADDRESS
HARVARD UNIVERSITY
1978

"A WORLD SPLIT APART"

I am sincerely happy to be here with you on the occasion of the 327th commencement of this old and illustrious university. My congratulations and best wishes to all of today's graduates.

Harvard's motto is "Veritas." Many of you have already found out and others will find out in the course of their lives that truth eludes us as soon as our concentration begins to flag, all the while leaving the illusion that we are continuing to pursue it. This is the source of much discord. Also, truth seldom is sweet; it is almost invariably bitter. A measure of bitter truth is included in my speech today, but I offer it as a friend, not as an adversary.

Three years ago in the United States I said certain things that were rejected and appeared unacceptable. Today, however, many people agree with what I then said. . . .

The split in today's world is perceptible even to a hasty glance. Any of our contemporaries readily identifies two world powers, each of them already capable of utterly destroying the other. However, the understanding of the split too often is limited to this political conception: The illusion according to which danger may be abolished through successful diplomatic negotiations or by achieving a balance of armed forces. The truth is that the split is both more profound and more alienating, that the rifts are more numerous than one can see at first glance. These deep manifold splits bear the danger of equally manifold disaster for all of us, in accordance with the ancient truth that a kingdom—in this case, our Earth—divided against itself cannot stand.

Contemporary Worlds

There is the concept of the Third World: Thus, we already have three worlds. Undoubtedly, however, the number is even greater; we are just too far away to see. Every ancient and deeply rooted self-contained culture, especially if it is spread over a wide part of the earth's surface, constitutes a self-contained world, full of riddles and surprises to Western thinking. As a minimum, we must include in this category China, India, the Muslim world, and Africa, if indeed we accept the approximation of viewing the latter two as uniform. For one thousand years Russia belonged to such a category, although Western thinking systematically committed the mistake of denying its special character and therefore never understood it, just as today the West does not understand Russia in Communist captivity. And while it may be that in past years Japan has increasingly become, in effect, a Far West, drawing ever closer to Western ways (I am no judge here), Israel, I think, should not be reckoned as part of the West, if only because of the decisive circumstance that its state system is fundamentally linked to religion.

How short a time ago, relatively, the small world of modern Europe was easily seizing colonies all over the globe, not only without anticipating any real resistance, but usually with contempt for any possible values in the conquered peoples' approach to life. It all seemed an overwhelming success, with no geographic limits. Western society expanded in a triumph of human independence and power, And all of a sudden the twentieth century brought the clear realization of this society's fragility. We now see that the conquests proved to be short-lived and precarious (and this, in turn, points to defects in the Western view of the world which led to these conquests). Relations with the former colonial world now have switched to the opposite extreme and the Western world often exhibits an excess of obsequiousness, but it is difficult yet to estimate the size of the bill which former colonial countries will present to the West and it is difficult to predict whether the surrender not only of its last colonies, but of everything it owns, will be sufficient for the West to clear this account.

Convergence

But the persisting blindness of superiority continues to hold the belief that all the vast regions of our planet should develop and mature to the level of contemporary Western systems, the best in theory and the most attractive in practice; that all those other worlds are but temporarily prevented (by wicked leaders or by severe crises or by their own barbarity and incomprehension) from pursuing Western pluralistic democracy and adopting the Western way of life. Countries are judged on the merit of their progress in that direction. But in fact such a conception is a fruit of Western incomprehension of the essence of other worlds, a result of mistakenly measuring them all with a Western yardstick. The real picture of our planet's development bears little resemblance to all this.

The anguish of a divided world gave birth to the theory of convergence between the leading Western countries and the Soviet Union. It is a soothing theory which overlooks the fact that these worlds are not at all evolving toward each other and that neither one can be transformed into the other without violence. Besides, convergence inevitably means acceptance of the other side's defects, too, and this can hardly suit anyone.

If I were today addressing an audience in my country, in my examination of the overall pattern of the world's rifts I would have concentrated on the calamities of the East. But since my forced exile in the West has now lasted four years and since my audience is a Western one, I think it may be of greater interest to concentrate on certain aspects of the contemporary West, such as I see them.

A Decline in Courage

A decline in courage may be the most striking feature that an outside observer notices in the West today. The Western world has lost its civic courage, both as a whole and separately, in each country, in each government, in each political party, and, of course, in the United Nations. Such a decline in courage is particularly noticeable among the ruling and intellectual elites, causing an impression of a loss of courage by the entire society. There remain many courageous individuals, but they have no determining influence on public life. Political and intellectual functionaries exhibit this depression, passivity, and perplexity in their actions and in their statements, and even more so in their self-serving rationales as to how realistic, reasonable, and intellectually and even morally justified it is to base state policies on weakness and cowardice. And the decline in courage, at times attaining what could be termed a lack of manhood, is ironically emphasized by occasional outbursts of boldness and inflexibility on the part of those same functionaries when dealing with weak governments and with countries that lack support, or with doomed currents which clearly cannot offer any resistance. But they get tongue-tied and paralyzed when they deal with powerful governments and threatening forces, with aggressors and international terrorists.

Must one point out that from ancient times a decline in courage has been considered the first symptom of the end?

Well-Being

When the modern Western states were being formed, it was proclaimed as a principle that governments are meant to serve man and that man lives in order to be free and pursue happiness. (See, for example, the American Declaration of Independence.) Now at last during past decades technical and social progress has permitted the realization of such aspirations: the welfare state. Every citizen has been granted the desired freedom and material goods in such quantity and of such quality as to guarantee in theory the achievement of happiness, in the debased sense of the word which has come into being during those same decades. (In the process, however, one psychological detail has been overlooked: The constant desire to have still more things and a still better life and the struggle to this end imprint many Western faces with worry and even depression, though it is customary to carefully conceal such feelings. This active and tense competition comes to dominate all human thought and does not in the least open a way to free spiritual development.) The individual's independence from many types of state pressure has been guaranteed; the majority of the people have been granted well-being to an extent their fathers and grandfathers could not even dream about; it has become possible to raise young people according to these ideals, preparing them for and summoning them toward physical bloom, happiness, the possession of material goods, money, and leisure, toward an almost unlimited freedom in the choice of pleasures. So who should now renounce all this, why and for the sake of what should one risk one's precious life in defense of the common good and particularly in the nebulous case when the security of one's nation must be defended in an as yet distant land?

Even biology tells us that a high degree of habitual well-being is not advantageous to a living organism. Today, well-being in the life of Western society has begun to take off its pernicious mask.

Legalistic Life

Western society has chosen for itself the organization best suited to its purposes and one I might call legalistic. The limits of human rights and rightness are determined by a system of laws; such limits are very broad. People in the West have acquired considerable skill in using, interpreting, and manipulating law (though laws tend to be too complicated for an average person to understand without the help of an expert). Every conflict is solved according to the letter of the law and this is considered to be the ultimate solution. If one is right from a legal point of view, nothing more is required, nobody may mention that one could still not be entirely right, and urge self-restraint or a renunciation of these rights, call for sacrifice and selfless risk: This would simply sound absurd. Voluntary self-restraint is almost unheard of: Everybody strives toward further expansion to the extreme limit of the legal frames. (An oil company is legally blameless when it buys up an invention of a new type of energy in order to prevent its use. A food product manufacturer is legally blameless when he poisons his produce to make it last longer: After all, people are free not to purchase it.)

I have spent all my life under a Communist regime and I will tell you that a society without any objective legal scale is a terrible one indeed. But a society with no other scale but the legal one is also less than worthy of man. A society based on the letter of the law and never reaching any higher fails to take advantage of the full range of human possibilities. The letter of the law is too cold and formal to have a beneficial influence on society. Whenever the tissue of life is woven of legalistic relationships, this creates an atmosphere of spiritual mediocrity that paralyzes man's noblest impulses.

And it will be simply impossible to bear up to the trials of this threatening century with nothing but the supports of a legalistic structure.

The Direction of Freedom

Today's Western society has revealed the inequality between the freedom for good deeds and the freedom for evil deeds. A statesman who wants to achieve something important and highly constructive for his country has to move cautiously and even timidly; thousands of hasty (and irresponsible) critics cling to him at all times; he is constantly rebuffed by parliament and the press. He has to prove that his every step is well-founded and absolutely flawless. Indeed, an outstanding, truly great person who has unusual and unexpected initiatives in mind does not get any chance to assert himself; dozens of traps will be set for him from the beginning. Thus mediocrity triumphs under the guise of democratic restraints.

It is feasible and easy everywhere to undermine administrative power and it has in fact been drastically weakened in all Western countries. The defense of individual rights has reached such extremes as to make society as a whole defenseless against certain individuals. It is time, in the West, to defend not so much human rights as human obligations.

On the other hand, destructive and irresponsible freedom has been granted boundless space. Society has turned out to have scarce defense against the abyss of human decadence, for example against the misuse of liberty for moral violence against young people, such as motion pictures full of pornography, crime, and horror. This is all considered to be part of freedom and to be counter-balanced, in theory, by the young people's right not to look and not to accept. Life organized legalistically has thus shown its inability to defend itself against the corrosion of evil.

And what shall we say about the dark realms of over criminality? Legal limits (especially in the United States) are broad enough to encourage not only individual freedom but also some misuse of such freedom. The culprit can go unpunished or obtain undeserved leniency—all with the support of thousands of defenders in the society. When a government earnestly undertakes to root out terrorism, public opinion immediately accuses it of violating the terrorists' civil rights. There is quite a number of such cases.

This tilt of freedom toward evil has come about gradually, but it evidently stems from a humanistic and benevolent concept according to which man—the master of this world—does not bear any evil within himself, and all the defects of life are caused by misguided social systems, which must therefore be corrected. Yet strangely enough, though the best social conditions have been achieved in the West, there still remains a great deal of crime; there even is considerably more of it than in the destitute and lawless Soviety society. (There is a multitude of prisoners in our camps who are termed criminals, but most of them never committed any crime; they merely tried to defend themselves against a lawless state by resorting to means outside the legal framework.)

The Direction of the Press

The press, too, of course, enjoys the widest freedom. (I shall be using the word "press" to include all the media.) But what use does it make of it?

Here again, the overriding concern is not to infringe the letter of the law. There is no true moral responsibility for distortion or disproportion. What sort of responsibility does a journalist or a newspaper have to the readership or to history? If they have misled public opinion by inaccurate information or wrong conclusions, even if they have contributed to mistakes on a state level, do we know of any case of open regret voiced by the same journalist or the same newspaper? No; this would damage sales. A nation may be the worse for such a mistake, but the journalist always gets away with it. It is most likely that he will start writing the exact opposite to his previous statements with renewed aplomb.

Because instant and credible information is required, it becomes necessary to resort to guesswork, rumors, and suppositions to fill in the voids, and none of them will ever be refuted; they settle into the readers' memory. How many hasty, immature, superficial, and misleading judgments are expressed every day, confusing readers, and are then left hanging? The press can act the role of public opinion or miseducate it. Thus we may see terrorists heroized, or secret matters pertaining to the nation's defense publicly revealed, or we may witness shameless intrusion into the privacy of well-known people according to the slogan "Everyone is entitled to know everything." (But this is a false slogan of a false era; far greater in value is the forfeited right of people *not to know*, not to have their divine souls stuffed with gossip, nonsense, vain talk. A person who works and leads a meaningful life has no need for this excessive and burdening flow of information.)

Hastiness and superficiality—these are the psychic diseases of the twentieth century and more than anywhere else this is manifested in the press. In-depth analysis of a problem is anathema to the press; it is contrary to its nature. The press merely picks out sensational formulas.

Such as it is, however, the press has become the greatest power within the Western countries, exceeding that of the legislature, the executive, and the judiciary. yet one would like to ask: According to what law has it been elected and to whom is it responsible? In the Communist East, a journalist is frankly appointed as a state official. But who has voted Western journalists into their positions of power, for how long a time, and with what prerogatives?

There is yet another surprise for someone coming from the totalitiarian East with its rigorously unified press: One discovers a common trend of preferences within the Western press as a whole (the spirit of the time), generally accepted patterns of judgment, and maybe common corporate interests, the sum effect being not competition but unification. Unrestrained freedom exists for the press, but not for the readership, because newspapers mostly transmit in a forceful and emphatic way those opinions which do not too openly contradict their own and that general trend.

A Fashion in Thinking

Without any censorship in the West, fashionable trends of thought and ideas are fastidiously separated from those that are not fashionable, and the latter, without ever being forbidden, have little chance of finding their way into peiodicals or books or being heard in colleges. Your scholars are free in the legal sense, but they are hemmed in by the idols of the prevailing fad. There is no open violence, as in the East; however, a selection dictated by fashion and the need to accommodate mass standards frequently prevents the most independent-minded persons from contributing to public life and gives rise to dangerous herd instincts that block successful development. In America, I have received letters from highly intelligent persons—maybe a teacher in a faraway small college who could do much for the renewal and salvation of his country, but the country cannot hear him because the media will not provide him with a forum. This gives birth to strong mass prejudices, to a blindness which is perilous in our dynamic era. An example is the self-deluding interpretation of the state of affairs in the contemporary world that functions as a sort of a petrified armor around people's minds, to such a degree that human voices from seventeen countries of Eastern Europe and Eastern Asia cannot pierce it. It will be broken only by the inexorable crowbar of events.

I have mentioned a few traits of Western life which surprise and shock a new arrival to this world. The purpose and scope of this speech will not allow me to continue such a survey, in particular to look into the impact of these characteristics on important aspects of a nation's life, such as elementary education, advanced education in the humanities, and art.

Socialism

It is almost universally recognized that the West shows all the world the way to successful economic development, even though in past years it has been sharply offset by chaotic inflation. However, many people living in the West are dissatisfied with their own society. They despise it or accuse it of no longer being up to the level of maturity attained by mankind. And this causes many to sway toward socialism, which is a false and dangerous current.

I hope that no one present will suspect me of expressing my partial criticism of the Western system in order to suggest socialism as an alternative. No; with the experience of a country where socialism has been realized, I shall certainly not speak for such an alternative. The mathematician Igor Shafarevich, a member of the Soviet Academy of Science, has written a brilliantly argued book entitled *Socialism;* this is a penetrating historical analysis demonstrating that socialism of any type and shade leads to a total destruction of the human spirit and to a leveling of mankind into death. Shafarevich's book was published in France almost two years ago and so far no one has been found to refute it. It will shortly be published in English in the U.S.

Not a Model

But should I be asked, instead, whether I would propose the West, such as it is today, as a model to my country, I would frankly have to answer negatively. No, I could not recommend your society as an ideal for the transformation of ours. Through deep suffering, people in our country have now achieved a spiritual development of such intensity that the Western system in its present state of spiritual exhaustion does not look attractive. Even those characteristics of your life which I have just enumerated are extremely saddening.

A fact which cannot be disputed is the weakening of human personality in the West while in the East it has become firmer and stronger. Six decades for our people and three decades for the people of Eastern Europe; during that time we have been through a spiritual training far in advance of Western experience. The complex and deadly crush of life has produced stronger, deeper, and more interesting personalities than those generated by standardized Western well-being. Therefore, if our society were to be transformed into yours, it would mean an improvement in certain aspects, but also a change for the worse on some particularly significant points. Of course, a society cannot remain in an abyss of lawlessness, as is the case in our country. But it is also demeaning for it to stay on such a soulless and smooth plane of legalism, as is the case in yours. After the suffering of decades of violence and oppression, the human soul longs for things higher, warmer, and purer than those offered by today's mass living habits, introduced as by a calling card by the revolting invasion of commercial advertising, by TV stupor, and by intolerable music.

All this is visible to numerous observers from all the worlds of our planet. The Western way of life is less and less likely to become the leading model.

There are telltale symptoms by which history gives warning to a threatened or perishing society. Such are, for instance, a decline of the arts or a lack of great statesmen. Indeed, sometimes the warnings are quite explicit and concrete. The center of your democracy and of your culture is left without electric power for a few hours only, and all of a sudden crowds of American citizens start looting and creating havoc. The smooth surface film must be very thin, then, the social system quite unstable and unhealthy.

But the fight for our planet, physical and spiritual, a fight of cosmic proportions, is not a vague matter of the future; it has already started. The forces of Evil have begun their decisive offensive. You can feel their pressure, yet your screens and publications are full of prescribed smiles and raised glasses. What is the joy about?

Short-Sightedness

Very well known representatives of your society, such as George Kennan, say: "We cannot apply moral criteria to politics." Thus we mix good and evil, right and wrong, and make space for the absolute triumph of absolute evil in the world. Only moral criteria can help the West against communism's well-planned world strategy. There are no other criteria. Practical or occasional considerations of any kind will inevitably be swept away by strategy. After a certain level of the problem has been reached, legalistic thinking induces paralysis; it prevents one from seeing the scale and the meaning of events.

In spite of the abundance of information, or maybe partly because of it, the West has great difficulty in finding its bearings amid contemporary events. There have been naive predictions by some American experts who believed that Angola would become the Soviet Union's Vietnam or that the impudent Cuban expeditions in Africa would best be stopped by special U.S. courtesy to Cuba. Kennan's advice to his own country—to begin unilateral disarmament—belongs to the same category. If you only knew how the youngest of the officials in Moscow's Old Square* roar with laughter at your political wizards!

---

*The Old Square in Moscow *(Staraya Ploshchad)* is the place where the headquarters of the central Committee of the CPSU are located; it is the real name of what in the West is conventionally referred to as the Kremlin.

As to Fidel Castro, he openly scorns the United States, boldly sending his troops to distant adventures from his country right next to yours.

However, the most cruel mistake occurred with the failure to understand the Vietnam war. Some people sincerely wanted all wars to stop just as soon as possible; others believed that the way should be left open for national, or Communist, self-determination in Vietnam (or in Cambodia, as we see today with particular clarity). But in fact, members of the U.S. antiwar movement became accomplices in the betrayal of Far Eastern nations, in the genocide and the suffering today imposed on thirty million people there. Do these convinced pacifists now hear the moans coming from there? Do they understand their responsibility today? Or do they prefer not to hear? The American intelligentsia lost its nerve and as a consequence the danger has come much closer to the United States. But there is no awareness of this. Your short-sighted politician who signed the hasty Vietnam capitulation seemingly gave America a carefree breathing pause; however, a hundredfold Vietnam now looms over you. Small Vietnam had been a warning and an occasion to mobilize the nation's courage. But if the full might of America suffered a full-fledged defeat at the hands of a small Communist half-country, how can the West hope to stand firm in the future?

I have said on another occasion that in the twentieth century Western democracy has not won any major war by itself; each time it shielded itself with an ally possessing a powerful land army, whose philosophy it did not question. In World War II against Hitler, instead of winning the conflict with its own forces, which would certainly have been sufficient, Western democracy raised up another enemy, one that would prove worse and more powerful, since Hitler had neither the resources nor the people, nor the ideas with broad appeal, nor such a large number of supporters in the West—a fifth column— as the Soviet Union possessed. Some Western voices already have spoken of the need of a protective screen against hostile forces in the next world conflict; in this case, the shield would be China. But I would not wish such an outcome to any country in the world. First of all, it is again a doomed alliance with evil; it would grant the United States a respite, but when at a later date China with its billion people would turn around armed with American weapons, America itself would fall victim to a Cambodia-style genocide.

Loss of Will

And yet, no weapons, no matter how powerful, can help the West until it overcomes its loss of will power. In a state of psychological weakness, weapons even become a burden for the capitulating side. To defend oneself, one must also be ready to die; there is little such readiness in a society raised in the cult of material well-being. Nothing is left, in this case, but concessions, attempts to gain time, and betrayal. Thus at the shameful Belgrade conference, free Western diplomats in their weakness surrendered the line of defense for which enslaved members of the Helsinki Watch Groups are sacrificing their lives.

Western thinking has become conservative: The world situation must stay as it is at any cost; there must be no changes. This debilitating dream of a status quo is the symptom of a society that has ceased to develop. But one must be blind in order not to see that the oceans no longer belong to the West, while the land under its domination keeps shrinking. The two so-called world wars (they were by far not on a world scale, not yet) constituted the internal self-destruction of the small progressive West which has thus prepared its own end. The next war (which does not have to be an atomic one; I do not believe it will be) may well bury Western civilization forever.

In the face of such danger, with such historical values in your past, with such a high level of attained freedom and, apparently, of devotion to it, how is it possible to lose to such an extent the will to defend oneself?

Humanism and Its Consequences

How has this unfavorable relation of forces come about? How did the West decline from its triumphal march to its present debility? Have there been fatal turns and losses of direction in its development? It does not seem so. The West kept advancing steadily in accordance with its proclaimed social intentions, hand in hand with a dazzling progress in technology. And all of a sudden it found itself in its present state of weakness.

This means that the mistake must be at the root, at the very foundation of thought in modern times. I refer to the prevailing Western view of the world which was born in the Renaissance and has found political expression since the Age of Enlightenment. It became the basis for political and social doctrine and could be called rationalistic humanism or humanistic autonomy: the proclaimed and practiced autonomy of man from any higher force above him. It could also be called anthropocentricity, with man seen as the center of all.

The turn introduced by the Renaissance was probably inevitable historically: The Middle Ages had come to a natural end by exhaustion, having become an intolerable despotic repression of man's physical nature in favor of the spiritual one. But then we recoiled from the spirit and embraced all that is material, excessively and incommensurately. The humanistic way of thinking, which had proclaimed itself our guide, did not admit the existence of intrinsic evil in man, nor did it see any task higher than the attainment of happiness on earth. It started modern Western civilization on the dangerous trend of worshiping man and his material needs. Everything beyond physical well-being and the accumulation of material goods, all other human requirement and characteristics of a subtler and higher nature, were left outside the area of attention of state and social systems, as if human life did not have any higher meaning. Thus gaps were left open for evil, and its drafts blow freely today. Mere freedom per se does not in the least solve all the problems of human life and even adds a number of new ones.

And yet in early democracies, as in American democracy at the time of its birth, all individual human rights were granted on the ground that man is God's creature. That is, freedom was given to the individual conditionally, in the assumption of his constant religious responsibility. Such was the heritage of the preceding one thousand years. Two hundred or even fifty years ago, it would have seemed quite impossible, in America, that an individual be granted boundless freedom with no purpose, simply for the satisfaction of his whims. Subsequently, however, all such limitations were eroded everywhere in the West; a total emancipation occurred from the moral heritage of Christian centuries with their great reserves of mercy and sacrifice. State systems were becoming ever more materialistic. The West has finally achieved the rights of man, and even to excess, but man's sense of responsibility to God and society has grown dimmer and dimmer. In the past decades, the legalistic selfishness of the Western approach to the world has reached its peak and the world has found itself in a harsh spiritual crisis and a political impasse. All the celebrated technological achievements of progress, including the conquest of outer space, do not redeem the twentieth century's moral poverty, which no one could have imagined even as late as the nineteenth century.

An Unexpected Kinship

As humanism in its development was becoming more and more materialistic, it also increasingly allowed its concepts to be used first by socialism and then by communism. So that Karl Marx was able to say, in 1844, that "communism is naturalized humanism."

This statement has proved to be not entirely unreasonable. One does see the same stones in the foundations of an eroded humanism and of any type of socialism: boundless materialism; freedom from religion and religious responsibility (which under Communist regimes attains the stage of anti-religious dictatorship); concentration on social structures with an allegedly scientific approach. (This last is typical of both the Age of Enlightenment and of Marxism.) It is no accident that all of communism's rhetorical vows revolve around Man (with a capital M) and his earthly happiness. At first glance it seems an ugly parallel: Common traits in the thinking and way of life of today's West and today's East? But such is the logic of materialistic development.

The interrelationship is such, moreover, that the current of materialism which is farthest to the left, and is hence the most consistent, always proves to be stronger, more attractive, and victorious. Humanism which has lost its Christian heritage cannot prevail in this competition. Thus during the past centuries and especially in recent decades, as the process became more acute, the alignment of forces was as follows: Liberalism was inevitably pushed aside by radicalism, radicalism had to surrender to socialism, and socialism could not stand up to communism. The Communist regime in the East could endure and grow due to the enthusiastic support from an enormous number of Western intellectuals who (feeling the kinship!) refused to see communism's crimes, and when they no longer could do so, they tried to justify these crimes. The problem persists: In our Eastern countries, communism has suffered a complete ideological defeat; it is zero and less than zero. And yet Western intellectuals still look at it with considerable interest and empathy, and this is precisely what makes it so immensely difficult for the West to withstand the East.

Before the Turn

I am not examining the case of a disaster brought on by a world war and the changes which it would produce in society. But as long as we wake up every morning under a peaceful sun, we must lead an everyday life. Yet there is a disaster which is already very much with us. I am referring to the calamity of an autonomous, irreligious humanistic consciousness.

It has made man the measure of all things on earth—imperfect man, who is never free of pride, self-interest, envy, vanity, and dozens of other defects. We are now paying for the mistakes which were not properly appraised at the beginning of the journey. On the way from the Renaissance to our days we have enriched our experience, but we have lost the concept of a Supreme Complete Entity which used to restrain our passions and our irresponsibility. We have placed too much hope in politics and social reforms, only to find out that we were being deprived of our most precious possession: our spiritual life. It is trampled by the party mob in the East, by the commercial one in the West. This is the essence of the crisis: The split in the world is less terrifying than the similarity of the disease afflicting its main sections.

If, as claimed by humanism, man were born only to be happy, he would not be born to die. Since his body is doomed to death, his task on earth evidently must be more spiritual: Not a total engrossment in everyday life, not the search for the best ways to obtain material goods and then their carefree consumption. It has to be the fulfillment of a permanent, earnest duty so that one's life journey may become above all an experience of moral growth: To leave life a better human being than one started it. It is imperative to reappraise the scale of the usual human values; its present incorrectness is astounding. It is not possible that assessment of the President's performance should be reduced to the question of how much money one makes or to the availability of gasoline. Only by the voluntary nurturing in ourselves of freely accepted and serene self-restraint can mankind rise above the world stream of materialism.

Today it would be retrogressive to hold on to the ossified formulas of the Enlightenment. Such social dogmatism leaves us helpless before the trials of our times.

Even if we are spared destruction by war, life will have to change in order not to perish on its own. We cannot avoid reassessing the fundamental definitions of human life and human society. Is it true that man is above everything? Is there no Superior Spirit above him? Is it right that man's life and society's activities should be ruled by material expansion above all? Is it permissible to promote such expansion to the detriment of our integral spiritual life?

If the world has not approached its end, it has reached a major watershed in history, equal in importance to the turn from the Middle Ages to the Renaissance. It will demand from us a spiritual blaze; we shall have to rise to a new height of vision, to a new level of life, where our physical nature will not be cursed, as in the Middle Ages, but even more importantly, our spiritual being will not be trampled upon, as in the Modern Era.

This ascension is similar to climbing onto the next anthropological stage. No one on earth has any other way left but—upward.

Lewis Thomas

Lewis Thomas

COMMENCEMENT ADDRESS
TRINITY COLLEGE
1980

"A LONG WAY TO GO"

Sometime towards the close of the 19th century Lord Kelvin, an eminence in the physics of that day, assured for himself a sort of immortality in his field by announcing that physics was now a finished science, that all the essential information in the field had been acquired, and that now all that remained was to tidy up a few loose ends here and there. Within the following several years, X-rays were discovered; then, quantum theory and relativity, and all the fundamental dogmas of classical physics were modified in a series of swift strokes. Biology and medicine have not yet been put through such a period, primarily because we have not learned enough yet to have achieved the illusory stability of Newtonian physics.

But we do have a tendency to talk like Kelvin from time to time and it must seem to some of our younger and brightest students that we are in possession of an almost finished science, knowing almost everything about everything. If we are not careful and honest, we can make it seem as though mastery of all today's enormous store of facts in biological science could settle the matter. Just by lining them up in our minds, one after the other, we would be able to comprehend life in all its essential details.

If I were a student today I would not be much attracted to such a field. I would look about for some less-settled discipline where there might be more room to move around — cosmology, say, or the famous social sciences where the answers to most important questions are still out there, totally unknown, waiting to be asked.

An intellectually fashionable view of man's place in nature today is that there's really no great problem, the plain answer is that it makes no sense, no sense at all. The universe is meaningless for human beings; we bumbled our way into the place by a series of random, senseless, biological accidents; the sky is not blue, it is black; you can walk on the moon if you feel like it, but there's nothing to do there except look at the earth and when you've seen one earth you've seen them all; the animals and the plants of the planet are at hostile odds with one another, each bent on elbowing any nearby neighbor off the earth; genes, tapes of polymer are the ultimate adversaries and, by random, the only real survivors.

Well, this grasp of things is sometimes presented as though based on science, with the implication that we already know most of the important, knowable matters and this is the way it all turns out. It is the wisdom of the 20th century, contemplating as its only epiphany the news that the world is an absurd apparatus and that we are stuck with it and in it. And, in the circumstance, we would surely have no obligations except to our individual selves and, of course, to the genes coding out the selves.

I believe something considerably less than this. I take it as an article of faith that we humans are a profoundly immature species, only now beginning the process of learning how to learn. Our most spectacular biological attribute, which identifies us as our particular sort of animal, is language. And the deep nature of this gift is a mystery. We are aware of our consciousness, but we cannot even make good guesses as to how this awareness arises in our brains or even, for that matter, that it does arise there for sure. We do not understand how a solitary cell fused from two can differentiate into an embryo and then into the systems of tissues and organs that become us. Nor do we know how a tadpole accomplishes his emergence, nor even a flea. We can make up instant myths, transiently satisfying but always subject to abandonment, about the origin of life on the planet. We do not understand why we make music or dance, or paint, or write poems. And we are bewildered, especially in this century, by the pervasive latency of love.

The thing about us that should astonish biologists more than it does is that we are so juvenile a species. By evolutionary standards of time we only just arrived on the scene, fumbling with our new thumbs, struggling to find our legs under the weight and power of our new brains. We are the newest and most immature of all significant animals perhaps a million or so years along as the taxonomists would like to define us, but probably only some thousands of years as the communal, speaking creatures uniquely capable of manufacturing metaphors and therefore recognizable as human.

Our place in the life of the world is still unfathomable because we have so much to learn, but it is surely not absurd. We matter. For a time anyway, it looks as though we might be responsible for the thinking of the system — which seems to mean at this stage a responsibility not to do damage to the rest of life if we can help it. This is itself an immensely complicated problem, in view of our growing numbers and the demands we feel compelled to make on the planet's resources. There is no hope of thinking our way through the quandry, except by learning more. And part of the learning — not all of it, mind you, but a good part — can only be achieved by science: more and better science, not for our longevity or our comfort or affluence, but for comprehension, without which our long survival is unlikely.

The culmination of a liberal arts education ought to include, among other matters, the news that we do not understand a flea, much less the making of a thought. We can get there someday if we keep at it, but we are nowhere near and there are mountains and centuries of work still to be done.

One major question needing to be examined is the general attitude of nature. A century ago there was a consensus about this: nature was read in tooth and claw; evolution was a record of open warfare among competing species; the fittest were the strongest aggressors, and so forth. Now it begins to look different. The tiniest and most fragile of organisms dominate the life of the earth. The chloroplasts inside the cells of plants, which turn solar energy into food and supply the oxygen for breathing, are the descendants of ancient, blue-green algae living now as permanent lodgers within the cells of what we like to call "higher forms." And the mitochondria of all nucleated cells which serve as engines for all the functions of life are the progeny of bacteria which took to living as cells inside cells long ago.

The urge to form partnerships, to link up in collaborated arrangements is perhaps the oldest, strongest, and most fundamental force in nature. There are no solitary, free-living creatures. Every form of life is dependent on other forms. The great successes in evolution, the mutants who have, so to speak, "made it" have done so by fitting in with and sustaining the rest of life. Up to now we might be counted among the brilliant successes, but we are flashy and somewhat unstable, and we should go warily into the future looking for ways to be more useful, listening more carefully for the signals, watching our step, and having an eye out for partners.

Partnerships have to have a certain steadiness and predictability to survive for any length of time. You can't have linkages between creatures that have nothing at all to offer to each other, and partners have to be equipped with accurate information about the identity of each other. There must exist, in short, an information system capable of emitting signals indicating usefulness. You can see this sort of system still conspicuously at work in the life of the sea. There are no unattached, isolated, animals. Creatures live on each other, next to each other, inside the same carapaces and, most commonly of all, inside each other. The emergence of mitochondria and chloroplasts as organelles is only one example, perhaps the earliest and most spectacular.

The greatest single invention of nature to date was surely the invention of the molecule of DNA. We have had it from the very beginning, built into the first cell to emerge, membranes and all, somewhere in the soupy water of a cooling planet, three thousand million years or so ago. All of today's DNA, strung through all the cells of the earth, is simply an extension and elaboration of that first molecule. In the fundamental sense we cannot claim to have made progress since the method used for growth and replication is essentially unchanged.

But we have made progress in all kinds of other ways. Although it is out of fashion today to talk of progress in evolution, if you use that word to mean anything like improvement, implying some sort of value judgment beyond the reach of science, I cannot think of a better term to describe what has happened. After all, to have come all the way from a system of life possessing only one kind of primitive microbial cell, living out colorless lives in hummocks of algal mats, to what we see around us today — this place, and the city of Paris, and the state of Iowa, and Woods Hole, and that succession of travertine-lined waterfalls and lakes like flights of great stairs in Plevlja in Yugoslavia, and the horse chestnut tree in my backyard, and the columns of neurons arranged in modules in the cerebral cortex of human beings — this has to represent improvement. We have come a long way on that old molecule.

To err is human, we say, but we don't like the idea much and it is harder still to accept the fact that erring is biological as well. We prefer sticking to the point and insuring ourselves against change. But there it is: we are here by the purest chance, and by mistake at that. Somewhere along the line nucleatides were edged apart to let new ones in. Maybe viruses moved in carrying bits of other foreign genomes; radiation from the sun or from outer space caused tiny cracks in the molecule, and humanity was invented.

And maybe, given the fundamental instability of the molecule, it had to turn out this way. After all, if you have a mechanism designed to keep changing the ways of living; and if all the new forms have to fit together as they plainly do with symbiotic living all over the place; and if every improvised new gene representing an embellishment in an individual is likely to be selected for the species if it turns out to be useful for others; and if you have enough time, maybe the system is simply bound to develop brains sooner or later — and awareness. Biology needs a better word than error for the driving force in evolution. Or perhaps error will do when you remember that it came from an old Indo-European root meaning to wander about looking for something.

I cannot make my peace with the randomness doctrine. I cannot abide the notion of purposelessness and blind chance in nature, and yet I do not know what to put in its place for the quieting of my mind. It is absurd to say that a place like this place is absurd when it contains in front of our eyes so many billions of different forms of life, each one in its way absolutely perfect, and all linked together to form what would surely seem to an outsider to be a huge spherical organism.

We talk, some of us anyway, about the absurdity of the human situation, but we do this because we do not know how we fit in or what we are for. Some people believe we are in trouble because of science and that we ought to stop doing science and go back to living in nature, with nature, and contemplating nature. It is too late for us to do this. Too late by several hundred years and there are now too many of us here — four billion already with the likelihood of doubling that population and doubling it again within the lifetime of some of the people here.

What I would like to know most about the developing earth is: does it already have a mind, or will it sometime gain a mind and are we a part of that? Are we a tissue for the earth's awareness? I like this thought, even though I cannot take it anywhere, and I must say it embarrasses me. I have that nagging hunch that it is a presumption, a piece of ultimate hubris. A single insect may have only two thoughts, maybe three, but there are a lot of insects. The million blind and almost mindless termites in a hill make up in their collective life an intelligence, a kind of brain now capable of building endless vaulted chambers and turning perfect arches, thinking all the way. I would like to know what whales are thinking about or dolphins, but if I were hoping to find out how intercommunication really works on this planet I would study beetles.

I'm willing to predict that there is one central, universal, aspect of human behavior genetically set by our very nature, biologically governed, driving each of us along. Depending on how one looks at it, it can be defined as the urge to be useful. This urge drives society along, sets our behavior as individuals and in groups, invents all our myths, writes our poetry, composes our music. This is why it is so hard being a juvenile species, still milling around in groups, trying to construct a civilization that will last. Being useful is easy for an ant. You just wait for the right chemical signal at the right stage in the construction of the hill and then you go looking for a twig of exactly the right size for that stage and carry it back up the flank of the hill and put it in place and then you go and do that thing again. An ant can dine out on his usefulness all his life and never get it wrong.

It is a different problem for us, carrying such risks of doing it wrong, getting the wrong twig, losing the hill, not even recognizing yet the outline of the hill. We are beset by strings of DNA, immense arrays of genes, instructing each of us to be helpful, impelling us to try our whole lives to be useful, but never telling us how. The instructions are not coded out in anything like an operator's manual. We have to make guesses all the time.

The difficulty is increased when groups of us are set to work together. I have seen and sat on numberless committees, not one of which intended anything other than great usefulness, and most of them ended up getting everything wrong — most of them useless. Larger collections of us, cities for instance, hardly ever get anything right. And of course there is the modern nation — probably the most stupefying example of biological error since the age of the great reptiles. Wrong at every turn and always felicitating itself loudly on its great usefulness.

It is a biological problem, as much so as a coral reef or a rain forest, but such things as happen to human nations, error piled on error, could never happen in a school of fish. It is, when you think about it, a humiliation. But then "humble" and "human" are cognate words, both derived from an old root meaning, simply, "earth." We are smarter than the fish, but their instructions come along in their eggs; ours we are obliged to figure out and we are, in this respect, slow learners and error-prone. We have come a long way but we may have, with a bit of luck, a much longer way to go.

Cyrus R. Vance

Cyrus R. Vance

Yours is the first Harvard class to graduate in the decade of the 1980s. The decisions our nation makes now will shape the future of that decade.

We can either work to shape, in a wise and effective manner, the changes that now engulf the world or, by acting unwisely, become shackled by them.

It is time to set and stick to basic goals. Neither we nor the world can afford an American foreign policy which is hostage to the emotions of the moment.

We must have in our minds a conception of the world we want a decade hence. The 1990 we seek must shape our actions in 1980, or the decisions of 1980 could give us a 1990 we will regret.

The decisions we make now should address four basic goals:

— preserving the military balance while effectively managing our competition with the Soviet Union;

— fostering strong alliances of free nations;

— supporting the efforts of Third World nations to preserve their independence and to improve the quality of life for their people, particularly those hovering at the edge of survival; and

— strengthening the health and well-being of our economic system within a strong international economy.

These goals are ambitious. It would be naive to think otherwise. But unless our reach is bold, our grasp will fall far short.

Let us keep in mind the world from which we start: a world undergoing rapid change, with growing expectations, better education, quickened communications; a world in which neither the United States nor any other country commands a preponderance of power or a monopoly of wisdom. It is a world of conflicts, among nations and values, among social systems and emerging new interests. It is a world in which competitive superpowers hold in their hands our common survival, yet paradoxically find it beyond their power to order events.

271

There is a disturbing fear in the land that we are no longer capable of shaping our future. Some believe that we have lost our military muscle; others worry that our political will has been sapped.

I do not accept this gloom. It discards the abiding, pragmatic philosophy that has characterized America ever since its founding.

I consider mistaken the view that we, and we alone, are responsible for all the confusing changes that we see around us. This is a serious misreading of our condition, a perverted hubris that overestimates our power and our responsibility for ill, and underestimates our capacity for good.

The international diffusion of power and intellect is a fact. It will not change. It requires fresh and vital forms of action, not regret and pining for supposed "good old days."

What *is* to be regretted is a reluctance to relate our basic purposes to these new conditions. Yesterday's answers will not provide tomorrow's solutions.

It seems to me that much of the current dissatisfaction with the world and our role in it rests on certain fallacies. These illusions must be exploded before our nation can chart a coherent and determined course in foreign policy.

The first fallacy is that a single strategy — a master plan — will yield the answers to each and every foreign policy decision we face. Whatever value that approach may have had in a bipolar world, it now serves us badly. The world has become pluralistic, exposing the inadequacy of the single strategy, the grand design where facts are forced to fit theory. Given the complexity of the world to which we have fallen heir, the effect of a single strategy is to blur this complexity and to divide nations everywhere into friends and enemies.

A second widely accepted fallacy is the fear of negotiation, the worry that somehow we will always come out second best in any bargain. This fallacy assumes we have a realistic alternative of going it alone, of not bothering to recognize the legitimate interests and desires of other peoples. Without the fair bargain, achieved through negotiation and diplomacy, there is only a misguided, failed effort to impose one will upon another.

This fallacy was at work in the emotion underlying the opposition to the Panama Canal and SALT II treaties. In each case, balanced agreements were negotiated that served the interests of others as well as ourselves. In each case, opposition in our own country was based, at least in part, on the view that such agreements are rewards or give-aways to small nations or adversaries. Denying others a fair bargain and its benefits will not alter their behavior or reduce their power; it will simply have the effect of denying ourselves the same advantages. If America fears to negotiate with our adversaries, or to bargain fairly with Third World nations, we will not have a diplomacy. And we, no less than others, will be the loser.

A third myth that needs to be exploded is that there is an incompatibility between the pursuit of America's values in our foreign policy, such as human rights, and the pursuit of our interests.

Certainly, the pursuit of human rights must be managed in a practical way. We must constantly weigh how best to encourage progress while maintaining an ability to conduct business with governments — even unpopular ones — in countries where we have important security interests.

But we must ultimately recognize that the demand for individual freedom and economic progress cannot be long repressed without sowing the seeds of violent convulsion. Thus it is in our interest to support constructive change, as we did, for example, in the Dominican Republic, and are seeking to do in Central America, before the alternatives of radicalism or repression force out moderate solutions.

We know from our own national experience that the drive for human freedom has tremendous force and vitality. It is universal. It is resilient. And, ultimately, it is irrepressible.

In a profound sense, then, our ideals and our interests coincide. For we have a stake in the stability that comes when people can express their hopes and build their futures freely.

Further is the dangerous fallacy of the military solution to non-military problems. It arises in particularly acute form at times of frustration, when the processes of negotiation are seen as slow-moving and tedious.

American military power is essential to maintaining the global military balance. Our defense forces must be modernized — and they will be. But increased military power is a basis, not a substitute, for diplomacy.

I have heard it argued that our response to a changing world must be a new emphasis on American military power and the will to use it. This is reflected in proposed new budget priorities in the Congress, in which unnecessary defense spending squeezes out domestic programs and foreign assistance. There is near consensus on the need for defense increases. But it is illusion to believe that they are a substitute for the diplomacy and resources needed to address such problems as internal change and basic need in other nations, or a battered international economy.

The use of military force is not, and should not be, a desirable American policy response to the internal politics of other nations. We believe we have the right to shape our future; we must respect that right in others. We must clearly understand the distinction between our readiness to act forcefully when the vital interests of our nation, our allies, and our friends are threatened and our recognition that our military force cannot provide a satisfactory answer to the purely internal problems of other nations.

Finally, there is a pervasive fallacy that America could have the power to order the world just the way we want it to be. It assumes, for example, that we could dominate the Soviet Union — that we could prevent it from being a superpower — if we chose to do so. This obsolete idea has more to do with nostalgia than with present-day reality.

Spread over the widest territory of any nation on earth, the Soviet Union has its own strategic interests and goals. From a state of underdevelopment and the ravages of war, it has built formidable military and industrial resources. We should not underestimate these resources any more than we should exaggerate them. We must preserve and manage a position of essential equivalence with the Soviet Union. It is naive to believe that the Russians will play by our rules, any more than we will accept theirs. It is naive to believe that they — any more than we — would willingly accept a position of second-best in military strength.

A dangerous new nostalgia underlies all these fallacies — a longing for earlier days when the world seemed, at least in retrospect, to have been a more orderly place in which American power could, alone, preserve that order. That nostalgia continually erodes confidence in our national leadership, for it encourages expectations that bear no relationship to reality. And it makes change in the world's condition seem all threat and no opportunity. It makes an unruly world seem more hostile than it is. The fact is that we are a people who not only have adapted well to change, but have thrived on it.

The new nostalgia leads us to simplistic solutions and go-it-alone illusions, diverting our energies from the struggle to shape change in constructive directions. It is selfindulgent nonsense, bound to lead us into error, if not disaster.

What course is open to us now?

Our real problems are long-term in nature. It will not do to reach for the dramatic act, to seek to cut through stubborn dilemmas with a single stroke. Against the real problems now facing us, this approach will not only fall far short, but also create new problems.

Obviously, immediate crises have to be dealt with as they occur. And we should learn from these events. But they should never be allowed to distort our foreign policy goals.

As a global power, the United States has an extraordinary range of interests. That is why we must make sure that our pursuit of the desirable does not interfere with our achievement of the essential.

If, by 1990, we have not made progress in the four basic areas I listed earlier, the world will indeed be the inhospitable place many now fear it is. In each area, we can make progress — if. If we listen to our hopes no less than our fears, if we are prepared to sacrifice now for our future good. And, most important, if we work with other nations to resolve problems none can solve alone.

First, we must preserve the global military balance and achieve, as well, balance in our political relations with the Soviet Union.

Our military strength is important to our own safety, to a strong foreign policy free from coercion, to the confidence of allies and friends, and to the future of reciprocal arms control and other negotiations. Our strength also buttresses regional balances that could be upset by the direct or indirect use of Soviet power.

Maintaining the military balance will be expensive. To limit the costs, and to increase our safety, we must have an effective arms control policy as an integral part of our security policy.

Yet when the historian of 1990 looks back upon the year 1980, I believe a profound mistake may well be identified: a failure to ratify the SALT II treaty. As a symbol of our hopes for a more peaceful world, as a commitment to work toward better security through arms control, and as a process of trying to work out differences with an adversary, this treaty stands at the very heart of a sensible and far-seeing American foreign policy.

Without this treaty, our efforts to prevent the spread of nuclear weapons will be in jeopardy. If the United States and the Soviet Union fail to make real headway toward controlling nuclear weapons and eliminating nuclear testing, nonnuclear nations will have less reason for their own restraint.

Without this treaty, both sides will have more nuclear weapons than with it. In particular, the Soviet Union will have thousands of additional nuclear warheads.

Without this treaty, it will be much more difficult for us to undertake reliable planning for our military forces, since we will not be in as good a position to know what is going on within the Soviet Union. The treaty bans practices that would prevent each side from being able to verify compliance with its terms.

Without this treaty, there is bound to be less emphasis placed in both of our societies on conciliation of differences without conflict. Political elements who wish to emphasize conflict over cooperation will be strengthened.

Without this treaty, the process of arms control might be dealt a blow from which it could not recover. Can anyone doubt that this will make the coming decade more dangerous? It is not too late. It may soon be. I believe that the Senate must move to ratify the SALT II treaty before the end of this year. Certainly we must continue our firm and sustained response to Soviet aggression against Afghanistan. But neither that aggression nor the fact that this is a political year are sufficient grounds for a failure to act in our own national interests. I am aware of the political difficulties in acting at this time. But if we fail to act, we will someday ask ourselves why we were blinded by considerations of the moment and lost a vital, long-term opportunity. It is far too easy, in an election year, to let what may seem smart politics produce bad policies.

Both the United States and the Soviet Union will have to work even harder in the years ahead to avoid extremely serious confrontations. How we conduct our relations with the Soviet Union will perhaps be the most significant test of our maturity of judgment, our clear-sighted recognition of real interests, and our capacity for leadership.

It is foolish and dangerous to believe that we can manage this relationship by deterrence alone. We also will need to provide positive incentives.

We must use both our strength and the prospects of mutually beneficial agreements to help shape competition with the Soviet Union. We must work for implicit if not explicit agreements to bound our competition by restraints, by a kind of common law of competition.

The means to implement this goal will rest on patience, steadiness, clarity, and consistency. In our approach toward Moscow, we cnanot afford wild swings from being too trusting to being hysterical. And even as we maintain a steady course, we must recognize that it will require constant effort to mold that common law of competition. That effort must include both deterrence and the possibility of cooperation where our interests coincide.

We must also think anew about how to manage our affairs with the People's Republic of China in relation to those with the Soviet Union. Even as we act to develop nonmilitary ties with China, we should strive to restore a more balanced approach to both countries.

A second and paramount goal for our nation should be to nuture strong alliances among free nations. Indeed we now have such alliances. Our

relationships with NATO, with Japan, with Australia, New Zealand, and others, are basically sound.

But there is no gainsaying that relations among the industrial democracies are uneasy. And we must address the causes for this; they may well be more fundamental in origin than we care to admit.

Our alliances must respond to recent developments in international politics:

— the shifts in relative power among allies;

— the growing importance of the Third World, and enhanced Soviet capabilities to extend its reach there; and

— a recognition that neither the United States nor any other nation, acting alone, is in a position to resolve the international problems which we confront.

These developments require a new understanding between us and our allies.

We must find better ways to coordinate our policies in areas beyond our territories, for it is there that we increasingly face new problems. While our immediate interests may sometimes diverge in such areas, our basic interests run in parallel, and accordingly should provide grounds for common action.

Our allies must recognize that while the American nuclear shield is unshakeable, and our commitment to the common defense is firm, they cannot expect America to bear a disproportionate share of the burdens of deterrence.

We, for our part, must accept the other side of the same coin. We need common efforts because we cannot bear all the burdens ourselves, nor do we have all the answers. The price to us will be a willingness to consult and adjust for the sake of allied agreement. Consultation cannot be a substitute for a clear sense of direction. But there is no point in consulting if we are unwilling then to adjust our course for the sake of a common purpose.

Partly because of the strength of our alliances, it is the Third World —more than our alliance areas — that is likely to be the cockpit of crises in the coming decade.

We must first be clear on the nature of our challenge there.

Certainly, as we have seen in Afghanistan and elsewhere in the Third World, Soviet actions pose threats we must meet.

But we will meet them ineffectually if we react only by imitating Soviet tactics — emphasizing the military at the expense of the political, and disregarding the indigenous yearning of Third World nations for true independence and economic justice.

We must recognize the strong sense of national pride — and fierce independence — of developing nations. Having fought to throw off the burden of outside domination, they will strenuously reject the efforts of other nations to impose their will. We should respect and reinforce that spirit of independence. Our interests are not served by their being like us, but by their being free to join with us in meeting the goals we share.

Support for the political independence and economic growth of the poorer nations is important primarily because these nations matter in their own right. Their conflicts could also become our wars. Our trade with them is increasing. Their instabilities can affect our interests in many ways.

Our own national interests are served when we support the security of Third World nations with our assistance. When we help them develop their economies, we not only meet pressing human needs, we invest in important trading relationships. Our interests are served by supporting peaceful change within those nations and by encouraging the peaceful resolution of their conflicts.

For example, our interests are clearly served by our efforts to help resolve the Arab-Israeli conflict and bring peace to this troubled and vitally important region.

In 1990, as in 1980, the problems of the Third World will remain a central challenge to our wisdom. No realistic plan yet exists to defuse the potential dangers or resolve all the anguish of hundreds of millions of people living in degrading poverty.

But over the next decade the United States can make a difference with regard to the severity of those problems — in helping create progress and hope, in not disregarding the violence and suffering of despair.

To make that difference, we must first accept our differences with Third World nations, yet work with them where our interests coincide. Peace came to Zimbabwe because of the ability of Britain and the United States to work with the African nations of the region. Had the opponents of improved relations with Mozambique, Zambia, Tanzania, and others had their way, the situation today might well have been far different. The logical corollary is clear; it makes no sense not to recognize the Government of Angola, a government with which we have cooperated in the search for peace in southern Africa despite fundamental differences on other issues.

It is imperative that we also put our resources behind our policies.

American aid programs comprise less than 1-1/2 percent of our federal budget. They — not rhetoric, not good will — are what make the most difference in supporting our Third World diplomacy and in addressing now the causes of later crises. Yet they are under constant assault in the Congress and elsewhere.

The result is — I can think of no other word — disgraceful.

Our security assistance has declined by 25 percent over the past twenty years.

The United States ranks thirteenth among the seventeen major industrial powers in percentage of GNP devoted to development assistance. We will likely soon drop another notch.

We are far in arrears in meeting the pledges we have made to the multilateral development banks — and likely to slip still farther.

It is not enough to strengthen our defenses. We must also increase the resources needed to support our diplomacy, a diplomacy designed to reduce the chances our military forces may be needed.

Other nations do not want the rhetoric of American leadership; they want its substance. And we must provide it. The UN Global Negotiations on relations between developed and developing countries — opening this fall in New York — offers a prime opportunity for us to demonstrate that leadership.

This brings me to a fourth goal for the decade: a strong American economy in a strong international economy.

I ask you to ponder the implications for our future of two stark statistics:

According to the International Energy Agency, based on current trends, by 1985 world demand for oil is likely to outstrip global oil production by two million barrels a day. Consider the implications of this fact for world oil prices . . . and our own economy . . .for the hard pressed economies of the poorer nations . . . for relations among the industrial nations if there is a new scramble for energy.

The other statistic is domestic in nature: Productivity in the United States declined in every quarter of 1979, after the rate of increase in our productivity had steadily slowed over the previous two decades. Decreasing productivity not only fuels inflation. It undercuts our trading position and the strength of the dollar. And declining productivity means increasing domestic pressures for protectionism.

In both cases — meeting the energy crisis and addressing the problem of productivity — we cannot rely on the genius of some economist with a new solution. We need acts of political will.

If the U.S. and the other industrial countries do not act decisively to reduce our levels of energy consumption, and particularly our demand for oil, we will stand on the brink of economic disaster by the end of the decade — or sooner. The effort must be made now.

The President recognized the danger posed by our energy dependence and, from the earliest days of the Administration, sought comprehensive legislation to deal with it. Public skepticism and Congressional inaction have delayed the full implementation of his program for three costly years. In the meantime, the oil exporters have added price increase after price increase at will, and used their oil power for political ends. This will not change unless we are willing to let domestic energy prices reflect the reality of the marketplace and to tax excessive use ourselves, instead of letting OPEC do it for us; unless we produce more energy efficient cars and houses and appliances and channel sufficient resources into developing alternative energy sources; unless we share equitably with other industrial countries the burden of conservation and stand together against unjustifiable price increases.

U.S. productivity declined in every quarter last year. Solving that problem will also be costly. But there must be reduced consumption and a higher rate of capital investment; a willingness to shift from obsolete industries instead of propping them up with protectionist trade barriers; incentives for innovation; responsible prices and wage demands by industry and labor. Each is at root a question not of economic theory, but of national will.

*   *   *   *   *

Meeting the four challenges I have described depends not on quick fixes, new gimmicks, bluffs, or threats. It requires steadiness, political will, and understanding of a world in change.

If we are prepared to accept the implications of a world of diffuse power, and work with others where we cannot succeed alone, there need be no insurmountable barriers to our progress.

There should be no mystery about how to manage EastWest relations with realism and prudence; creating more cooperative alliances; addressing the problems of Third World nations; and acting now to strengthen our economy for later.

The mystery will be for the historian of 1990, if — blinded by the new nostalgia — we fail now to shape our future. The puzzle will be why we reacted against change in the world and did not seek to shape it.

The historian will then conclude that ours was a failure not of opportunity, but of seeing opportunity; a failure not of resources, but of the wisdom to use them; a failure not of intellect, but of understanding and of will.

It need not be so. For now, as always before, our destiny is in our hands.

Thomas Voss

Thomas Voss

COMMENCEMENT ADDRESS
MERCY COLLEGE
August 20, 1978

"YOUR LAST LECTURE"

My thanks to President Grunewald for this invitation and my congratulations to the administration and faculty of this college for making it, in a few years, a hallmark among independent urban colleges for its excellence in meeting the educational needs of its communities. But I am here to talk with the graduates.

Commencement addresses this year tend to be of three types A) Theme I: The Moral Degeneration of America e.g. Solzhenitzyn at Harvard and various divines at various small church colleges.. B) Theme II: "Small is Beautiful" a reassessment of American life in terms of a decreased standard of living in the 1980's and 1990's e.g. Robert Strauss and various economists at various colleges.. C) Theme III: "Renewal and Commitment": American will again be a number one power or is a number one power: e.g. President Carter at Annapolis and Cabinet Officers at various colleges.

In all those addresses, there is an underlying anxiety about controlling our life. This anxiety is peculiar because as of now, there is no war in which we are directly involved, no troops walk about on our streets, and campuses are not being held captive by their students. *But* don't you feel the concern that something is wrong? This apprehension is particularly reflected in our inability to control inflation. We can't seem to cope with change in mores and movements and we now believe in our polled objectivity that government no longer can solve our problems — so we retreat into our personal lives and cope as best we can. To heighten our anxieties, we are informed by the Carnegie Committee on Policy Studies and by the government agencies, that facing us is a new world of work; so profound will be the changes that predictions are bordering on dogma.

It is said that manufacturing will no longer by the nation's major employer in 25 years, but service-oriented and special skills companies will be. They say by 2010 that heavy industry and manufacturing will be primarily foreign-based and they refer to the plight of American steel as a present day indication.

It is said that economic growth will be around 3% then, instead of about 4.5% which it is today and therefore, job choices will be harder. Yet with a more educated populace at an average age of 35 in 2010, unlike 29 today, labor shortages will become a way of life.

We will be, they say, in a post-industrial society with short work weeks and a leisure ethic. Computers will replace the post office through terminals in our homes and also handle our banking and shopping; indeed, our fingers will do the walking.

But for those of you my age or over, you will remember the clarity of the American purpose, as well as the great depression and the great society, and the Hudson automobile, the Truman Doctrine and World War II ration books.

However, many of you here cannot remember those days because you were not born and that may or may not be advantageous to you, as you face running this complex and noisy society, which has survived a decade of confusion.

My question to you and my topic for you as you commence is: "What will be your place in this society and how will you cope with it?"

In the early 1900's the great grandson of John Adams, named Henry Adams, wrote a semi-autobiography about how he coped with his times and his civilization. He chose, unlike others in his Brahmin family, study and art as his fields of interest, rather than politics and banking. While being a university professor, he studied his times and what had influenced him as a 20th century man. He constructed a vision of himself, *for himself,* using symbols and personalities for the union of societal functions in the past and the diffusion of societal structure in his present.

He found the obvious transformation from the importance of the spiritual life to that of the secular, and the concomitant change to self-interest regulated by other self-interests. Throughout, he is a confused, *but* a compelling protagonist who endeavors to understand his place in his time, but more importantly, *what* has shaped his destiny as it unfolds for him.

Most of us do not formulate ourselves; indeed, it is considered somewhat unfashionable. Yet, your now-completed structured education assumes a comprehension of your self as a prerequisite for your commencement. With the onslaught of statistics, information, sensationalism and the currents of daily demands, one finds it difficult to do that in college and virtually impossible after. Yet, we yearn for this cohesiveness — this synthesis of self — in order to find our *personal place* in history.

As your last lecturer, what I am asking you is: "Who will you use as your models, your heroes, your symbols . . . who will lend credence to your beliefs and give you a purpose for which to die — as you decide your place in our times?"

Many of us have lived half of our allotted span and have seen, but not heard a great deal; have not fathomed much from our experiences, and often laboured in recreating the wheel or building a temple of words.

As a boy, I found my life was full of heroes and models, from political figures like Roosevelt to religious figures like Pius XII; their clay feet only came to light by social anthropologists some 30 years after they seem to have functioned quite well in difficult times. But it was hard to emulate people of such distinguished degree, so, many of us found it easier to find a more approximate hero. My neighborhood was working class and we honored a now-forgotten working class outfielder with the Chicago Cubs, a consistent player named Andy Pafko. Pafko never was a Ted Williams, nor a Joe DiMaggio but the kind of player who hits in the man on third and catches the fly ball — the backbone of the team. I never knew Pafko's salary nor his agent's name, if he had one. I never heard him endorse an aftershave lotion, or an automobile.

Now we have superstars at super salaries and our executive leaders are known to have clay feet before they become presidents, or cabinet members or supreme court justices. No-fault insurance, no-fault divorce, no-fault grading (pass-fail) highlight our life today; our responsibilities are weakened, our rights sometimes seemingly over-guaranteed and our standards are decided daily.

Therefore, let me ask if you will pay my social security benefits, those intergenerational taxes, in the year 2010, as I am paying for others in 1978? Let me ask if you will begin a policy of euthanasia to limit society numerically when I am 80 years of age in 2018? Will you work over one-third of a year to pay taxes for governmental and social services to benefit me as I do now? Will you bear arms to keep Papua New Guinea free if invaded? What about West Germany? South Carolina?

I have always thought that at commencements, the class should be asked to stand and recite the Athenian Oath, as they did in Athens, Greece over 2000 years ago. After completing a strict regimen and obtaining adulthood, they were asked to rise and proclaim that they would make their society the better for their being its new citizens.

However, such a pledge these days would probably not be fashionable and possibly, not even legal. I don't know what your futures are, but I do hope you will not fall victim to lives of quiet desperation or lives of quiet boredom as the social complexity and confusion mount. You must decide; Henry Adams did —Andy Pafko did.

Future generations will be judged by your success with yourselves and therefore, with our society. You *will to be* heroes. You have no choice and I have no choice. To parody an old Beatle's song "Will you love me, will you help me, when I'm 64?" *Good luck* to you *and* to all of us.

John William Ward

John William Ward

COMMENCEMENT ADDRESS
SUFFOLK UNIVERSITY
June 14, 1981

A Commencement speaker enjoys an advantage and suffers a disadvantage. The advantage is that no one will long remember what a Comencement speaker says. The moment is conventional; in another sense of that word, so are the speeches. For occasions like this, you should know I get considerable help at home. I was once a college president and had to give commencement addresses, so one of my sons suggested that I simply take all the talks I have given, extract the third paragraph from each one, and run them all together. He said, they all sound the same, anyway, and graduates are probably thinking about other things. So, hard as it is on one's ego, there is a certain advantage in being a Commencement speaker. It doesn't matter much what you say.

The disadvantage is more particular: we do not know one another. By "we" I mean the graduates. It is you I wish to speak to; others may listen in, of course, but it is your day and to you I want to talk. But, as I say, we don't know each other, have not shared in a common enterprise, have not gained a sense of each other in the classroom or over coffee. That makes it hard to know where you are "coming from," as the cant expression has it, what is on your minds, what stirs your feelings, That makes it hard to know what to say to you.

There is, however, one thing we do have in common, a *zip* code — 02114, Beacon Hill. Our apartment is on Pinckney Street which teeters on the downward slope of the unfashionable North side of the Hill, once the rear entrances to the stables and gardens, the service entries of the stately mansions of Mount Vernon Street. Suffolk University, and especially the Law School which came first, has been deeply involved in the ebb and flow of history which has physically as well as socially shaped and re-shaped Beacon Hill. Further, the founders of Suffolk University self-consciously placed it near the State House and the Court House, the political and legal institutions which are central to the liberal sense of a just and fair society. For the past two years, I have been much involved in that world, too, along with your own Professor Fran Burke, serving on a Special Commission to see if it might be possible to make government somewhat better and behavior somewhat more lawful. So, with this cluster of associations, I thought I would talk about the one thing we do have in common, Beacon Hill.

The Hill itself provides a convenient text, the words of John Winthrop which are cast in bronze on a tablet placed on the Common's side of Beacon Street as you mount the hill from Charles Street, a memorial tablet on the occasion of the three hundredth anniversary of the founding of Massachusetts Bay Colony in 1630. The tablet does not say, but Winthrop's words are taken from "A Modell of Christian Charity," his lay sermon on the Puritan theory of state and society:

> ". . . wee must consider that wee shall be as a City
> upon a Hill, the eies of all people are upon us; so
> that if we shall deal falsely with our god in this
> work we have undertaken . . . we shall be made a
> story and a by-word through the world."

Even one who does not know John Winthrop's writings will recognize the tradition out of which he speaks, the notion that the new world, America, is to be a model, an example to the rest of the world, a patent and a symbol of the good society. In more recent times, that other and Irish son of the Puritans, John Fitzgerald Kennedy, used Winthrop's very words, we shall be as a city upon a hill, to define his own vision of a new frontier in American politics. There was, to be sure, a literal beacon set atop the hill to warn the colonists of attack upon the infant settlement, but Beacon Hill quickly became metaphor, a light in the new world which would be a guiding beacon to the promised land, what Lincoln was to call the last, best hope of mankind.

The tradition has its ugly side, to be sure. It was used to rationalize the decimation and the destruction of the native Americans who were here long before Columbus sailed the ocean blue to discover, as we like to put it, the new world. It underlies the moral arrogance of American superiority in much of its dealings with the rest of the world. But it would be an unwise historian, or citizen, for that matter, who neglected the emotional appeal of the ancient vision that the historical mission, the destiny of American society, was no less than the millenial dream of creating on earth a good and just society. In our last presidential campaign, Mr. Reagan, you will recall concluded his televised debate with Mr. Carter with a rhetorical appeal to this tradition of manifest destiny, the notion that providence had preserved the new world, a virgin land, to provide a home for free and equal and independent Americans. We call it "the American Dream."

John Winthrop's 'Model of Christian Charity" has long been one of my favorite texts in American history. You must remember where and when he gave it to catch the full irony of its meaning. Winthrop delivered his political sermon to the settlers of the Massachusetts Bay Colony while still at sea, aboard the ship, Arabella, which bore the colonists to their new home from old England. As their political leader, Winthrop was reminding his fellow colonists of their obligation one to another. The promise was great, but so was the possibility of failure, and Winthrop knew why. The words etched in bronze today on Beacon Hill come from the peroration of Winthrop's address. But there were more words still to come. Winthrop ended with these: "But if our hearts shall turn away so that we . . . shall be seduced and worship . . . other Gods, our pleasures and profits, and serve them . . . we shall surely perish out of the good land . . . we pass over this vast sea to possess."

Before the settlers had even landed, while still at sea in 1630, Winthrop already saw the dilemma. The ideal was that a new start, a fresh beginning, free from all the corruptions and complexities of the old world, would lead to the good society where, in Winthrop's words, "we must be willing to abridge ourselves of our superfluities for the supply of others necessities . . . we must delight in each other, make others conditions our own, rejoice together, mourn together, labor and suffer together, always having before our eyes . . . our community as members of the same body." But, ahead, lay also the open land of a new world, a continent to conquer, commerce to be developed, riches to be made, the lure, as Winthrop saw, of personal pleasure and private profit.

Nostalgia for the good old days when things were somehow better has been a constant refrain in American thought, but here is Winthrop, even before setting foot on land, apprehensive that the American dream might already be behind him, behind somewhere there in the wake of the Arabella, if his fellow settlers, seeking their own pleasure and profit, were to value their own "superfluities," to use his word, to value their own higher, personal standard of living, and come to neglect the necessities of others, the common good, the social welfare.

Thus far the lesson, as Puritan preachers liked to say. What of its application? What does the ancient text have to do with us today? Let us begin with Suffolk University and its graduates. Gleason Archer placed Suffolk University where it is because he wished to reach the very people who were left out, who did not belong to the privileged world of the Mount Vernon proprietors or in the genteel confines of Harvard Yard. Suffolk University was for the many ethnic groups, East European Jews, Italians, Poles, Irish, people who — in the words of Mr. David L. Robbins's Heritage publication about Suffolk University — "people who had fled European shores in search of the American dream." (p. 20) The school was built near cheap public transportation and classes were held at night so working-class immigrants could find both education and opportunity.

But working-class immigrant students found few champions. One member of Boston's legal establishment contemptuously remarked, to make attorneys of them was "like trying to turn cart horses into trotters." (Boston Bar Journal,

May 1979, p. 17) After two gubernatorial vetoes, the charter to give Suffolk degree-granting powers was not enacted until the first Irish Governor of the Commonwealth of Massachusetts, David I. Walsh, sat in the governor's office in 1914. The power of votes and the leadership of immigrant political bosses like Martin Lomasney led to that charter, to be sure, but more than harsh reality was involved. Ideals played their part. Suffolk University may take pride that, as an institution, it embodied at its founding the dream which brought John Winthrop to Boston, the ideal that as a community, as members of the same body, we have an obligation to others and not just to our own pleasures and profits.

What of today? When I am asked to give talks like this, I like to do my homework. I did not have today's Commencement program, so I used last year's, on the assumption it fairly represents the present. After today's ceremony is over, you can test the numbers against today's program. Last year, Suffolk University awarded 454 law degrees; 57 were to residents of Suffolk County, of Boston. Of the 640 degrees in Business Administration, 104 went to Boston residents. To put it another way, 88% of the Law degrees and 84% of the Business degrees went to students who live outside of Boston. To use Mr. Robbins's pamphlet again, the present student body of Suffolk University comes from families who "have been able to leave the inner city and the contiguous suburbs for the more middle-class suburbs. For the most part, they are no longer people on the outside of the American dream looking in, but people living that dream." (p. 26)

Perhaps, but some times our very success creates problems. The history of Suffolk University may symbolize the failure of the City on a Hill. I say "may" not does. If the American dream is to mean no more than individual success, personal pleasure and private profit, as Winthrop had it, if from the comfort of middle-class suburbs one forgets those who are left behind, those who are still outside looking in, then the dream of the good society will become a social nightmare.

The history of Suffolk University represents a major national trend and points to an even more major social problem. The Census of 1980 is, for historians, remarkable because it is the first census in the history of the United States since the Census of 1810 where, proportionately, more people moved toward rural areas than toward urban areas. Whether the Census of 1980 represents a trend or indicates a temporary phenomenon will depend upon the viability of our major cities; that is, will depend upon mass transport, essential services, and personal safety, if the flight from the cities is to be reversed. And it is a flight. Along with a shift in population, accompanied by a comparable shift in capital, from the Northeast quadrant of the United States to the

Southwest, the older cities of America have in the past ten years shown an absolute decline in real numbers, not just proportionately. The last census shows negative numbers, a decline in metropolitan population for Massachusetts, Connecticut, New York, New Jersey, and Pennsylvania, and bare stability in mid-western states. Industry, which once provided the economic base for these older cities, has moved south or overseas. The American economy has become a service economy. In the national labor market, agriculture, industry, and construction, all three together, account for less than a third of all jobs; the service sector provides employment for about 70% of the entire work force. The word "service" usually summons up images of fast-food chains and drycleaning establishments, but remember that it includes distribution services, communications, accounting, banking and legal services, and the entire nonprofit and governmental sector of the economy. What skills are needed for success in that world? Clearly, the ability to deal with words and abstractions and to solve problems in a rapidly changing environment: in other words, a highly educated work force. Around Boston, everyone knows this, of course. In shorthand, the shift from shoes and textiles and machine shops to wordprocessing equipment and computers, from physical labor to intellectual skills.

Now, what of the city? Who is left behind? Who is left out of the educated, middle-class American dream now resident in the suburbs? Take out the educated middle-class and the answer is obvious. The cities are now the homes of the brown and the black, the poor and the undereducated, the elderly and welfare recipients. There are reverse eddies, to be sure, as on Beacon Hill and in the Back Bay of young, two-income couples, just starting out, or older couples, children grown and gone, moving back into the city, but statistically these are miniscule trends compared with the larger social forces affecting all the major cities of the United States. It was not only Boston whose white population declined 25% in the past ten years. New York declined 30%; Philadelphia, 23%; Baltimore, 28%; Chicago, 33%; and San Francisco, 23%. If one combines the black population with "Hispanic" and other non-white categories used by the U. S. Census, the non-white population is already a majority in the cities of New Orleans, Atlanta, the District of Columbia, Baltimore, and Chicago, and the white population is a bare majority in St. Louis and Memphis.

One needs to be precise, to be careful, when talking about "white flight" from the cities. It is, more properly, a middle-class flight. In 1978, almost half, more than four out of ten black families in cities were headed by a woman, and such families represent the lowest median income of all categories of families in the United States. Of households where family income is more than $15,000, three city families migrated out of the city for every one which moved in. That category of more affluent families includes black families as well as white families. The black middle-class is also migrating out, except that the black middle-class, depending upon both wife and husband working to make it, is in every sense of the word a minority, and the flight from the cities may fairly be called a white flight.

What, then, of our "city upon a hill" the millenial dream of a good and just and fair community of equal citizens? We can shrug, of course, and say it was just a dream. The reality is a city of the poor and undereducated. In Boston, a fourth of the population is on some form of welfare, in a city where the public school system is a mockery of the traditional role of public education as the vehicle for equality and opportunity, with transportation and basic services in steady decline, and old neighborhoods bisected by the turnpikes and highways which carry the successful from shining towers downtown back to the distant suburbs in the evening. We can, as I say, shrug, and close our minds and harden our hearts and say, that's tough, but that's reality.

Or, in the tradition of Suffolk University, we can confront reality and can change it. We can dream that impossible dream. But not if we define the American dream as private, individual success. On this festive day, you who graduate have every reason to take pride and pleasure in what you have accomplished. Only remember you did not get to this day alone. That is why, at the start, I asked parents to stand and receive your thanks. That is why I remind you of the essential meaning of the institution from which you graduate, an urban university which refused to accept the inevitability that some should be hewers of wood and drawers of water.

Today you receive degrees and the titles of Doctors, Masters, Bachelors. Those degrees carry, in the customary language of their bestowal, certain rights and responsibilities. But in a democratic society, the greatest title of them all is "citizen." And the essential responsibility of the citizen, whatever one's calling, wherever life takes one, is to have the moral imagination to see, and the will to act on the age old dream that, yes, we are a community, members of the same body, bound together in a common enterprise, the creation of a decent and humane society.

As Fran Burke always used to say on our Commission, I wanted to share that with you. Thank you.

Jessamyn West

Jessamyn West

COMMENCEMENT ADDRESS
JUNIATA COLLEGE
May 24, 1981

"SHARING YOUR BEING WITH OTHERS — THROUGH WORDS"

Ladies and Gentlemen, Members of the Graduating Class of 1981:

I am going to speak to you this morning about our opportunities and responsibilities as users of words — of our responsibilities to the words and to each other.

I do this fully aware that we are celebrating today the successful concludsion by the class of 1981 of four years of listening to lectures. I know also that there have been delivered in the United States since its inception as a nation in 1776, two million, three hundred and ninety-four thousand, seven hundred and thirty-five commencement addresses, and this number does not include speeches made to other than those being graduated from institutions of higher learning.

Now I have been conducting a private poll of my own and I have found that not a single word of these speeches has been rememberd by a graduate at any level — let alone the names of those who spoke the words that have been forgotten. This is not to be wondered at — nor does it mean that memorable words have not on occasion been spoken in celebration of these rites of passage.

What it means is that this is quite like a poor time to ask students who have just finished four years of listening to lectures, to listen to one more of the same.

If we were a less civilized people, or perhaps more, we would probably celebrate this occasion without words: we would meditate, or feast, or dance or sing or chant, or perhaps pray. The tradition, however, is for a speaker to give these already word-saturated young people more words.

There is even a tradition as to what a speaker should say on these occasions. He should look into the smiling and comely young faces below him and say, "You are the hope of the world. You will green the earth, you will stamp out bigotry. You will establish peace; banish poverty and eradicate cruelty."

Well, tradition or no tradition, I can't say those words. I do not know. You will, alas, mature and with luck, even age. And we all know that faces just as smiling, just as comely as yours went on after their graduation to build Andersonville Prison; to operate Treblenka and Auschwitz, where final solutions were implemented; they went on, these idealistic and hopeful young people, to massacre six thousand Huguenots; and under the leadership of Cromwell, to destroy such visions of eternity in stone as Tintern and Melrose Abbeys.

Young people graduating today have at their command the ability to prevent such act as these. Will they do so? I do not know. But I do know that no speech made today will affect acts which twenty years of learning — or of refusing to learn — have programmed them for in the future.

William Gass, the critic, writes, "It may be a country-headed thing to say that literature is language; that stories and the people and places in them are made up of words."

Like Gass, I am country-headed. Like him, I also believe that the word is the world's beginning for the writer — and the reader.

Now I am back to the place I should, perhaps, never have left: that is a consideration of the responsibilities and opportunities of users of words — not just as writers, but as human beings. As human beings, we have the opportunity through the responsible use of words to convey to others not only our own vision of the unique world in which each of us lives — alone — but to convey to others the only true treasure each of us possesses, that is our unique selves.

This speech is in fact an invitation — no, that is too weak a word — it is an urgent call to join the largest mutual aid society in the world — the society of those who are willing, in the words of Martin Buber, the great Hasidic philosopher, "To make the effort to impart one-self to others as one is." And this in spite of the fact that about half the population appears about half the time to be using words to hide who they truly are.

This is not a question, Buber warns, of saying everything that occurs to one (and I shall try to remember this as I speak). But it is a question of the verity of what is between us — and without which we can experience no authentic human existence.

"Something human," said the little mermaid in this fairy tale," "is dearer to me than any pearl."

In the aridity, the dehumanization of our communicating today, we live like that mermaid; caught up in the inhumanity of a great mechanical fairy tale offered pearls — great big lustrous production number pearls, when what we long for is something a good deal less large, a good deal less lustrous — and a good deal less fishy — something, in fact, human.

John Woolman on his Western travels often spoke to audiences of Indians. The chief of a tribe of these Indians, a man by the name of Paupenhang, said to Woolman when he was finished speaking, "I love to feel where your words come from."

What did Paupenhang mean by this? He meant, I believe, that he felt that peace, that refreshment, that contentment that we all feel in the presence of someone who makes the effort to impart himself to us as he is. "One loves to feel where words come from." When we do not feel this, we are denied authentic human existence — which according to Buber, occurs only when persons who are communicating, permit each other to partake of their being.

Ideally, one's words and one's life should be so much of a piece that one could no more open his mouth than he could open his veins without giving of his essence.

Though the comparison is not apt. We are human beings not by virtue of the blood in our viens but by virtue of the words in our mouths. By blood kinship we are kin to our animal brothers; by word kinship, we can be united to each other.

Emerson said, "Let every word cover a thing." By this, he was urging not only a concrete and therefore a poetic language, but an exact language.

What exactitude do we have now, when "message" means, "I'm going to try to sell you something." That is, a commercial.

When *Zest* is a soap.

When *My Sin* is a perfume.

When *Charm* is a brassiere.

When *Joy* is a dishwashing liquid.

When *Pride* is a furniture polish.

When *Old Quaker* is not an octogenarian member of the religious society of Friends, but a medium-priced blend of bourbons.

Well, God send us another Emerson, and send him soon. Otherwise, we will not be able to understand a word he says.

Emerson in one of his journals prayed that his days be "loaded and fragrant." What modern readers make of this, I know not, unless they believe that Emerson wanted to be scented with *My Sin* and filled with *Old Quaker*.

This is the lighter side of our responsibility in the use of words. But when we use sham words, we do make life shoddy. When we use graceless words, we do make life awkward. When we use evil words, if we use them with power and persuasiveness, we can make life hell.

And we can, if we use fair words to hide black deeds, undermine concepts of right and wrong won by men through centuries of attempting to discriminate.

With the disappearance of any exactitude in language, accompanied as this is by the disappearance of any possibility of reliance on what anyone says (the speaker may not know what he is saying himself), men tend to put their reliance on that language whose nature is unchanging — and whose meaning is clear to all — force.

A high school principal taked to me recently of the problem he was having with a teacher.

"Why don't you, " I asked "say so-and-so and so-and-so to her?"

"Certainly not," said the principal. "She would think I was getting personal."

What a sad commentary this is on the ways we have responded to one another in the past: to have caused the word personal to mean vindictive, prying, accusing, something to be avoided.

How pitiful it is that we taught each other to fear the personal. That we say, in effect, do not treat me as a person, treat me as a senior citizen, a teacher, a student, a Democrat, a Republican.

Use impersonal, sham, reality-hiding words. Become an object, a label, a thing, a black, a white. Computer will then speak to computer. Robot will embrace robot.

We have been impersonal with each other for so long that a whole profession has come into being whose function it is to listen to us when we find that we can no longer endure the impersonality of our lives and must speak personally to someone.

We then pay $20 to $50 an hour to someone whose profession it is to listen to those of us who are trying to escape from our straightjackets of schizophrenic impersonality.

We all nowadays, as Marshal McLuhan said, are members of a global village. As residents of this village, we will all be happier, not by all becoming alike but by all of us recognizing and cherishing and thanking God for our rich, subtle and invigorating differences. And these differences require strong honest words if they are to be communicated and if we are to be saved from living only as labels, professions, nationalities, ages, colors.

It may seem simple. First, to have the character to use the words that make it possible for others to share your being. And second, to have the craft to know what these words are. It isn't. It is neither simple nor easy.

In the first place, it does take character to share your being. Most of us don't want to give ourselves away. A real person must do that. We must be willing to stick our necks out. And perhaps discover that we are fools. We must give ourselves away. What else do we have to give?

These are perilous times. Perilous in every way. I have asked myself and you may be asking yourselves, how I can recommend in such times a cause with all the difficulty and all the significance too, you may feel, of counting the number of angels that can dance on a pinhead. Is it folly, stupid folly, to say anything so simple and personal as, respect words? To say, try to use words so that you impart yourself to others as you are?

Try to use words so that you honor the million-year history of man's struggle to think which our language represents.

At the beginning of this speech — which was quite a few minutes ago and quite a few words back — so that you may have forgotten it, I said that I was issuing an urgent invitation to you to join the largest mutual aid society in the world: the society of those willing to make the effort to impart oneself as one is to others.

Where's the mutual aid in that? Will it deflate inflation? Increase jobs? Discover more oil? Reconcile Arab and Jew? Or even Republican and Democrat?

I'll tell you what it will do. It will prevent us from becoming mass-men, herdsmen, anonymous man. It will prevent us from becoming faceless members of a mob, responding to mass sounds, or responding to mass signs: heil Hitlers or clenched fists.

By such sounds and signs, we shuck off our responsibilities and opportunities as individuals. We become party members, not persons.

What are we? Rubber stamps? Robots? Parrot squawkers?

Or human beings treating language once again as people did for tens of thousands of years, as a holy instrument to be used to see the reality and hence the wonder of the world.

Biologists believe the gift of language is the single human trait that marks us all genetically, setting us apart from all the rest of life.

Language is, they say, like nest building, or hive making, the universal and biologically specific activity of human beings. We cannot be human without it, and if we were to be separated from it, our minds would die as surely as bees lost from the hive. Language is at the core of our existence holding us together.

So let's keep talking. Let's keep writing and reading. Let's keep building that hive, language, which is our home as rational human beings, and let's fill it with the purest honey of honest communications.

Morris L. West

Morris L. West

COMMENCEMENT ADDRESS
MERCY COLLEGE
May 30, 1982

Mr. President, ladies and gentlemen: I am honored to be with you today. I am grateful for the honor you have bestowed upon me.

I face you with a certain amount of trepidation. I asked instruction about the audience which I was about to address. I sought the information from one of the worthy gentlemen sitting before you. This is what he told me.: "Your audience will be pragmatic, skeptical, sharp-edged, attentive, street-wise, striving for success, searching for increased self-esteem, trying to find for themselves a summer place in a darkening world. Some of them will bear the scars of economic and racial battles. All of them will have some sense of what you are talking about, when you address yourself to the questions of freedom and self-respect."

These definitions did not deter me, rather they encouraged me. You see, I am 66 years old, I was born at a time when the advertisements for employment carried always the subscription: "no Catholics, no Irish, no Jews, need apply"; when it was the avowed policy of my country — against which, in later life, I fought many a bitter battle — to keep Australia white!

So I know what this university is about and I have shared some of the struggles which many of you have undergone and which you will face in the future. I was threatened, my family was threatened, because I spoke loudly against the forthcoming war in Vietnam, because I said white men should never fight Asians in Asia and that you will never stop an idea with a bomb.

What have I to offer you today? Only some thoughts which I would like to buzz around in your heads like gadflies. I am not here to teach you anything. I am here only to share with you, fraternally, some of the experience of a lifetime.

Let us talk for a moment about freedom. Freedom is something which is largely preached in the United States of America. It is spoken about in this country as if it were the natural heritage of every citizen. Constitutionally it may be; factually, as you know, it is not. The true country of freedom is the country of the mind. In the most libertarian society the geography of freedom is always limited for many. There are those who are house-bound by illness;

307

there are those who are handicapped by mental infirmity; they are not free. There are those for whom the mechanism of justice has proved inadequate; they are not free. Freedom can only be preserved, only be cultivated, in the mind of man and woman. Liberty is you. Liberty is the plant which will grow inside you, regardless of geography. Only inside a man or a woman will it preserve its true and recognizable form.

What this university, I believe, has done for you, and must do for generations to come, is give you the key to the country of the mind; so that you can open your own minds which, too often, and, too long, remain a closed country - to new ideas, to new implantations, to new risks. That is the first thought I'd like to leave with you.

The second is this: we take language for granted. We accept it, as the ancients did, as a divine gift, like the Promethean gift of fire. Language is not a gift. Language is a human construct; and, like every human construct, it is both useful and terribly dangerous. In this country — more perhaps than in any other — language is in a state of debasement. It is so because of the huge immigrant influx and the necessity of imposing on a polyglot population, in the shortest possible time, a lingua franca, a common tongue, sufficient for the commerce of ordinary life; of buying and selling, and eating and drinking, and marrying and giving in marriage, and supplying the normal social institutions.

That, as you are very well aware, is not enough for the whole commerce of human life. I quote you only one example. In the last tragic weeks we have had a word bandied about between nations; the word is "sovereignty," "Sorranita." Has anybody ever told you, have you ever bothered to inquire — and I give it to you as a challenge — the generic meaning of the word sovereignty? It is seen as a word meaning to rule. It is seen and bandied about as a word connoting imperium, domination. It has lost its generic meaning, which is self-determination, the God-like quality of free will, the God-like quality of being able to take or to leave, to receive or to offer. If there is such a concept as sovereignty, if that concept is in fact a reality in human life, then it must carry within itself all the qualities of self-determination: right to abdicate, for instance: to abdicate normal rights. I am free to relinquish that which is mine by right, in favor of someone who is more needy than I.

This lack of knowledge of the tool, the weapon which we have in our hands, is highly dangerous to us all; because, we live in a society, ladies and gentlemen, in which we have, without question, relinquished our control of the greatest network of communications — the world. Into whose hands? The makers of cornflakes, the sellers of razor blades and sanitary pads! You hear the news of the world by courtesy of soap-makers! You can't change that situation now. Or can you? The possession which was once yours, of the air you breathe, has not been extended to the air waves which carry the communications from one man to one woman to another.

This bastardization of communication, this pollution of the wells of thought, can only be offset by you; in the humbler commerce of the hearth, the house-hold; in the speech between men and women in private places over a meal; in the loud speech of men and women in private places in protest.

We do not have to be right, but we have to be free. In order to be free we have to be knowing — and to be knowing, ladies and gentlemen, we have to be very, very patient, and very, very conscientious.

Another word which has been bandied about for which men are dying, even as I speak is the word "principle." Dear God, how many times have I heard it spoken and how many men have I seen die for principle? And how few times have I heard the word questioned? The word, "principle," ladies and gentlemen, derives from a Latin word, "principia": the beginnings of things, the roots of heaven, the roots of earth, the roots of our very existence.

These roots are not discovered by mere nomenclature. By giving them a name you do not know them. You have to search them out; which is what this institution and others, please God, mean.

Search them out! Think about them! Make pilgrimage to find them, as men once made pilgrimage to find the Holy Grail. And remember, you will not find the roots of heaven, you will not find the beginnings of things, unless you are like the old Grail searchers of the legend, pure of heart.

If you think that sounds like a bad joke, in today's pornographic age, it isn't. Because, if your search is polluted by a grasping for unjust settlements in your own life or in public life, the principles will elude you. You will never see them except in figment and in illusion. You will always be the victims of the hucksters, the peddlers of illusion.

One last word, ladies and gentlemen! Unless you make this patient search for the roots of things, the beginnings, the principles, unless you have the patience to learn to live by the principles you will discover, then we shall all have the dubious privilege of dying for them.

Go with God!